Strategies for Success on the SAT*: Mathematics Section

Teacher Consultants:

Walter Hamera

B.S., Economics, Purdue University
M.S., Applied Mathematics, California State University, San Francisco
Mathematics Department Chair, Laguna Beach High School, Laguna Beach, California

Gary Shapiro

B.S., Mathematics, Worcester Polytechnic Institute
M.Ed., Boston University
Mathematics Instructor and Former Mathematics Department Chair, Laguna Beach High School,
    Laguna Beach, California

Valorie Quigley

B.S., Business Administration, University of Kansas
M.A., Mathematics Education, University of Kansas
Mathematics Instructor and Former Mathematics Department Chair, Laguna Beach High School,
    Laguna Beach, California

Acknowledgements:

iUniverse: Susan Driscoll, Dan Silvia, Jessica Florez, Joyce Greenfield and Sally Peterson

FreelancePermissions.com: Natalie Giboney and Melissa Flamson

Avant Productions, Inc. (graphics): Clark Severson, Jeriann Severson and Olivia Klaus

Avalon Marketing & Communications: Patty Lavelle

Kleinworks Agency: Judy Klein

The author expressly thanks Lauren Meggison, MA, MFA, Ph.D., Director, Cambridge Academic Services & Consulting, Inc. and the *Lyceum for Elementary Enrichment & Test Prep* (4th – 6th grades), Laguna Beach, California, for her dedicated assistance and support. The author also gratefully acknowledges the contributions and efforts of Shane Andrade, Manuela Andronic, Michelle Ha, Susan Li, Courtney Taylor, Evan Miyazono, Jennifer Owens, Nicole Edwards and Mariana Aguirre.

The author extends her deepest personal thanks to Maurice L. Muehle for his invaluable guidance and assistance.

Strategies for Success on the SAT: Mathematics Section

by

Lisa Muehle

Director, Cambridge Academic Services & Consulting, Inc. and the *Colloquium Test Prep Course for the SAT*
(Long-term SAT training for $7^{th} - 11^{th}$ grade students)
Laguna Beach, California

iUniverse Star
New York Lincoln Shanghai

Strategies for Success on the SAT: Mathematics Section

iUniverse Star
an iUniverse, Inc. imprint

iUniverse books may be ordered through booksellers or by contacting:

iUniverse
2021 Pine Lake Road, Suite 100
Lincoln, NE 68512
www.iuniverse.com
1-800-Authors (1-800-288-4677)

Because of the dynamic nature of the Internet, any Web addresses or links contained in this book may have changed since publication and may no longer be valid.

Further information:
Lisa Muehle, Director
Lauren Meggison, MFA, Ph.D., Director
Cambridge Academic Services & Consulting, Inc.
303 N. Broadway Plaza, Suite 204
Laguna Beach, California 92651
(949) 443-2700
www.e-cambridgetutors.com
E-mail: cambridge@e-cambridgetutors.com

The author gratefully acknowledges the following sources and appreciates permission granted to reprint material used in this book:

Information gathered from The MacTutor History of Mathematics Archive, School of Mathematics and Statistics, University of St. Andrews, Scotland. http://www-history.mcs.st-andrews.ac.uk/

Page 57: From "The Origin of the Word 'Algebra'" by Dr. John Dawson, www.mathforum.org. Reprinted by permission of the author.

Page 121: From Chicago Bulls, 1987-88 NBA Season Statistics, http://www.statsc.freeservers.com/nba/nba87-88.html.

Page 145: "The Origin of the Rhombus" by Pat Ballew, www.pballew.net/rhomb.html. Reprinted by permission of the author.

ISBN: 978-1-58348-013-7 (pbk)
ISBN: 978-0-595-82416-8 (ebk)

Printed in the United States of America

<u>Dedication</u>

This book is dedicated to my partner Lauren Meggison,
my mother Adrienne Ruth Brown Gillett,
and my father Maurice Lee Muehle.

- Lisa Muehle

Table of Contents

BASIC INFORMATION ABOUT THE SAT

SAT Format, Content & Scoring

Section of SAT	Format & Question Types	Content	Score Range
Mathematics	❑ Two 25-minute sections ❑ One 20-minute section *(Total of 70 minutes)* Mostly multiple-choice questions; some student-produced response questions.	❑ Arithmetic and Number Operations ❑ Algebra I & II ❑ Plane Geometry ❑ Coordinate Geometry ❑ Data Analysis, Statistics and Probability	M 200–800 (Lowest possible score = 200, median score = 500, "perfect" score = 800.)
Critical Reading	❑ Two 25-minute sections ❑ One 20-minute section *(Total of 70 minutes)* All multiple-choice questions.	❑ Sentence Completions ❑ Critical Reading: Reading passages ranging from 400–850 words with several accompanying questions. Short reading passages of approximately 100 words followed by one or two questions. Dual passages followed by questions about the individual passages as well as questions comparing the two passages. *Passage Subject Matter:* Natural Sciences Humanities Social Science Literary Fiction	M 200–800 (Lowest possible score = 200, median score = 500, "perfect" score = 800.)
Writing	❑ One 25-minute essay ❑ One 25-minute multiple-choice section ❑ One 10-minute multiple-choice section *(Total of 60 minutes)*	❑ Written Essay ❑ Improving Sentence Errors ❑ Improving Sentences ❑ Improving Paragraphs *Areas of Focus:* Grammar Usage Word Choice Writing Process	W 200–800 (Lowest possible score = 200, median score = 500, "perfect" score = 800.) *Two subscores are given for the writing section: a multiple-choice subscore on a scale of 20–80, and an essay subscore on a scale of 0–12. These subscores are combined and converted to the 200–800 point scale, with the essay counting for approximately 1/3 of the available Writing section points.*

Total testing time for the SAT is 3 hours and 45 minutes, which includes a 25-minute experimental section. (The experimental section is not scored.) A total of 2,400 points are available (800 points per section).

Understanding the Guessing Penalty for Wrong Answers on the SAT

The following table summarizes scoring for the SAT mathematics section:

	Question is Answered Correctly	Question is Left Blank	Question is Marked with Wrong Answer
Multiple-Choice Math Question with Answer Choices (A) – (E)	+ 1 point	0 points	$-\dfrac{1}{4}$ point
Student Produced Response Question (Grid-in Questions)	+ 1 point	0 points	0 points

For student produced response questions, there is no penalty for a wrong answer. For multiple-choice questions, you will lose $\dfrac{1}{4}$ of a point for each wrong answer.

The guessing penalty actually sounds scarier than it is. If you were to randomly guess the answers to five different SAT multiple-choice questions, the odds are that you would get four questions wrong and one right (according to the basic rules of probability). These questions would be scored as follows:

$$4 \text{ questions wrong} \bullet (-\tfrac{1}{4}\text{ point}) \quad = -1 \text{ point}$$

$$1 \text{ question right} \quad\quad\quad\quad\quad = +1 \text{ point}$$

$$\overline{\hspace{6cm}}$$

$$0 \text{ points}$$

So you would not have experienced any loss of points if you had guessed the answers to five questions and gotten only one right answer. This means that the "guessing penalty" is really a misnomer.

If you are able to eliminate two or even three wrong answer choices, your odds will have improved considerably. For example, if you were to guess between two answer choices on ten different questions (one of which was the correct answer), odds are that you would have answered five questions correctly (+5 points) and missed the other five questions (-1.25 points) for a net gain of 3.75 points. 3.75 points is considerably better than the zero points you would have had if you had left those questions blank.

Educated guessing on the SAT can help improve your score considerably. If you are stumped on a question but you can eliminate even one answer choice, you may want to guess. If you can eliminate two or more answer choices, you would be well advised to make your best educated guess. **Using process of elimination to make sound educated guesses remains the most important success strategy on the SAT.**

Calculator Use on the SAT

Calculators are allowed on the SAT. Use of a graphing calculator is strongly advised for many of the exam's Algebra-II level problems. The graphing calculator instructions and associated key sequences provided in this guide as well as the graphing calculator screen graphics are based upon a Texas Instruments graphing calculator (model TI-83). The TI-84 Plus Silver Edition is compatible to the TI-83 Plus Silver Edition. Texas Instruments and other companies offer a wide variety of graphing calculators with strong applications to the SAT and other important exams (SAT II, ACT, AP, etc.).

Suggested Study Plan

It is best to start as early as possible in studying for the SAT. To get the most out of this book, you may wish to utilize one of the following study plans:

8-week plan: Complete one lesson per week   *4-week plan:* Complete two lessons per week

Lesson #	Approximate Time Needed	Chapter #s	Chapter Topics	Instructions
1	2.5 hours	1 & 2	• Introduction & Strategies • Arithmetic & Basic SAT Math	• Read & highlight text • Do all practice exercises presented in text
2	2.5 hours	3	• Algebra	• Read & highlight text • Do all practice exercises presented in text
3	1 hour	7A	• *Practice Exercises* Algebra & Number Operations	• Do all practice exercises • Review answer explanations
4	2.5 hours	4	• Coordinate Geometry & Graphs in a Coordinate Plane	• Read & highlight text • Do all practice exercises presented in text
5	2.5 hours	5	• Plane & Solid Geometry	• Read & highlight text • Do all practice exercises presented in text

6	2 hours	7B & 7C	• *Practice Exercises*
			  • Plane & Coordinate Geometry and Graphs
			  • Mixed Practice
				• Do all practice exercises
				• Review answer explanations

7	1.5 hours	6	• Miscellaneous Math Topics	• Read & highlight text • Do all practice exercises presented in text
8	1 hour	7D	• *Practice Exercises* "Math Hall of Fame" for the SAT (Classic SAT Math Problems)	• Do all practice exercises • Review answer explanations

Mathematics
Chapter 1
Introduction & Strategies

1. The Two Math Question Types on the SAT

2. Tips, Pointers and Approaches for Certain SAT Math Question Types

3. Calculators and the SAT

4. Hints for Grid-In Success

5. Avoid "*The Lights of Las Vegas*": Attractive but Wrong Answer Choices

6. "*Paint by Numbers*": Substitute Numbers for Variables in the Answer Choices

7. "*Throw it in Reverse*" and Solve Backwards

8. Eliminating Obviously Wrong Answer Choices

9. Guesstimating

Tips & Strategies for Mathematics Success on the SAT

✓ **Mathematics Strategy #1:**
• **Understand the Two Math Question Types that Appear on the SAT**

MATH QUESTION TYPE #1:

Most math problems on the SAT follow a multiple-choice format with five answer choices, (A) – (E). Here is an example:

How many distinct prime factors exist for the number 30?

    (A)   2
    (B)   3
    (C)   4
    (D)   5
    (E)   6

The answer is (B); the prime factors of 30 are 2, 3 and 5.

MATH QUESTION TYPE #2:

A few math problems on the SAT require student-produced responses. There are no answer choices provided for these questions. Answers to these problems are entered into an answer grid. Here is an example:

If $\dfrac{5}{8}x = 25$, what does x equal?

The answer to this question is 40 (divide 25 by $\dfrac{5}{8}$ to find x). You would enter the number 40 into the answer grid corresponding to the question; refer to the section later in this chapter about grid-in problems.

At the beginning of every math section on the SAT, a geometry reference chart with diagrams is provided that includes the following information and formulas:
- ➤ Area and circumference of a circle
- ➤ Area of a rectangle and of a triangle
- ➤ Volume of a rectangular solid and of a cylinder
- ➤ The Pythagorean Theorem for finding the lengths of the legs or the hypotenuse in a right triangle
- ➤ The relationships in special right triangles (45°-45°-90° and 30°-60°-90°)
- ➤ Degree measures of a circle and a straight line, and the sum of the measures of the interior angles of a triangle

---

✓ Mathematics Strategy #2:

• Tips, Pointers and Approaches for Certain SAT Math Question Types

---

Certain SAT math questions involve concepts with which students may lack familiarity. Other problems are best solved via specific approaches that avoid SAT "traps." The purpose of this section is to provide useful strategies and techniques for some of these problem types. Formal definitions and complete explanations of these topics are found in subsequent chapters. If you are unfamiliar with a given topic, study it first in more detail in the chapter in which it is more thoroughly presented.

Sets
(see Arithmetic & Basic Math chapter, page 27)

A **set** is a group or collection of numbers or other items usually listed within braces.

Examples:

$$A = \{2, 7, 9, 11\} \qquad B = \{2, 5, 9, 15\}$$

- If you were asked to find the **intersection** of sets A and B (A ∩ B), you would specify the elements the two sets have in common. A ∩ B = {2, 9}

- If you were asked to find the **union** of sets A and B (A ∪ B), you would specify the combined elements of the two sets. A ∪ B = {2, 5, 7, 9, 11, 15}
  (Do not double list values that are contained in both sets.)

- Remember, the symbol "∪" resembles the letter "u" (as in "union").

Absolute Value
(see Algebra chapter, pages 66 – 70)

The **absolute value** of x is denoted $|x|$. The absolute value of a non-zero number is always <u>positive</u> but there are always <u>two different numbers</u> that can be placed inside the absolute value sign that will yield the same absolute value outcome:

(1) A specific real number *and*
(2) That number's additive inverse.

Example: The solution set for the equation $|x| = 9$ is {-9, 9}.

A problem type you may encounter on the SAT:

If j and k are integers such that $2 < |j| < 7$ and
$1 < |k| < 6$, what is the least possible value of $j + k$?

The potential traps:

- Forgetting to consider the negative values for *j* or for *k*. **Because this is an absolute value expression, the least possible value of *j* or of *k* is the additive inverse of its greatest possible positive value.**

- Not interpreting the inequality sign and incorrectly deciding that the greatest value of *j* is 7 or that the greatest value of *k* is 6. **The "<" sign means "less than," not "less than or equal to."** This means that the least possible value of *j* is -6, not -7, and the least possible value of *k* is -5, not -6.

The least possible value of *j* + *k* is -6 + -5 = -11.

<u>Radical Equations</u>
(see Algebra chapter, pages 71 – 73)

A **radical equation** includes at least one term containing a variable in a radicand (under the square root sign).

A problem type you may encounter on the SAT:

If $10 + 4\sqrt{x} = 16$, what is the value of *x*?

The approach: **Take the same initial steps for solving a linear equation with a single variable.** Isolate the term containing the variable in the radicand (under the square root sign) on one side of the equation and then divide through the equation by the radicand's coefficient:

$$10 + 4\sqrt{x} = 16$$

$$4\sqrt{x} = 6$$

$$\sqrt{x} = \frac{6}{4} = \frac{3}{2}$$

Now square both sides of the equation to find *x*:

$$\left(\sqrt{x}\right)^2 = \left(\frac{3}{2}\right)^2$$

$$x = \frac{9}{4}$$

Caution: Squaring both sides of an equation containing a radical expression does not always produce equivalent equations! Check all potential solutions in the original equation.

<u>Negative & Fractional Exponents</u>
(see Algebra chapter, pages 77 – 79)

SAT math problems may include expressions with **negative** *or* **fractional exponents** (*examples:* x^{-3} and $16^{\frac{1}{4}}$).

What you may see on the SAT:

$$\text{If } y^{-\frac{3}{2}} = \frac{1}{8}, \text{ what does } y \text{ equal?}$$

The key: Raise each side of the equation to the $\left(-\dfrac{2}{3}\right)$ power, the reciprocal of the existing exponent. This will remove the exponent from the variable term:

$$y^{\left(-\frac{3}{2}\right)\left(-\frac{2}{3}\right)} = \frac{1}{8}^{\left(-\frac{2}{3}\right)}$$

Use your calculator to evaluate $\dfrac{1}{8}^{\left(-\frac{2}{3}\right)}$: $y = \dfrac{1}{8}^{\left(-\frac{2}{3}\right)} = 4$

<u>Function Terms and Notation</u>
(see Algebra chapter, pages 82 – 83)

A **function** is a set of ordered pairs $(x,\ y)$, or $(x,\ f(x))$ such that for every x-value there is exactly one corresponding $f(x)$ or y-value. The **domain** of a function is the set of all of its x-values. The **range** of a function is the set of all of its $f(x)$ or y-values.

Function notation and the coordinate plane: Points in the xy-plane may be specified with function notation. *Example:* $f(3) = 1$ specifies the ordered pair $(3, 1)$.

Tips for identifying a function's domain and range:

- **The domain for almost all functions that appear on the SAT is the set of all real numbers.** There are <u>two exceptions</u> that you might encounter on the SAT for which the domain of the function is **not** the set of all real numbers:

    1. Functions that contain the **square root form of a radical expression.**
       Example: $f(x) = \sqrt{x+5}$

    2. Functions that contain a **rational expression** (the quotient of two polynomials).
       Example: $f(x) = \dfrac{2x+3}{5x-4}$

- **If a function does contain a rational expression, its domain cannot contain any values that will make it "undefined"** (cause the denominator to equal zero). Set the denominator equal to zero to find any restrictions for the domain. For $f(x) = \dfrac{2x+3}{5x-4}$, $5x-4$ cannot equal 0, so x cannot equal $\dfrac{4}{5}$. The domain of this function is, therefore, the set of all real numbers except $\dfrac{4}{5}$.

- **If a function contains the square root form of a radical expression, the domain cannot include any values of x that will yield a negative number in the radicand (under the square root sign).** For the function $f(x) = \sqrt{x+5}$, any number less than -5 will yield a negative value in the radicand. The domain is, therefore, the set of all real numbers greater than or equal to -5.

- **The range of a function includes all values greater than or equal to its minimum y-value and less than or equal to its maximum y-value.** A graphing calculator is very useful in identifying the range of a function.

A problem type you might see on the SAT:

> If a function f is defined as $f(x) = 3x + 2$, and the domain of the function is $-2 \le x \le 4$, what is the range of the function?

Because this is a linear equation, you can substitute the minimum and maximum values of the domain to find the minimum and maximum values of the range:

$$f(-2) = 3(-2) + 2 = -4$$
$$f(4) = 3(4) + 2 = 14$$

The range of f is $-4 \le y \le 14$.

Identifying Graphs of Functions
(see Coordinate Geometry chapter, pages 102 – 105; 109 – 115)

It is essential that you become familiar with the following four functions and their graphs:

1. Linear function: $f(x) = ax + b$
(a and b are real number constants.)
The graph of a linear function is a line. (The graph of a linear inequality is a dotted or solid line with shading above or below the line.)

Example: $f(x) = 2x - 1$

Graphing Calculator Screen:
$f(x) = 2x - 1$

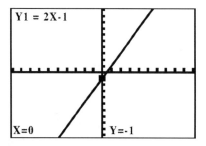

2. Quadratic Function: $f(x) = ax^2 + bx + c$
(a, b, and c are real number constants, and $a \neq 0$.)
The graph of a quadratic function is a parabola.

Example: $f(x) = x^2 + 5$

Graphing Calculator Screen:
$f(x) = x^2 + 5$

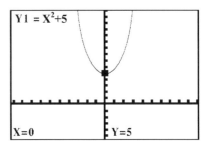

3. Exponential function: $f(x) = a^x$
(a, the base, is a positive real number not equal to 1.)
The graph of an exponential function is an exponential curve. This function is so named because the variable is in the exponent. A quantity grows exponentially when its increase is proportional to an existing amount. Common examples include compound interest accrued by invested principal (e.g., any amount invested at 7% per year annual compound interest will approximately double in 10 years) and population growth (a population that grows at 7% per year will also approximately double in 10 years).

Example: $f(x) = 3^x$

Graphing Calculator Screen:
$f(x) = 3^x$

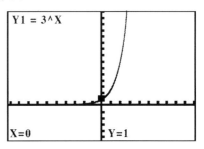

4. Absolute Value Function: $f(x) = |x|$
Its graph resembles a "V."

Example: $f(x) = |x - 2|$

Graphing Calculator Screen:
$f(x) = |x - 2|$

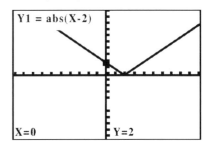

Comparing Graphs of Functions
(see Coordinate Geometry chapter, pages 110 – 111)

You can use your graphing calculator to compare the graphs of functions. Compare the location of each graph's minimum or maximum point, if any.

Compare the orientation of each graph. Most non-linear graphs you encounter will open either upward or downward with respect to the *y*-axis.

Graphing Calculator Screen:
The graph of $f(x) = x^2$ opens upward and the graph of $f(x) = -x^2$ opens downward.

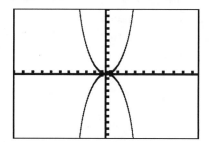

Compare the shape of each graph. Graphs may be dilated (vertically stretched or vertically compressed).

Graphing Calculator Screen:
The inner curve represents $f(x) = x^2$ and the outer curve represents $f(x) = \dfrac{1}{2}x^2$.

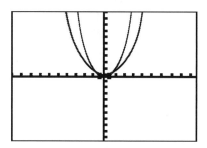

<u>**Slope of a Line**</u>
(see Coordinate Geometry chapter, pages 98 – 101)

If the equation of a line is stated in standard form, you can determine its slope by simple inspection. For any non-vertical line specified by standard form:

$$ax + by + c = 0,$$

The slope of any line when written in standard form $= -\dfrac{a}{b}$.

Example:

The slope of the line represented by the equation $4x - 3y - 6 = 0$ is $\dfrac{4}{3}$.

Any line **parallel** to this line will have the same slope of $\dfrac{4}{3}$.

Any line **perpendicular** to this line will have the negative reciprocal slope of $-\dfrac{3}{4}$.

Finding Midpoint and Distance
(see Coordinate Geometry chapter, pages 105 – 108)

If you are asked to find the distance between two points in a coordinate plane and you cannot remember the distance formula, sketch a right triangle in the margin of your test booklet in which the "hypotenuse" connects the two points and horizontal and vertical "legs" complete the triangle.

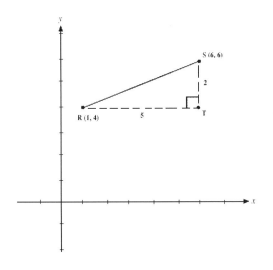

In the figure shown, the segment $\overline{RS}$ is the "hypotenuse" connecting R (1, 4) and S (6, 6). Segment $\overline{ST}$ represents the vertical "leg" and segment $\overline{RT}$ represents the horizontal "leg."

Apply the **Pythagorean Theorem:**

$$5^2 \quad + \quad 2^2 = (\text{distance } RS)^2$$

x units y units

$$29 = (\text{distance } RS)^2 \qquad \sqrt{29} = RS$$

The same sketch can be used to visually determine the **midpoint** of $\overline{RS}$.

The x-coordinate halfway between 1 and 6 is $(1 + 6) \div 2$, or $\dfrac{7}{2}$.

The y-coordinate halfway between 4 and 6 is 5.

The midpoint of $\overline{RS}$ is $(\dfrac{7}{2}, 5)$.

✔ Mathematics Strategy #3:

- ### Calculators and the SAT

Graphing Calculator: A "Must-Have" for the SAT

A graphing calculator will prove very valuable when you take the SAT. The exam includes certain second-year Algebra concepts that can be more quickly and easily solved with a graphing calculator than with a scientific calculator or four-function calculator.

Graphing calculators allow you to input various functions or equations into an equation editor, after which you can evaluate a function at a specified value, graph it, or create a table of *x*- and *y*-values. Because the equation editor allows you to enter and graph several equations at a time, you can compare various graphs. The **table** feature allows you to compare $f(x)$ or *y*-values for different equations at specified *x*-values. The **data editor** can be used to enter a set of data points that are then plotted, revealing the associated graph. **The visual screen provided by a graphing calculator makes it easy to identify domain and range, intersection points, minimum and maximum points, and zeroes of functions.**

Graphing calculators are also very useful and efficient for solving certain non-graphing problems. Graphing calculators are easy to use in working with absolute value expressions, exponents, square roots, cube roots, trigonometry applications, and scientific notation. As with scientific calculators, graphing calculators can change fractions into decimals and vice versa.

It is important that you become proficient with your graphing calculator's operations well in advance of your actual test date. You must also bear in mind that no calculator is going to think for you. You will still have to know how to set up a particular problem and correctly input the data presented. **Any calculator is a tool, not a test taker.**

General Calculator Tips

Be sure to read over the following chart and make certain that your calculator meets specifications for the exam:

CALCULATORS AND THE SAT

Allowed	Not Allowed
Calculators with graphing capabilities	Calculators with "QWERTY" style keypads
Scientific calculators	Noise-making calculators (music, talking, beeping or other noise or sound effects)
Simple four-function (addition, subtraction, multiplication, division) calculators	Electronic "pads" with electronic "pens" or similar devices
	Laptops or mini-computers
	Any device that requires electricity
	Output devices such as printers or paper tapes
	PDAs or pocket organizers

Important tips for calculator success on the SAT:

❑ **Many of the math problems on the SAT do not require the use of a calculator.** Before 1994, calculators were not even allowed on the SAT. Common sense and logical reasoning are more important than any sort of calculator in solving SAT math problems.

❑ **When you approach a math problem, do not just start punching a bunch of numbers into your calculator.** Think the problem through before you perform any calculator operations. You may save yourself needless steps if you think carefully about what the question is asking.

❑ **Make sure you understand your calculator and how it handles the order of operations.** The acronym for the correct order of mathematical operations is "PEMDAS": Parenthetical Terms, Exponential Terms, Multiplication and Division (left to right), Addition and Subtraction (left to right).

❑ **When you use your calculator to perform a series of operations for one problem, use the parenthetical keys on your calculator to appropriately group terms.** This will help your calculator understand the order that you want it to perform operations.

❑ **The SAT does not usually include very many problems that require lengthy calculations.** If you find yourself repeatedly performing extensive calculator operations, you may be on the wrong track.

❑ **Always do "scratch work" in the margins of your test booklet to set problems up and to make notes between calculator steps.** Write down intermediate results.

❑ **Practice with your calculator extensively before exam day.** Make sure you understand all of its features.

❑ **Take two:** Although a graphing calculator is a very valuable tool for the SAT, the exam also presents problems involving simple operations that are sometimes more easily performed by a scientific calculator. The advantageous **[a b/c]** key for entering fractions is found on most scientific calculators but not on graphing calculators. **It is best to be equipped with both a graphing calculator as well as a scientific calculator when you take the SAT**; each type will be better suited to assist you in solving specific SAT math problems quickly and accurately. Additionally, in the event that one of the calculators fails to function properly on exam day, you will have an alternate.

❑ **Be sure to put fresh batteries into your calculator(s) before exam day.**

✔ **Mathematics Strategy #4:**

• **Hints for Success on Grid-In Problems**

The SAT includes a few math problems for which no multiple-choice answers are provided. The following graphic illustrates the components of the answer grid provided for these questions:

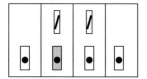

←The top row of the answer grid contains four empty boxes in which to write the numerical answer to a given question.

The appropriate ovals below (containing fraction bars, decimal points and digits) are then darkened to reflect the answer written in the top row of boxes. In this example, the answer 2.01 is correctly entered and gridded.

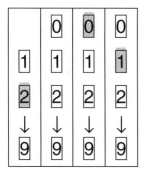

←The second row of the answer grid contains fraction bars.

←The third row contains decimal points.

←The rows of ovals beneath the decimal points contain the digits 0 through 9.

- Any of the four boxes in the top row can contain a single numerical digit; a fraction bar or a decimal point can be entered in specified boxes.

- **The middle two columns of the grid's second row contain ovals featuring fraction bars.** This makes it possible to grid fractions containing up to three total digits in the numerator and denominator combined. The following are examples of fractions that the grid will accommodate:

11/2 (representing $5\frac{1}{2}$)   2/25   4/9

- **The grid's third row has ovals containing decimal points.** The decimal point located in the fourth column is never used. The following are examples of decimals that the grid will accommodate:

.4   .42   .425

GRID-INS: POSSIBLE & IMPOSSIBLE ANSWERS

Possible Answers (Those the Grid Can Accommodate)	Impossible Answers (Those the Grid Cannot Accommodate)
Any number between .001 and 9,999	Any number larger than 9,999 or smaller than .001
Positive numbers or zero	Negative numbers
Whole numbers, fractions or decimals	Answers that include variables

Answers that do not occupy the entire four spaces can be entered in any position in the answer grid.

.34 can be entered as:

or

5/7 can be entered as:

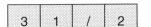

or

Mixed fractions cannot be entered directly. $3\frac{1}{2}$ **cannot be entered as:**

The scanner would read the answer immediately above as $\frac{31}{2}$, or $15\frac{1}{2}$. $3\frac{1}{2}$ must be entered as the improper fraction 7/2 or as the decimal 3.5:

| 7 | / | 2 | |

| 3 | . | 5 | |

or

or

| | 7 | / | 2 |

| | 3 | . | 5 |

Study the following chart to understand specific rules regarding entering answers correctly into the answer grid.

GRID-IN RESPONSE GUIDE

Answer Type	Tip	Answer to Problem	Correctly Gridded	Incorrectly Gridded
Mixed Fraction	Do not grid as a mixed fraction.	$3\frac{1}{2}$	3.5 7/2	31/2
Simple Fraction	If the fraction is a repeating decimal, the answer may be entered as a fraction or as a decimal. Decimal answers must be entered to occupy all available boxes.	$\frac{2}{3}$	2/3 .666 .667	.6 .66 .67
Non-terminating Decimal	Do not truncate the decimal prematurely. Do not make a rounding error.	.8574111...	.857	.8 .85 .858
Percents	Do not convert the percent to a decimal.	85%	85	.85
Dollar amounts	Do not enter dollars as cents or vice versa.	$3.46	3.46	346
A range of numbers	Grid in one possible answer. Correctly interpret inequality signs.	$\frac{1}{2} < x < \frac{3}{4}$	.51 .6 .7	.5 .75 (The inequality is a "less than" sign, not a "less than or equal to" sign. The number must be *between* .5 and .75)

GRID-IN SUMMARY

1. **Change mixed fractions into improper fractions or decimals.**
2. **If the answer is a repeating or non-terminating decimal, put a decimal point in the far left box and then fill in all three remaining boxes with digits.** Do not truncate the decimal prematurely after one or two digits.
3. **You do not have to round lengthy decimal answers.** Simply truncate decimals after the third digit.
4. The grid does not include dollar or percent signs. Grid these answers without the corresponding sign.
5. **Be sure to fill in the oval that corresponds with the number above it.** The scanner does not read the numbers you write in the boxes – only the bubbled ovals below them.
6. **Make sure that you fill in only one oval per column.** No double bubbles!
7. **Be neat and be bold.** Fill in ovals neatly and completely. Use dark pencil. No scruffy bubbles!
8. It is unnecessary to put implied zeroes in a decimal number. For example, grid .4, not 0.4 or 0.40.
9. **There is no guessing penalty for grid-in problems.** If you have no idea what the answer is, take your best educated guess.
10. If the answer to a problem falls within a range or is one of multiple possibilities, correctly grid in just one of the possible answers.

✓ **Mathematics Strategy #5:**

• **Avoid "The Lights of Las Vegas"**
  (Attractive but Incorrect Answer Choices)

When you drive into Las Vegas, each hotel's display of bright, flashing lights competes for your attention. "Come in here," the neon lights blink. "Lose your money here," they wink. Those are the "Lights of Las Vegas," the tantalizing visual display used by a hotel to lure you into its casino instead of one of the others. The brighter its lights, the more apt you are to end up inside.

Evidently the folks who write SAT questions have been to Las Vegas and have noticed the competing neon light displays, because they have applied the same principle to SAT answer choices. **The test writers put attention-grabbing answer choices – often in (A), sometimes in other choices – that they think you will be tempted to choose.** "Lose your points here," choice (A) screams out. It is a fine-looking answer choice. But in actuality, it can be a mirage. It can be (and often is) incorrect! Here is a perfect example:

> The boys in a chemistry class averaged 80% on a recent test. The girls in the
> class averaged 90% on the same test. If there are 10 boys and 15 girls enrolled
> in the class, what was the class average?
>
> (A)   85%
> (B)   86%
> (C)   87%
> (D)   88%
> (E)   90%

Do you see the "Lights of Las Vegas" in answer choice (A)? 85% is a very, very attractive looking answer for this problem, because it is the simple average of 80% and 90%. But this problem presents a *weighted* average in which there are more girls than boys, and the answer actually turns out to be 86%, or (B).

Many SAT math questions are written in such a way as to trick students into selecting answer choices that look good – but are absolutely wrong! Here are some tips for avoiding the "Lights of Las Vegas" on the SAT:

1. **Any time you select (A) as an answer for a math question, be sure to double-check the other choices.** (A) is the first choice you see, and if you are in a hurry or are not sure how to do the problem, you might fall for a wrong answer.

2. **Be suspicious of numbers repeated from the problem.** In the weighted average question above, choice (E) contains 90%, a number that was used in the problem. Numbers that appear in the problem look familiar and can serve as attention-getting (but incorrect) answer choices.

3. **Calculate carefully and perform operations in the correct order.** Watch for wrong answers you would get if you made calculation errors or if you performed the operations in the wrong order.

✔ **Mathematics Strategy #6:**

• **"Paint by Numbers"**
(Substitute Numbers for Variables in the Answer Choices)

Many SAT math problems contain complex algebraic expressions as answer choices. These answer choices are too abstract to grasp. For these problems, it is best to utilize a time-honored strategy that we'll call "Paint by Numbers." To use this method, **replace the variables with easy-to-use numbers and calculate a result; then substitute these same numbers into the algebraic expressions in the answer choices and look for a match.**

Be sure to assign user-friendly integers to represent the variables in the problem. Good small numbers to use are 2, 3, 4, 5, and 10. Good large numbers to use are typically 20 or 25 as well as their multiples (50, 100 or 200). Avoid choosing prime numbers over 10, such as 13, 17, 19 or 23. Generally speaking, it is also best not to select 0 or 1, as these numbers have special properties that can skew the results. *Example*:

> At Camp Caitlin, s cans of soup are needed to serve lunch to c campers for d days. If 15 campers do not attend the camp, for how many days will s cans of soup provide lunch for the campers?
>
> (A) $s(c - 15)$
>
> (B) $\dfrac{cs}{c - 15}$
>
> (C) $\dfrac{cs}{15}$
>
> (D) $\dfrac{c - 15}{s}$
>
> (E) $\dfrac{s}{c - 15}$

Assume there are 200 cans of soup that will feed 25 campers lunch for 8 days. Those are good numbers to use, because that means that one can of soup is used per camper per day. If 15 campers do not attend, then there would be only 10 campers present. 200 cans of soup would provide lunch for those 10 campers for 20 days, so the MAGIC NUMBER to look for when these numerical values are substituted into the answer choices is 20. Replace s with 200 and c with 25 in the answer choices to find out which choice produces 20:

> (A) $200(25 - 15) = 2{,}000$
>
> (B) $\dfrac{25 \cdot 200}{25 - 15} = 500$
>
> (C) $\dfrac{25 \cdot 200}{15} = 333.\overline{3}$
>
> (D) $\dfrac{25 - 15}{200} = \dfrac{1}{20}$
>
> (E) $\dfrac{200}{25 - 15} = 20$ *(THIS IS THE ANSWER)*

→**Success Strategy**←

With "Paint by Numbers," it is important to try every answer choice to make sure that there are not two different choices that produce a correct result. If that happens, re-assign numbers to the variables in the remaining answer choices and work through the problem again!

PRACTICE: "PAINT BY NUMBERS"

The St. Claire library charges $.50 a day the first day a library book is overdue and $.10 a day thereafter. What will the charge be if a book is turned in d days late?

(A) $.10d + .50$

(B) $.50d + .10$

(C) $.50 + .10(d - 1)$

(D) $.10 + .50(d - 1)$

(E) $d(d + .10) + .50$

Solution:

"Paint by Numbers": Assign a number for d and figure out what the late charges would be for that number of days. Assume that the book is 5 days late. The late charges would be .50 for the first day and $4 \cdot .10$ for the remaining days. This makes a total fine of .90.

In each answer choice (A) – (E), replace d with 5 to see which choice produces .90:

(A) $.10(5) + .50 = 1.00$

(B) $.50(5) + .10 = 2.60$

(C) $.50 + .10(5 - 1) = .90$ *(THE ANSWER)*

(D) $.10 + .50(5 - 1) = 2.10$

(E) $5(5 + .10) + .50 = 26.00$

"Paint by Numbers" is an excellent strategy for solving certain math problems such as the following question regarding exponential growth.

PRACTICE: "PAINT BY NUMBERS"

A financial investment doubled in value every six years. If the initial investment was $1,000, what was its value after t years?

(A) $1000 \cdot 2^{6t}$

(B) $1000 \cdot 6^{t-1}$

(C) $1000 \cdot 2^{\frac{6}{t}}$

(D) $1000 \cdot 2^{\frac{t}{6}}$

(E) $1000 \cdot 6^{\frac{t}{6}}$

Solution:

"Paint by Numbers:" Assign a number for t and determine what the value of the investment will be at the end of that many years. Let $t = 24$ years, a multiple of the 6 year increments by which the investment doubles.

Year	Value
Beginning	$1,000
6 years later	$2,000
12 years later	$4,000
18 years later	$8,000
24 years later	$16,000

Now substitute 24 for t in each answer choice and find the choice that simplifies to 16,000:

(A) $1000 \cdot 2^{(6 \cdot 24)} = 2.2 \cdot 10^{46}$

(B) $1000 \cdot 6^{(24-1)} = 7.9 \cdot 10^{20}$

(C) $1000 \cdot 2^{\frac{6}{24}} = 1,189.2$

(D) $1000 \cdot 2^{\frac{24}{6}} = 16,000$ *(THE ANSWER)*

(E) $1000 \cdot 6^{\frac{24}{6}} = 1,296,000$

✓ **Mathematics Strategy #7:**

- **"Throw it in Reverse"**
  (Solve Backwards)

Many word problems on the SAT can be solved by using the math strategy "Throw it in Reverse" – by testing each answer choice to find the one that works. This strategy works very well on challenging word problems or "brain teasers" that offer integers as answer choices.

Because the answer choices for most SAT math problems are usually arranged in increasing order from (A) – (E), it is usually best to start with answer choice (C) when you "Throw it in Reverse." If (C) does not work, it is important to decide if the value in choice (C) was too large or too small. If choice (C) turns out to be too big, then try (B). If choice (B) is still too big, then try (A). If, on the other hand, choice (C) turns out to be too small, then try choice (D). If choice (D) is still too small, then try (E). By testing the answer choices in this sequence [(C) → (E) or (C) → (A)], you will not have to try more than three answer choices!

Example:

> Andrew is currently twice Nicole's age. Five years ago, he was three times her age then. What is Nicole's current age?
>
> (A)   5
> (B)   10
> (C)   15
> (D)   20
> (E)   25

First try the value in answer choice (C) to determine if it works:

(C)   15   If Nicole's current age were 15, then Andrew's current age would be 30. This means that 5 years ago, Nicole would have been 10 and Andrew would have been 25. Because 25 is not three times 10, choice (C) is not the answer. We can conclude that 15 is TOO BIG to be Nicole's current age in comparison to Andrew's, because 25 is <u>less</u> than 3 times the age Nicole would have been 5 years ago. This means that we should try a SMALLER ANSWER CHOICE, so we will proceed to (B).

(B)   10   If Nicole were currently 10 years old, then Andrew would be 20. Five years ago Nicole would have been 5 years old and Andrew would have been 15, or three times her age. THIS IS THE ANSWER!

> *Note that only two answer choices were actually tested because it was possible to determine that choice (C) was TOO BIG. If choice (B) had also been TOO BIG, we would have known by default that the answer was (A)!*

"Throw it in Reverse" is a good approach for many math problem types, including the following linear inequality.

PRACTICE: "THROW IT IN REVERSE"

Given the inequality $3x - 4y > 2$, which of the following ordered pairs (x, y) is included in the solution set?

(A)   (0, 0)

(B)   (-3, -2)

(C) $(0, -\frac{1}{2})$

(D)   (5, -1)

(E)   (-7, 1)

"Throw it in Reverse." In this case, it does not matter which choice you begin with, as choices (A) through (E) do not present a set of increasing (or decreasing) values. Substituting each answer choice back into the original inequality reveals that choice (D) contains the only ordered pair that works: $3(5) - 4(-1) > 2$.

✓ Mathematics Strategy #8:

• Eliminating Obviously Wrong Answers

On many SAT multiple-choice math questions, there are answers that are so unreasonable (or even inconceivable) that they can be eliminated from consideration. Common sense can assist you in ruling out answer choices containing numbers that are clearly too large or too small.

Example:

Five goats at a county fair weigh 67, 52, 36, 49 and 71 pounds. What is their average weight?

(A)   31 pounds
(B)   48 pounds
(C)   55 pounds
(D)   69 pounds
(E)   79 pounds

The average of any set of numbers must fall within the actual range of the numbers; this means that the answer to this problem must be between 36 and 71. Choices (A) and (E) can be eliminated. Further, choice (D) is probably too large; four of the numbers listed are smaller than 69 and only one is slightly larger. If you were not sure how to do this problem, you should guess either (B) or (C).

If answer choices contain radicals, it may be helpful to convert them into rational number approximations. This will make it easier to identify unreasonable answers. For example, if an answer choice contains $5\sqrt{3}$, multiply 5 by the approximate value of $\sqrt{3}$, which is 1.732, to obtain the more comprehensible number 8.66 or 8.7.

✓ **Mathematics Strategy #9:**

• **Guesstimating**

Many SAT geometry problems lend themselves to estimating and approximating techniques.

⇨ **Some figures in geometry problems are drawn to scale.** Unless there is a disclaimer indicating that a figure is not drawn to scale, unknown lengths and angle sizes in polygons can often be approximated by comparing them with specified lengths and angles sizes.

⇨ **If the lengths of two sides of a triangle are provided, the third length must be between the sum and the difference of the lengths of the known sides.** *Example*: If two of a triangle's sides are 6 and 10, the third side must be between 4 *(or 10 – 6)* and 16 *(or 10 + 6).*

⇨ **Study the chart below to become familiar with the sizes of commonly encountered angles.** Apply this knowledge when approximating the sizes of other angles.

COMMON ANGLES AND THEIR SIZES

Angle	Angle Size
30°	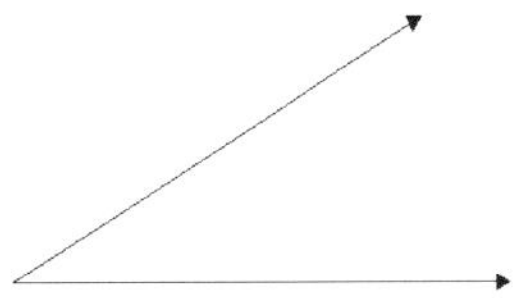
45°	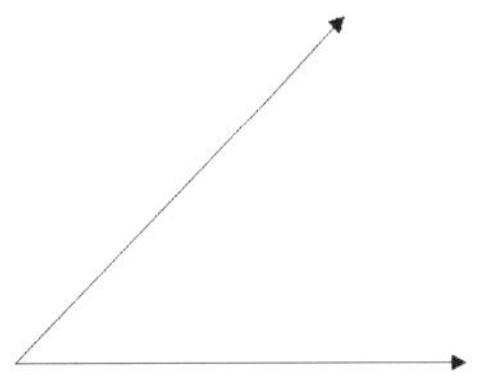
60°	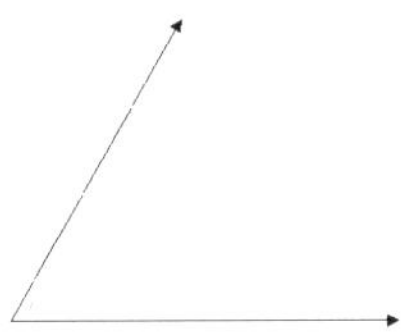

Angle	Angle Size
90°	
180°	

⇨ **π equals approximately 3.14.** For the purposes of the estimating, the area of any circle is about 3 times the square of its radius and a circle's circumference is about 6 times its radius.

⇨ **In order to find the "shaded region" (partial area) of a triangle, parallelogram, or circle,** you can sometimes draw equal subdivisions (wedges or triangles) within the figure to assist in finding the shaded area.

Example:

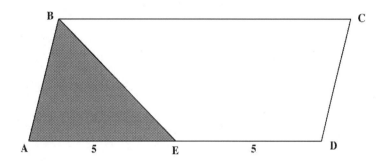

The area of parallelogram $ABCD = 40$, E is the midpoint of $\overline{AD}$ and $AE = 5$. What is the area of the shaded region?

The problem is asking for the area of a shaded region within a parallelogram of known area. Because E is the midpoint of $\overline{AD}$, triangles of equal size can be drawn within the parallelogram, dividing it into four equal parts:

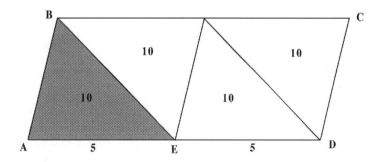

The four triangles shown in the figure above have equal areas, so the area of the shaded region (ΔABE) is 10.

Mathematics
Chapter 2
Arithmetic & Basic SAT Math

1. Sets

2. Number Properties & Operations

3. Scientific Notation & Place Value

4. Prime Numbers, Factors & Divisibility

5. Fractions

6. Ratio & Proportion

7. Percents

8. Averages

9. Measurement Conversions

ARITHMETIC TOPIC #1:
SETS

> A **set** is a group or collection of numbers or other items usually listed within braces. For example, the set of integers may be represented as follows: $\{...-3, -2, -1, 0, 1, 2, 3...\}$

> Any item in a set is referred to as an **element** or member of the set. The symbol for element is "$\in$." $-3 \in \{...-3, -2, -1, 0, 1, 2, 3...\}$

> A portion of a set, or two or more elements of a set, is called a **subset.** The symbols used to represent subset are "$\subset$" or "$\subseteq$." $\{0, 1, 2\} \subset \{...-3, -2, -1, 0, 1, 2, 3...\}$

> The elements that two different sets share or have in common is referred to as the **intersection** of those sets. The symbol for intersection is "$\cap$." $\{3, 4, 5, 6\} \cap \{1, 3, 5, 7\} = \{3, 5\}$

> The combined elements of two sets is called the **union** of those sets. The symbol for union is "$\cup$." $\{\text{Even Integers}\} \cup \{\text{Odd Integers}\} = \{\text{All Integers}\}$

> The **empty set** refers to the one set containing no elements. The empty set can be noted in two ways: $\{ \ \}$ or $\varnothing$

SAT PRACTICE: SETS

$A = \{-7, -4, -3, -1, 0, 1, 2, 4\}$
$B = \{-4, -2, 2, 5\}$
$C = \{-4, 3, 5\}$

With respect to the three sets specified above, how many elements are contained in $(A \cap B) \cup C$?

(A)   2
(B)   3
(C)   4
(D)   5
(E)   6

Solution:

$(A \cap B) = \{-7, -4, -3, -1, 0, 1, 2, 4\} \cap \{-4, -2, 2, 5\} = \{-4, 2\}$

$$(A \cap B) \qquad \cup \qquad \qquad C$$
$$\downarrow \qquad\qquad\qquad\qquad \downarrow$$
$$\{-4, 2\} \qquad \cup \qquad \{-4, 3, 5\} = \{-4, 2, 3, 5\}$$

There are four elements in the final result, so the answer is (C).

ARITHMETIC TOPIC #2
NUMBER PROPERTIES & OPERATIONS

The word "integer" has a Latin etymology that traces back to 1508. It originally meant "whole" or "complete." The use of the word as a noun meaning "a whole number" (as opposed to a fraction) was first recorded in 1571.

Number Properties & Operations: Basic Definitions

An **integer** is a member of the set of positive whole numbers {1, 2, 3, . . . }, negative whole numbers {. . . -3, -2, -1}, and zero {0}.

A **rational number** is a number that can be expressed as a ratio *a/b*, in which *a* and *b* are integers and $b \neq 0$.

Examples: 7.2 $\dfrac{1}{2}$ $-3\dfrac{2}{11}$

An **irrational number** is a number that cannot be written as the ratio of two integers.

Examples: $\sqrt{3}$ π

The set of **real numbers** is the union of the set of rational numbers and the set of irrational numbers.

Order of Operations: In order to correctly simplify a mathematical expression, a specific order of operations must be followed. "PEMDAS" is an acronym for the correct order of operations: **P**arentheses, **E**xponents, **M**ultiplication and **D**ivision (in order from left to right), **A**ddition and **S**ubtraction (in order from left to right).

Example: Simplify: $12 \div 6 + 3^2(9 - 5) - 3 \cdot 2$

- Simplify within **P**arentheses: $12 \div 6 + 3^2(4) - 3 \cdot 2$
- Apply **E**xponents: $12 \div 6 + 9(4) - 3 \cdot 2$
- **M**ultiplication and **D**ivision, in order from left to right: $2 + 36 - 6$
- **A**ddition and **S**ubtraction, in order from left to right: 32

Number line: The number line is used to express units of distance in both a positive and negative direction. To find the **distance between two points**, either count the spaces between them or subtract one of the coordinates (numbers) from the other. The absolute value of this number will equal the distance between the two points.

Example:

The distance between points *A* and *B* on the number line above is $|-7 - 5| = 12$.

To determine the **midpoint** between two points on a number line, add the two coordinates and divide by 2. The coordinates of the midpoint of $\overline{AB}$ on the number line above is $(-7 + 5) \div 2 = -1$.

Operations with Signed Numbers

OPERATION	THE CORRECT APPROACH	EXAMPLES:
Addition (Both numbers have the **same sign**).	Ignore the signs associated with each number and add the number parts. The answer will keep the sign associated with the original numbers.	$(+3) + (+4) = +7$ $(-3) + (-4) = (-7)$ *In each case, the initial operation is 3 + 4 = 7. The correct sign is then applied to the answer.*
Addition (The two numbers have **different signs**).	Ignore the signs associated with each number and subtract the smaller number from the larger. Keep the sign of the number with the larger absolute value (additive inverse).	$(+10) + (-2) = +8$ $(-10) + (+2) = -8$ *In each case, the initial operation is 10 – 2 = 8. The correct sign is then applied to the answer.*
Subtraction	Subtracting a positive number is the same as adding a negative number. Subtracting a negative number is the same as adding a positive number.	$(-9) - (+5)$ becomes $(-9) + (-5) = -14$ $(+13) - (-7)$ becomes $(+13) + (+7) = 20$
Multiplication & Division	If all factors are positive, the answer is positive. If an even number of the factors is negative, the answer is positive. If an odd number of the factors is negative, the answer is negative.	$(+2)(+3)(+4) = +24$ $(+24) \div (+6) = +4$ $(+7)(-3)(-2) = +42$ $(-42) \div (-6) = +7$ $(+4)(-5)(-3)(-2) = -120$ $(-18) \div (+2) = -9$

SAT PRACTICE: NUMBER PROPERTIES & OPERATIONS

For any real number *x,* which of the following are true?

I. $x > x - 1$

II. $x^2 > x$

III. $x > \dfrac{1}{x}$

(A)   I only
(B)   I and II
(C)   I and III
(D)   II and III
(E)   I, II & III

Solution:

Consider each of the statements I, II and III.

I. $x > x - 1$ Any real number x will be greater than $x - 1$. Statement I is TRUE.

II. $x^2 > x$ This is one of the SAT writers' favorite traps. x^2 is greater than x when x is greater than 1 or when x is negative. But the squares of fractions between 0 and 1 are always smaller than the original numbers, and the squares of 0 and 1 are equal to the original numbers. Statement II is FALSE.

III. $x > \dfrac{1}{x}$ This inequality is not true if x is a fraction between 0 and 1 or if x is less than or equal to -1. Statement III is FALSE.

Because only statement I is true, the answer is (A).

SAT PRACTICE: NUMBER PROPERTIES & OPERATIONS (COUNTING CONSECUTIVE INTEGERS)

Consecutively numbered raffle tickets were sold at the county fair. The first ticket on the roll was number 22. If 356 tickets were sold, what was the number of the last ticket purchased?

(A)   334
(B)   335
(C)   356
(D)   377
(E)   378

Solution:

(Last ticket #) – (1ˢᵗ ticket #) + 1 = # tickets sold
       ↓   ↓   ↓   ↓
       x –   22   + 1 =   356

$x = 377$
The answer is (D).

> **→Success Strategy←**
>
> To count consecutive integers inclusively, subtract the smaller number from the larger and then add 1. It is easy to discern this pattern by simply counting with small numbers. *Example:* How many tickets on a roll are numbered 2 through 6? *The tickets that are numbered 2, 3, 4, 5, and 6, or 5 tickets, which is the same result as* (6 – 2) + 1 = 5

ARITHMETIC TOPIC #3
SCIENTIFIC NOTATION & PLACE VALUE

When **scientific notation** is used, numbers are expressed using powers of the base number 10.

Examples:

$3.25 \times 10^4 = 32{,}500$ (decimal is moved 4 places to the right)

$4.638 \times 10^{-5} = .00004638$ (decimal is moved 5 places to the left and zeroes are added as placeholders)

SAT questions may ask also you about the **place value** of various digits in a specified number. Remember that units to the right of the decimal point end in **-th**.

SAT PRACTICE: SCIENTIFIC NOTATION & PLACE VALUE (SCIENTIFIC NOTATION)

$(5 \cdot 10^4) + (2.2 \cdot 10^2) + (4.5 \cdot 10^{-3}) =$

(A)   5,202.245
(B)   50,022.045
(C)   50,220.045
(D)   50,220.0045
(E)   50,022.0045

Solution:

Expand the individual terms and add them up! *Use your calculator's scientific notation keys to perform these operations quickly and accurately.*

$$5 \cdot 10^4 \;=\; 50,000$$
$$2.2 \cdot 10^2 \;=\; 220$$
$$4.5 \cdot 10^{-3} \;=\; \underline{\quad .0045}$$
$$50,220.0045$$

The answer is (D).

> →SUCCESS STRATEGY←
>
> Your graphing or scientific calculator can be used to easily solve problems regarding scientific notation. On a graphing calculator, press **[MODE]** and select **[Sci]**. On a scientific calculator, simply use the **[EE]** key.

SAT PRACTICE: SCIENTIFIC NOTATION & PLACE VALUE (PLACE VALUE)

In which of the following numbers is the digit 9 found in both the thousandths place and the hundreds place?

(A)   9,494.9494
(B)   4,949.4949
(C)   9,449.4994
(D)   4,994.4994
(E)   9,999.4444

Solution:

Underline the thousandths place and the hundreds place in each answer choice. Remember not to confuse "thousandths" with "thousands". The only answer choice that has a 9 in both the hundreds and the thousandths place is (D).

ARITHMETIC TOPIC #4
PRIME NUMBERS, FACTORS & DIVISIBILITY

The 17th century French philosopher and mathematician Marin Mersenne met and corresponded with other eminent mathematicians of the time and played a significant role in disseminating mathematical knowledge throughout Europe at a time when scientific journals had not yet been established. Mersenne was intrigued by prime numbers of the following form:

$$2^p - 1, (p \text{ is prime})$$

For example, $2^5 - 1 = 31$, which is prime. Today we refer to prime numbers of this form as "Mersenne Primes." Mersenne Primes include the numbers 3, 7, 31 and 127.

Prime Numbers, Factors & Divisibility

A **prime number** is a positive integer greater than 1 that has no positive integer divisors other than 1 and itself. The following are the prime numbers between 1 and 20:

2, 3, 5, 7, 11, 13, 17, 19

A **composite number** is a positive integer other than 1 that is not a prime number.

To determine the **prime factorization** of a number, break it down into factors until all of the factors are prime. For example, to find the prime factorization of 60, you could start by finding any two numbers whose product is 60, such as 4 and 15. Then you would further break down these factors into their prime factors:

$$4 = 2 \cdot 2 \text{ and } 15 = 3 \cdot 5$$

So the prime factorization of $60 = 2^2 \cdot 3 \cdot 5$

Factors of a Number: All of the numbers (both positive and negative) that divide evenly (without remainders) into another number are called the "factors" of that number. For example, the factors of 36 are as follows: $\pm 1, \pm 2, \pm 3, \pm 4, \pm 6, \pm 9, \pm 12, \pm 18$ and ± 36.

DIVISIBILITY GUIDE

Factor	Description of Numbers that the Factor Will Divide Into Evenly
2	Even numbers (those that end in 0, 2, 4, 6 or 8).
3	The sum of the number's digits is divisible by 3. *Example:* 34,725 is divisible by 3 because 3 + 4 + 7 + 2 + 5 = 21, and 21 is divisible by 3.
4	The number's last two digits form a number that is divisible by 4. *Example:* 67,936 is divisible by 4 because its last two digits form a number (36) that is divisible by 4.
5	The number ends in 5 or 0.
6	The number is even and is also divisible by 3.
9	The sum of the number's digits is divisible by 9. *Example:* 14,985 is divisible by 9 because 1 + 4 + 9 + 8 + 5 = 27, and 27 is divisible by 9.
10	The number ends in 0.

The **Greatest Common Factor (GCF)** is the largest integer that divides without a remainder into a set of two or more integers. To find the Greatest Common Factor of two numbers, list the prime factors of each number and then multiply the factors that both numbers have in common. If there are no common prime factors, the GCF is 1.

Example: Find the Greatest Common Factor of 30 and 42.

$$30 = 2 \cdot 3 \cdot 5$$

$$42 = 2 \cdot 3 \cdot 7$$

The common prime factors are 2 and 3, so the GCF of 30 and 42 is $2 \cdot 3 = 6$.

The **Least Common Multiple (LCM)** is the smallest number that two or more numbers will divide into evenly. To find the Least Common Multiple of two numbers, first find their Greatest Common Factor. Multiply the two numbers and then divide their product by their Greatest Common Factor.

Example: Find the Least Common Multiple of 30 and 42.

As shown above, the GCF for 30 and 42 is 6:

$(30 \cdot 42) \div 6 = 210$, so 210 is the Least Common Multiple of 30 and 42.

Note: You may use a graphing calculator to find the GCF or LCM directly. These operations are found in the **[NUM]** subdirectory of the **[MATH]** key menu.

SAT PRACTICE: PRIME NUMBERS, FACTORS & DIVISIBILITY

Which of the following is NOT a factor of $10q$ if q is a prime number greater than 5?

(A) $2q$
(B) $5q$
(C)   10
(D)   5
(E) q^2

Solution:

Factor $10q$: $10q = 2 \cdot 5 \cdot q$

The factors of $10q$ are $\pm q$, ± 2, ± 5, ± 10, $\pm 2q$, $\pm 5q$ and $\pm 10q$. The only answer choice not listed as a factor is q^2. The answer is (E).

SAT PRACTICE: PRIME NUMBERS, FACTORS & DIVISIBILITY

Let A be the set of distinct positive factors of 48 and B be the set of distinct positive factors of 60. The number of distinct positive factors found in both sets A and B (factors in common) is:

(A)   3
(B)   4
(C)   5
(D)   6
(E)   7

Solution:

Identify the positive factors of each number:
    The following are the positive factors of 48: 1, 2, 3, 4, 6, 8, 12, 16, 24 and 48
    The following are the positive factors of 60: 1, 2, 3, 4, 5, 6, 10, 12, 15, 20, 30 and 60
    There are 6 common positive factors for 48 and 60: 1, 2, 3, 4, 6, and 12
The answer is (D).

SAT PRACTICE: PRIME NUMBERS, FACTORS & DIVISIBILITY

An integer J is divisible by 2, 3 and 5. If $K = J + 10$, then which of the following must be true?

        I. K is divisible by 2
        II. K is divisible by 10
        III. K is divisible by 15

(A)   I only
(B)   II only
(C)   III only
(D)   I and II
(E)   I, II & III

Solution:

If *J* is divisible by 2, 3 and 5, then it follows that *J* is a multiple of $2 \cdot 3 \cdot 5$, or 30.
So *J* is a multiple of 30 (such as 60, 90, 120…).

To find possible values of *K*, add 10 to possible values for *J* (multiples of 30):

Now consider each of the statements I, II and III with respect to the values for *K* established in the table above.

Value of *J*	Corresponding Value of *K* (*J* + 10)
30	40
60	70
90	100
120	130

I.   40, 70, 100 and 130 are all divisible by 2. Statement I appears to be TRUE.
II.   40, 70, 100 and 130 are all divisible by 10. Statement II appears to be TRUE.
III.   40, 70, 100 and 130 are not divisible by 15. Statement III is FALSE.

Because both statements I and II appear to be true and statement III is false, choose (D).

SAT PRACTICE: PRIME NUMBERS, FACTORS & DIVISIBILITY (DIVISIBIILITY VARIANT: REMAINDERS)

When an integer *m* is divided by 6, the remainder is 2. What is the remainder when 5*m* is divided by 6?

(A)   1
(B)   3
(C)   4
(D)   5
(E)   6

Solution:

Pick a number for *m*. Because dividing *m* by 6 leaves a remainder of 2, choose any multiple of 6 and add 2. 6 is the smallest multiple of 6 and the easiest to use:

$6 + 2 = 8$. Let $m = 8$.
$5m = 5 \cdot 8 = 40$
$40 \div 6 = 6$ remainder 4 (because $6 \cdot 6 = 36$ and $36 + 4 = 40$).

The answer is (C).

ARITHMETIC TOPIC #5
FRACTIONS

→ SUCCESS STRATEGY ←

For operations with fractions, your calculator may speed the process and insure accuracy.

Scientific Calculator

- Use the **[a b/c]** key to enter fractions.

    To enter $5\frac{1}{2}$, press **5 [a b/c] 1 [a b/c] 2** .

- Press the **[=]** to reduce any entered fractions.
- Press **[2ⁿᵈ] [a b/c]** to change mixed numbers into improper fractions and vice versa.
- Press **[2ⁿᵈ] [←]** to change fractions into decimals and vice versa.

Graphing Calculator

- Enter fractions using the parentheses and division keys.

    For example, to enter $\frac{1}{4}$, press **(1 ÷ 4).**

Once a decimal answer is displayed, press **[MATH]**, select **1:> Frac** and press **[ENTER]**. This will change a decimal answer to a fraction.

Fraction Basics
(Remember that you can use your calculator to perform all of these operations!)

Adding or Subtracting Fractions	Find equivalent fractions with a common denominator, then add or subtract the numerators.	$\dfrac{5}{8}+\dfrac{1}{12}=\dfrac{15}{24}+\dfrac{2}{24}=\dfrac{15+2}{24}=\dfrac{17}{24}$
Multiplying Fractions	Multiply the numerators and then multiply the denominators. (Before you multiply, you can cancel any common factors in the numerators and denominators.)	$\dfrac{2}{3}\bullet\dfrac{4}{7}=\dfrac{2\bullet 4}{3\bullet 7}=\dfrac{8}{21}$ $\dfrac{1}{\not{2}}\bullet\dfrac{\not{2}}{\not{3}}\bullet\dfrac{\not{3}}{\not{4}}\bullet\dfrac{\not{4}}{5}=\dfrac{1}{5}$
Dividing Fractions	Invert the second fraction and multiply.	$\dfrac{1}{4}\div\dfrac{2}{7}=\dfrac{1}{4}\bullet\dfrac{7}{2}=\dfrac{1\bullet 7}{4\bullet 2}=\dfrac{7}{8}$
Reducing Fractions	Factor the numerator and the denominator. Cancel out the Greatest Common Factor.	$\dfrac{12}{18}=\dfrac{2\bullet\not{6}}{3\bullet\not{6}}=\dfrac{2}{3}$

Changing a Mixed Number to an Improper Fraction	Multiply the whole number by the denominator, add the numerator, and place this result over the denominator.	$3\dfrac{2}{5} = \dfrac{(5\cdot 3)+2}{5} = \dfrac{17}{5}$
Finding a Reciprocal	Obtain the reciprocal (multiplicative inverse) of a fraction by switching the numerator and the denominator. The product of reciprocals equals 1.	The reciprocal of $\dfrac{2}{5}$ is $\dfrac{5}{2}$. The reciprocal of $-1\dfrac{1}{3}$ is $-\dfrac{3}{4}$.
Comparing Fractions	To determine whether one fraction is greater than, less than, or equal to another fraction, turn both fractions into decimals and make the comparison. Use your calculator!	Compare $\dfrac{2}{7}$ and $\dfrac{1}{4}$. $\dfrac{2}{7}$ $\qquad$ $\dfrac{1}{4}$ $\downarrow$ $\qquad$ $\downarrow$ $.286 > .25$
Converting Fractions to Decimals and Percents	To change a fraction to a decimal, divide the numerator by the denominator. Turn the decimal into a percent by moving the decimal two places to the right and adding the percent sign.	$\dfrac{3}{8} = 3 \div 8 = .375$ $.375 = 37.5\%$

SAT PRACTICE: FRACTIONS (ADDITION & SUBTRACTION)

In the equation $\dfrac{3}{2} - \dfrac{y}{9} = \dfrac{7}{6}$, y equals:

(A) -6
(B) -3
(C) -2
(D)   3
(E)   6

Solution:

$-\dfrac{y}{9} = \dfrac{7}{6} - \dfrac{3}{2}$ $\qquad\qquad$ ← Isolate the variable term

$-\dfrac{y}{9} = -\dfrac{1}{3}$ $\qquad\qquad$ ← Simplify

Now cross multiply and solve for *y*:

$$-3y = -9$$
$$y = 3$$

The answer is (D).

Note: You could also "Throw it in Reverse" and work backwards from the answer choices!

SAT PRACTICE: FRACTIONS (MULTIPLICATION & DIVISION)

For any real number *x*, *x* divided by $\dfrac{3}{5}$ and then multiplied by $\dfrac{2}{5}$ equals:

(A)   *x* divided by $\dfrac{2}{3}$

(B)   *x* divided by $\dfrac{1}{5}$

(C)   *x* multiplied by $\dfrac{2}{3}$

(D)   *x* multiplied by $\dfrac{3}{2}$

(E)   *x* multiplied by $\dfrac{6}{5}$

Solution:

Perform each operation as indicated:

$$x \div \frac{3}{5} = x \bullet \frac{5}{3} = \frac{5}{3}x \qquad \frac{2}{5} \bullet \frac{5}{3}x = \frac{10}{15}x = \frac{2}{3}x$$

The answer is (C).

SAT PRACTICE: FRACTIONS (WORD PROBLEM – FINDING FRACTIONAL PART)

A woman leaves $\dfrac{1}{2}$ of her estate to her son and the remainder in equal shares to her three nieces. If the son gives $\dfrac{1}{5}$ of his share of the estate to the woman's youngest niece, what fractional part of the estate will the youngest niece then possess?

(A) $\dfrac{4}{15}$

(B) $\dfrac{11}{30}$

(C) $\dfrac{13}{30}$

(D) $\dfrac{8}{15}$

(E) $\dfrac{7}{10}$

Solution:

Draw a pie graph to represent the division of the estate among the four individuals.

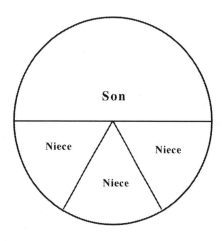

The son receives $\dfrac{1}{2}$ of the estate. Each niece receives $\dfrac{1}{3}$ of the other $\dfrac{1}{2}$.

$$\dfrac{1}{3} \cdot \dfrac{1}{2} = \dfrac{1}{6}$$ of the estate is given to each niece.

The son then gives the youngest niece $\dfrac{1}{5}$ of his $\dfrac{1}{2}$ of the estate:

$$\dfrac{1}{5} \cdot \dfrac{1}{2} = \dfrac{1}{10}$$

Youngest niece's original share of estate		Portion of estate that son gives youngest niece		Youngest niece's final share of estate
↓		↓		↓
$\dfrac{1}{6}$	$+$	$\dfrac{1}{10}$	$=$	$\dfrac{4}{15}$

The youngest niece ends up with $\dfrac{4}{15}$ of the total estate. The answer is (A).

SAT PRACTICE: FRACTIONS (WORD PROBLEM – FINDING WHOLE AMOUNT)

A bag contains marbles, $\frac{2}{3}$ of which are red and $\frac{1}{3}$ of which are yellow. After 20 yellow marbles are added to the bag, $\frac{1}{2}$ of the marbles in the bag are red and $\frac{1}{2}$ are yellow. How many marbles were in the bag to begin with?

(A)   40
(B)   60
(C)   80
(D)   100
(E)   120

Solution:

Determine the ratio of the original number of red marbles to the original number of yellow marbles:

$$\frac{\frac{2}{3} \text{ red marbles}}{\frac{1}{3} \text{ yellow marbles}} = 2$$

• For every two red marbles originally in the jar, there was one yellow marble. If there were x yellow marbles to begin with, there were $2x$ red marbles.

• After 20 marbles are added, the red and yellow marbles are equal in number:

Yellow marbles		Added marbles		Red marbles
↓		↓		↓
x	+	20	=	$2x$

$x = 20$

So there were originally x, or 20 yellow marbles in the jar, and $2x$, or 40 red marbles. $20 + 40 = 60$ total marbles to begin with. The answer is (B).

Note: Once again, you could "Throw it in Reverse" and work backwards from the answer choices. Answer choices (A), (C), and (D) can be eliminated because they contain numbers that cannot be divided evenly into thirds. Begin by testing choice (B):

$$\frac{2}{3} \cdot 60 = 40 \text{ red marbles}$$

$$\frac{1}{3} \cdot 60 = 20 \text{ yellow marbles}$$

After 20 yellow marbles are added, there are 40 yellow and 40 red marbles in the bag ($\frac{1}{2}$ of each color).

SAT PRACTICE: FRACTIONS (COMPARING FRACTIONS)

In which of the following groups are the fractions arranged in increasing order?

(A) $\dfrac{4}{9}, \dfrac{3}{7}, \dfrac{11}{21}$

(B) $\dfrac{11}{21}, \dfrac{4}{9}, \dfrac{3}{7}$

(C) $\dfrac{3}{7}, \dfrac{11}{21}, \dfrac{4}{9}$

(D) $\dfrac{4}{9}, \dfrac{11}{21}, \dfrac{3}{7}$

(E) $\dfrac{3}{7}, \dfrac{4}{9}, \dfrac{11}{21}$

Solution:

Convert each fraction to a decimal and make the comparison.

$$\frac{4}{9} \qquad\qquad \frac{3}{7} \qquad\qquad \frac{11}{21}$$
$$\downarrow \qquad\qquad \downarrow \qquad\qquad \downarrow$$
$$.\overline{4} \qquad\qquad .429\ldots \qquad\qquad .524\ldots$$

So $\dfrac{3}{7} < \dfrac{4}{9} < \dfrac{11}{21}$ The answer is (E).

SAT PRACTICE: FRACTIONS (RECIPROCALS)

If $\dfrac{1}{x} = z$ and $\dfrac{1}{y} = 2z$, what is the value of $x - y$ when $z = -\dfrac{1}{3}$?

(A)   -9

(B) $-4\dfrac{1}{2}$

(C)   -3

(D) $-1\dfrac{1}{2}$

(E)   3

Solution:

First, find the reciprocal of z to find x:

If $z = -\dfrac{1}{3}$, then x (its reciprocal) = -3

Next find the reciprocal of $2z$ in order to find y:

$$\text{If } z = -\frac{1}{3} \text{ then } 2z = -\frac{2}{3}$$

$$y \text{ (the reciprocal of } 2z) = -\frac{3}{2}$$

Determine the value of $x - y$:

$$x - y = -3 - \left(-\frac{3}{2}\right) = -3 + \frac{3}{2} = -1\frac{1}{2}$$

The answer is (D).

ARITHMETIC TOPIC #6
RATIO & PROPORTION

The ancient Greeks were fascinated with what is known as the **Golden Rectangle**. If the largest possible square is cut from a golden rectangle, the resulting smaller rectangle is similar to the original rectangle. In the diagram shown, assume that the value of y is 1. The following **Golden Ratio** then exists:

$$\frac{1}{x} = \frac{x}{1+x}$$

The value of x in the above proportion is represented by the Greek letter Phi (ϕ) and is an irrational number equal to approximately 1.618.

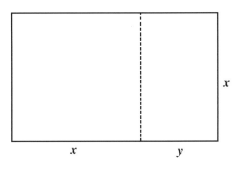

The Golden Ratio has many intriguing applications found throughout the natural world. Its value is encountered in population growth, the ratio of various human body parts, the formation of a snail's spiral, and in the number of seeds packed within flowers.

Ratio & Proportion Basics

Ratios express the relationship between two quantities, usually a part to another part or a part to the whole. Ratios can be expressed in different ways. The ratio of a to b can be written:

a to b or $a:b$ or $\dfrac{a}{b}$ or $a \div b$

Ratios (like fractions) should always be expressed in their simplest form.

A proportion expresses the equivalence of two ratios in which the first term divided by the second term equals the third term divided by the fourth:

$$\frac{w}{x} = \frac{y}{z}$$

In the proportion above, the second and third terms, in this case x and y, are known as the **means** of the proportion. The first and fourth terms, in this case w and z, are known as the **extremes** of the proportion. The relationship between w and x is proportional to the relationship between y and z. In any proportion, the product of the means is equal to the product of the extremes. In the proportion above, $x \bullet y = w \bullet z$.

SAT PRACTICE: RATIO & PROPORTION (SIMPLE RATIOS)

Of 200 vehicles in a parking lot, 165 are cars and the remainder consists of motorcycles. Which of the following expresses the ratio of the number of motorcycles to the number of cars?

(A) $\dfrac{7}{40}$

(B) $\dfrac{7}{33}$

(C) $\dfrac{33}{40}$

(D) $\dfrac{33}{7}$

(E) $\dfrac{40}{7}$

Solution:

200 vehicles – 165 cars = 35 motorcycles

$$\frac{\text{Motorcycles}}{\text{Cars}} = \frac{35}{165} = \frac{7 \bullet 5}{33 \bullet 5} = \frac{7}{33}$$ The answer is (B).

SAT PRACTICE: RATIO & PROPORTION (RATIO APPLICATIONS)

If the ratio of men to women at a fundraiser is 5:4, which of the following could NOT be the number of people at the fundraiser?

(A)   18
(B)   56
(C)   63
(D)   225
(E)   729

Solution:

Add the two parts of the ratio (men and women) together. The number of people at the fundraiser must be a multiple of this sum.

$$5 \text{ men} + 4 \text{ women} = 9$$

The total number of people at the fundraiser must be a multiple of 9. The only number listed in the answer choices that is not a multiple of 9 is 56. The answer is (B).

SAT PRACTICE: RATIO & PROPORTION (WORD PROBLEM-PROPORTIONAL DISTRIBUTION)

A grant of $2,700,000 is to be disbursed to three colleges in the ratio of 5:4:3. What is the least amount that will be given to one of the colleges?

(A) $125,000
(B) $225,000
(C) $675,000
(D) $900,000
(E) $1,125,000

Solution:

Create a ratio of the least part of the ratio to the whole.

$$\frac{3}{5+4+3} = \frac{3}{12} = \frac{1}{4}$$

Multiply this fractional part by the value of the estate to find the smallest share:

$$\frac{1}{4} \cdot 2{,}700{,}000 = 675{,}000$$

The answer is (C).

SAT PRACTICE: RATIO & PROPORTION (TRIPLE RATIOS)

In Alex's aquarium, the ratio of guppies to angelfish is 7:4 and the ratio of angelfish to swordfish is 2:3. What is the ratio of guppies to swordfish?

(A)   7:3
(B)   21:4
(C)   7:6
(D)   4:3
(E)   7:12

Solution:

Set up and multiply the ratios to cancel factors containing the type of fish that does not appear in the final ratio:

$$\frac{7 \text{ guppies}}{4 \;\langle \cancel{\text{angel fish}} \rangle} \cdot \frac{2 \;\langle \cancel{\text{angel fish}} \rangle}{3 \text{ swordfish}} = \frac{14 \text{ guppies}}{12 \text{ swordfish}}$$

Reduce the final ratio: $\dfrac{14}{12} \div \left[\dfrac{2}{2}\right] = \dfrac{7}{6}$, or 7:6.   The answer is (C).

SAT PRACTICE: RATIO & PROPORTION (DIRECT PROPORTION)

If 3 liters of chlorine are required to purify every 375 cubic meters of water, how many liters would be required to clean a swimming pool 25 meters long, 15 meters wide, and filled 6 meters deep with water?

(A)   12
(B)   15
(C)   18
(D)   21
(E)   25

Solution:

Volume of water in the swimming pool = 25 • 15 • 6 = 2,250 cubic meters

$$\frac{\text{liters of chlorine}}{\text{cubic meters of water}} = \frac{3}{375} = \frac{x}{2,250}$$

Cross-multiply to solve for x: $375x = 3 • 2250$ $x = 18$ liters of water

The answer is (C).

SAT PRACTICE: RATIO & PROPORTION (INVERSE PROPORTION)

A rancher has enough hay to feed 45 cows for 15 days. If he wants to feed 30 additional cows from this same quantity of hay, for how many days will the hay supply feed the total number of cows?

(A)   2
(B)   5
(C)   9
(D)   10
(E)   12

Solution:

This problem presents an inverse proportion:
Number of cows to be fed • Number of days the food will last = A constant value

Use this relationship to make an equation to solve for the unknown quantity.

# of cows	# of days food will last	=	# of cows	# of days food will last
↓	↓		↓	↓
45 •	15	=	75 •	x

$45 • 15 = 75x$

$x = \dfrac{675}{75} = 9$ The answer is (C).

ARITHMETIC TOPIC #7
PERCENTS

To solve **percent problems,** use this proportion: $\dfrac{\text{part}}{\text{whole}} = \dfrac{n\%}{100\%}$

Cross-multiply to solve for the missing quantity: part • 100% = $n\%$ • whole

A second way to solve percent problems is to translate the problem into a "Number Sentence."

Example: Find 26% of 400.

"Find" means the same thing as "what equals":

$$
\begin{array}{cccc}
\text{Find} & 26\% & \text{of} & 400? \\
\downarrow & \downarrow & \downarrow & \downarrow \\
n & = .26 & \bullet & 400 \\
n & = 104 & &
\end{array}
$$

SAT PRACTICE: PERCENTS (FINDING TOTAL AMOUNT)

27% of the books in a library are novels, 12% are biographies, 56% are general non-fiction, and the remaining 1,265 are children's readers. How many total books are there in the library?

(A)   1,332
(B)   5,060
(C)   20,350
(D)   23,500
(E)   25,300

Solution:

Subtract the percentages of novels, biographies and general non-fiction from 100% to determine the percentage of books that are children's readers:

$$100 - 27 - 12 - 56 = 5$$

The 1,265 children's readers represent 5% of all of the books in the library.

$$\frac{1,265}{\text{total books } (b)} = \frac{5}{100}$$

1,265 • 100 = 5b
Total books = 25,300   The answer is (E).

SAT PRACTICE: PERCENTS (PERCENT INCREASE)

The number of tourists who visited a national park in 2000 was 25% greater than the number who visited in 1990. If 200,000 people visited the national park in 2000, how many tourists visited it in 1990?

(A)   50,000
(B)   150,000
(C)   160,000
(D)   175,000
(E)   250,000

Solution:

$$\frac{200,000}{1990 \text{ tourists } (t)} = \frac{100 + 25}{100}$$

$200,000 \cdot 100 = 125t$
$t = 160,000$

The answer is (C).

> **→SUCCESS STRATEGY←**
>
> For percent increase problems, use the following equation:
>
> $$\frac{\text{Increased amount or price}}{\text{Original amount or price}} = \frac{100\% + \% \text{ increase}}{100\%}$$

Note: Be aware that on this problem you cannot simply find 25% of 200,000 and subtract that amount from 200,000. That incorrect process would produce 150,000, the incorrect answer found in (B).

SAT PRACTICE: PERCENTS (PERCENT DECREASE)

Justin bought a jacket on sale for $ 40.00, which represented a 20% markdown from the original price. What was the original price of the jacket?

(A) $ 32.00
(B) $ 44.00
(C) $ 48.00
(D) $ 50.00
(E) $ 56.00

Solution:

$$\frac{40}{\text{original price } (p)} = \frac{100 - 20}{100}$$

$40 \cdot 100 = 80p$

Original price = $50.00

The answer is (D).

> **→SUCCESS STRATEGY←**
>
> For percent decrease problems, use the following equation:
>
> $$\frac{\text{Decreased amount or price}}{\text{Original amount or price}} = \frac{100\% - \% \text{ decrease}}{100\%}$$

Note: As with the previous problem regarding percent increase, to solve this problem you cannot calculate 20% of $40.00 and add that result to $40.00. That method would produce $48.00 as the original price, the incorrect answer found in (C).

SAT PRACTICE: PERCENTS (PERCENT INCREASE/DECREASE COMBINATION)

Casey purchased a new boat in 1995. Four years later he sold it to Eric for 30% less than he paid for it in 1995. After refurbishing the boat, Eric sold it to Shane for 20% more than Eric had paid Casey for it. The price that Shane paid for the boat was what percent of the original price that Casey paid for it in 1995?

(A)   70 percent
(B)   80 percent
(C)   84 percent
(D)   90 percent
(E)   91 percent

- Assume that Casey purchased the new boat for $100.

- Casey sold Eric the boat for 30% less than what Casey paid for it:

$$30\% \cdot \$100 = \$30 \qquad \$100 - \$30 = \$70$$

  Casey sold Eric the boat for $70.

- Eric then sold the boat to Shane for 20% more than Eric paid for it:

$$20\% \cdot 70 = \$14 \qquad \$70 + \$14 = \$84$$

Shane bought the boat for $84, which represents 84% of the original price. The answer is (C).

→SUCCESS STRATEGY←

Start with 100!

For percent increase/decrease combination problems that ask about percent changes with respect to an unspecified original amount, always start with a base number of 100 – even if 100 does not realistically fit the situation described in the problem. Because such problems are based on a relative change in amount, any starting number can be used. 100 is the least complicated number to start with when solving these problems.

Note: For percent increase/decrease combination problems, it is incorrect to simply subtract the decrease from the increase to obtain the final result. In this problem, you cannot just combine a decrease of 30% with an increase of 20% to obtain a net decrease of 10%. The problem must be performed in two steps, because the second percentage change is based on a different amount than the first.

ARITHMETIC TOPIC #8
AVERAGES

Mean, median and mode are the three measurements of "central tendency." All three have made appearances in SAT math questions.

Mean: Commonly known as the simple average, the mean is calculated by dividing the sum of a group of terms by the number of terms present.

Median: The middle value of the set when all of terms are listed in increasing order. If there is an even number of values, the median is the average (mean) of the two middle terms (add the two middle terms together and divide by two).

Mode: The value appearing the most frequently in a set of data.

Averages: Summary and Examples

Find the mean, median, and mode of the following set of numbers:

$$2, 3, 3, 4, 6, 8, 9$$

Mean: $\dfrac{\text{Sum of terms}}{\text{Number of terms}} = \dfrac{2+3+3+4+6+8+9}{7} = \dfrac{35}{7} = 5$

Median = 4, as it is the middle value among the terms.

Mode = 3, as it is the most frequently occurring term.

$$
\begin{array}{ccccccccc}
 & & \textbf{Mode} & & \textbf{Mean} & & & & \\
 & & \downarrow & & \downarrow & & & & \\
2, & 3, & 3, & 4, & (5), & 6, & 8, & 9 & \\
 & & & \uparrow & & & & & \\
 & & & \textbf{Median} & & & & &
\end{array}
$$

SAT PRACTICE: AVERAGES (TERMS WITH ALGEBRAIC EXPRESSIONS)

What is the average (arithmetic mean) of $3x + 1$, $5x - 3$, and $-2x + 2$?

(A) $3x + 1$

(B) $x - 3$

(C) x

(D) $2x$

(E) $2x + 2$

Solution:

Add the three algebraic expressions (combine like terms) and divide by 3:

$$\frac{(3x+1)+(5x-3)+(-2x+2)}{3} = \frac{6x}{3} = 2x$$

The answer is (D).

SAT PRACTICE: AVERAGES (FINDING A MISSING TERM)

GRID-IN PROBLEM:

The average of Maya's first three test scores was 86%. The average of her next two test scores was 89%. If the final exam is weighted as two tests, what percentage will Maya have to score on the final exam to achieve an average test score of 90%?

Solution:

Because the final exam counts as two tests, the total number of tests is 7. Let x stand for the final exam score:

$$\frac{(3 \bullet 86)+(2 \bullet 89)+2x}{7}=90$$

$$436 + 2x = 90 \bullet 7$$
$$2x = 630 - 436$$
$$2x = 194$$
$$x = 97$$

Grid-in 97.

SAT PRACTICE: AVERAGES (WEIGHTED AVERAGE)

7 women in a bowling league have an average score of 179. If the overall average of the league's 20 bowlers is 205, what is the men's average bowling score?

(A)   192
(B)   202
(C)   211
(D)   219
(E)   226

Solution:

> →SUCCESS STRATEGY←
>
> To find a "weighted" average, use the following equation:
> Weighted average for Group A and Group B =
>
> $$\frac{(\text{Group A's average} \bullet \#\text{of members in group A})+(\text{Group B's average} \bullet \#\text{of members in group B})}{\#\text{of members in A}+\#\text{of members of B}}$$

The problem above involves a "weighted average" because there are more male bowlers than female bowlers:
20 total bowlers – 7 female bowlers = 13 male bowlers

women's   # of   men's   # of
average   women   average   men
↓   ↓   ↓   ↓

$$\frac{(179 \quad \bullet \quad 7) + (\text{Average of men } (m) \quad \bullet \quad 13)}{7 + 13} = 205$$

$(179 \bullet 7) + 13m = 205 \bullet 20$

$1{,}253 + 13m = 4{,}100$

$13m = 2{,}847$

$m = 219$

The answer is (D).

SAT PRACTICE: AVERAGES (MEDIAN & MODE)

10, 20, 20, 30, 30, 30, 40, 40, 40, 40, 50, 50, 50, 50, 50

Given the series of meter readings above, which of the following statements are true?

I.   The median and the mode are both greater than the mean.

II.   The median and the mode are equal.

III.   The mean is one of the numbers listed as a meter reading.

(A)   I only

(B)   II only

(C)   III only

(D)   I and II

(E)   none are true

Solution:

Find the mean, median and mode for the set of numbers.

$$\textbf{Mean: } = \frac{10 + 20 + 20 + 30 + 30 + 30 + 40 + 40 + 40 + 40 + 50 + 50 + 50 + 50 + 50}{15} = \frac{550}{15} = 36.\overline{6}$$

The **mean** is $36.\overline{6}$. The **median** is the middle term when the numbers are arranged in increasing order and the **mode** is the most frequently occurring term.

Mean   Median   Mode
↓   ↓   ↓

$10, 20, 20, 30, 30, 30, \underset{(36.\overline{6})}{}, 40, \overset{}{40}, 40, 40, 50, 50, 50, 50, 50$

Only statement I is true. The answer is (A).

ARITHMETIC TOPIC #9:
MEASUREMENT CONVERSIONS

Make sure that you know the following metric and English measurement conversions:

Metric

1 kilo-(meter/liter/gram) =
   1,000 meters/liters/grams
1 meter/liter/gram =
   100 centi- or 1,000 milli-(meters/liters/grams)

Linear Measure

12 inches = 1 foot
36 inches = 3 feet = 1 yard
5,280 feet = 1,760 yards = 1 mile

Square Measure

1 square foot = 144 square inches (12 • 12)
1 square yard = 9 square feet (3 • 3)

Volume

1 cubic foot = 1,728 cubic inches (12 • 12 • 12)
1 cubic yard = 27 cubic feet (3 • 3 • 3)

Dry Measure

16 ounces = 1 pound
2000 pounds = 1 ton

Liquid Measure

3 teaspoons = 1 tablespoon
8 ounces = 1 cup
32 ounces = 4 cups = 2 pints = 1 quart
4 quarts = 1 gallon

SAT PRACTICE: MEASUREMENT CONVERSION

A length of ribbon measuring 3 yards 2 feet 3 inches is cut into two pieces, the shorter of which is $\frac{2}{3}$ the length of the longer piece. How long is the shorter piece of ribbon?

(A)   1 yard 9 inches
(B)   1 yard 1 foot 6 inches
(C)   1 yard 1 foot 9 inches
(D)   2 yards 9 inches
(E)   2 yards 1 foot 6 inches

Solution:

First, convert the length of the ribbon into inches.

$$(3 \text{ yards} \bullet 36 \text{ inches}) + (2 \text{ feet} \bullet 12 \text{ inches}) + 3 \text{ inches} = 135 \text{ inches}$$

For the short piece of ribbon to be $\frac{2}{3}$ the length of the longer piece, the pieces exist in a 2:3 ratio.

Divide the ribbon into 5 parts as shown:

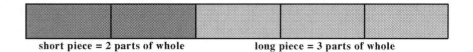

short piece = 2 parts of whole   long piece = 3 parts of whole

Set up a proportion to solve for the shorter length of ribbon:

$$\frac{\text{short piece}}{\text{total length}} = \frac{2}{5} \qquad \frac{\text{short piece } (s)}{135} = \frac{2}{5}$$

$$5s = 2 \bullet 135$$

$$s = 54$$

54 inches = 1 yard 1 foot 6 inches   (36 + 12 + 6 inches)

The answer is (B).

Mathematics
Chapter 3
Algebra

This chapter presents various SAT algebra topics. The graphs of algebraic equations and functions (linear and quadratic equations and absolute value functions) are presented in the next chapter.

ALGEBRA TOPIC #1:
ALGEBRA FUNDAMENTALS

Algebra was first practiced in Egypt and Arabia over two millennia ago. The word "algebra" has its origins in the Arab term "al-jabr." According to Dr. John W. Dawson, Jr., Professor of Mathematics at Penn State University (York campus), ancient Middle Eastern mathematicians used this medical term as an analogy:

> *The early use of "al-jabr" was in the sense of "the resetting of bones," and this term was adopted by the early algebraists of the Mashreq as an analogy for what we today call "combining like terms."*
>
> *It's worth noting in that regard that a parallel usage still persists in English between the medical term "reduction" of a fracture and the mathematical term "reduction" of an equation. Of course, the original meaning of "calculus," as a "pebble," also persists in modern medical English (where a kidney stone, for example, is technically known as a "urinary calculus").*

Math problems on the SAT may require you to simplify or rearrange algebra expressions, solve various algebraic equations, and to solve word problems algebraically. Some problems focus on very basic algebra concepts.

Algebra Basics

An **algebraic expression** consists of one or more algebraic terms in a phrase. It can include variables (usually represented by letters), constants or coefficients (numbers), and operating symbols (plus and minus signs).

Solving for One Variable in Terms of Another

The objective is to isolate a specific variable on one side of the equation.

Example: The formula for area of a triangle is $A = \frac{1}{2}bh$. Solve for b.

To solve for base, isolate b:

$A = \frac{1}{2}bh$ ←Write the formula

$2A = bh$ ←Multiply both sides of the equation by 2

$\frac{2A}{h} = b$ ←Divide by h

Solving a Linear Equation with a Single Variable

The general steps for solving an equation with a single variable are as follows:

1. Combine all variable terms on one side of the equation (using addition or subtraction).
2. Combine all constant terms on the side opposite of the variable (using addition or subtraction).
3. Divide through the equation by the variable's coefficient.

Example

$$\text{Solve:}\quad 4x + 2 = 6x - 10$$

$$-2x + 2 = -10 \quad \leftarrow \text{Subtract } 6x \text{ from both sides}$$

$$-2x = -12 \quad \leftarrow \text{Subtract } 2 \text{ from both sides}$$

$$x = 6 \quad \leftarrow \text{Divide both sides by -2}$$

→SUCCESS STRATEGY←

Solving an equation with a single variable is the process of performing PEMDAS backwards! You are simply "undoing" the usual order of operations by systematically combining like terms to solve for the variable.

SAT PRACTICE: BASIC ALGEBRA (WORD PROBLEM FOR EQUATION IN A SINGLE VARIABLE)

The sum of x and 3 is 17 less than the product of x and 6. x equals:

(A) $-2\dfrac{4}{5}$

(B) $-2\dfrac{6}{7}$

(C) 0

(D) 2

(E) 4

Solution:

Translate the problem into a "Number Sentence."

The sum of x and 3   is   17 less than   the product of x and 6.
$$\downarrow \qquad\qquad \downarrow \qquad\qquad \downarrow$$
$$x + 3 \quad = \quad -17 \quad + \quad 6x$$

Solve for x:

$$
\begin{aligned}
x + 3 &= 6x - 17 \\
20 &= 5x \\
4 &= x
\end{aligned}
$$

The answer is (E).

SAT PRACTICE: BASIC ALGEBRA (EXPRESSIONS WITH TWO VARIABLES)

If a and b are each positive integers and $ab = 12$, then which of the following could not be a possible value of $5a + 7b$?

(A)   42
(B)   44
(C)   52
(D)   67
(E)   89

Solution:

List all of the possible combinations for a and b such that $ab = 12$.

If $ab = 12$ and a and b are both positive integers, then the possible values for a and b and the corresponding values of $5a + 7b$ are as follows:

a	b	Value of $5a + 7b$
1	12	$5(1) + 7(12) = 89$
2	6	$5(2) + 7(6) = 52$
3	4	$5(3) + 7(4) = 43$
4	3	$5(4) + 7(3) = 41$
6	2	$5(6) + 7(2) = 44$
12	1	$5(12) + 7(1) = 67$

42 is the only answer choice that is not a listed value for $5a + 7b$. The answer is (A).

SAT PRACTICE: BASIC ALGEBRA (SOLVING FOR A VARIABLE)

(Note: This problem represents the most challenging of this type.)

If r and y are positive integers in the equation $\dfrac{sy}{rs + y} = \dfrac{1}{r}$, then $s =$

(A) $\dfrac{y}{ry - r}$

(B) $\dfrac{1 - y}{r}$

(C) $\dfrac{1 - r}{y}$

(D) ry^2

(E) $\dfrac{y}{r - y}$

Solution:

Take systematic steps to isolate *s* on one side of the equation:

$$\frac{sy}{rs + y} = \frac{1}{r}$$

$$rsy = rs + y \qquad \leftarrow \text{Cross-multiply}$$

$$rsy - rs = y \qquad \leftarrow \text{Gather all terms containing s on one side of the equation}$$

$$s(ry - r) = y \qquad \leftarrow \text{Factor out } s$$

$$s = \frac{y}{ry - r} \qquad \leftarrow \text{Divide both sides by } (ry - r)$$

The answer is (A).

SAT PRACTICE: BASIC ALGEBRA (MULTIPLE ALGEBRAIC EQUATIONS)

GRID-IN PROBLEM:

a, *b* and *c* are positive real numbers such that $ab = 200$, $\dfrac{c}{b} = 50$, and $b^2 = \dfrac{1}{4}$. What is the value of $\dfrac{a}{c}$?

Solution:

- Solve for *a*: $ab = 200 \qquad a = \dfrac{200}{b}$

- Solve for *c*: $\dfrac{c}{b} = 50 \qquad c = 50b$

- Solve for *b*: $b^2 = \dfrac{1}{4} \qquad b = \sqrt{\dfrac{1}{4}} = \dfrac{1}{2}$

- Now find *a* and *c* by replacing *b* with $\dfrac{1}{2}$: $a = \dfrac{200}{\dfrac{1}{2}} = 400 \qquad c = 50 \cdot \dfrac{1}{2} = 25$

- Therefore: $\dfrac{a}{c} = \dfrac{400}{25} = 16$

Grid-in 16.

SAT PRACTICE: BASIC ALGEBRA (MULTIPLE ALGEBRAIC EQUATIONS)

If $s = y - 1$ and $t = \dfrac{z}{y^2}$, then $\dfrac{1}{st} =$

(A) $\dfrac{y}{z-1}$

(B) $\dfrac{yz}{z-y^2}$

(C) $\dfrac{1}{y^2 z}$

(D) $\dfrac{y^2}{yz-z}$

(E) $\dfrac{1-z}{y-1}$

Solution:

Multiply equivalent expressions for s and t to find st:

$$\overset{\overset{s}{\downarrow}}{(y-1)} \bullet \overset{\overset{t}{\downarrow}}{\dfrac{z}{y^2}} = \dfrac{z(y-1)}{y^2} = \dfrac{yz-z}{y^2}$$

$$st = \dfrac{yz-z}{y^2}$$

Find the reciprocal of st: $\dfrac{1}{st} = \dfrac{y^2}{yz-z}$

The answer is (D).

Inequalities

The first use of inequality signs can be traced back to the 16th century English mathematician and astronomer Thomas Harriot. Following his undergraduate education at St. Mary's Hall at Oxford, Harriot managed various aspects of Sir Walter Raleigh's navigational expeditions and accompanied Raleigh on one of his voyages to Virginia.

Harriot's mathematical achievements included helping to give algebra its modern form. He founded the English school of algebra and invented the signs of inequality "<" and ">" (although he may have used different symbols). He is considered by many to be the greatest mathematician that Oxford has ever produced.

Solving a Linear Inequality with a Single Variable

Follow the same steps as for solving a linear equation with a single variable, but remember that if you multiply or divide by a negative number, you must invert the inequality sign.

Example

Solve: $2x + 8 > 5x - 7$

$-3x + 8 > -7$ ← Subtract $5x$ from both sides

$-3x > -15$ ← Subtract 8 from both sides

$x < 5$ ← Divide both sides by -3 and invert the inequality sign

The solution set for this inequality would be graphed on a number line as follows:

SUMMARY OF GRAPHING
A LINEAR INEQUALITY WITH A SINGLE VARIABLE

Expression	**Sign**	**Description of Graph**	**Graph on a Number Line**
"greater than"	>	open dot with arrow pointed to the right	o———————▷
"greater than or equal to"	≥	solid dot with arrow pointed to the right	•———————▷
"less than"	<	open dot with arrow pointed to the left	◁———————o
"less than or equal to"	≤	solid dot with arrow pointed to the left	◁———————•

Example: Linear Inequality with a Single Variable

Which of the following characterizes the number line graph for the solution set of the inequality $\frac{2}{3}x > \frac{5}{6}x - 2$?

(A)   solid dot on the coordinate 12 with an arrow pointed to the right

(B)   open dot on the coordinate 12 with an arrow pointed to the right

(C)   open dot on the coordinate -12 with an arrow pointed to the left

(D)   open dot on the coordinate 12 with an arrow pointed to the left

(E)   solid dot on the coordinate 12 with an arrow pointed to the left

Solution:

Solve the inequality.

$$\frac{2}{3}x > \frac{5}{6}x - 2 \quad \leftarrow \text{Write the inequality}$$

$$-\frac{1}{6}x > -2 \quad \leftarrow \text{Subtract } \frac{5}{6}x \text{ from both sides of the inequality}$$

$$x < 12 \quad \leftarrow \text{Multiply both sides by -6 and invert the inequality sign}$$

"<" indicates that there will be an open dot on the coordinate 12 with an arrow pointed to the left. The answer is (D).

ALGEBRA TOPIC #2:
MONOMIALS AND POLYNOMIALS

Many classic SAT algebra problems involve operations with monomials and polynomials. A **monomial** is an algebraic expression consisting of a constant, a variable, or the product of a constant and one or more variables.

Examples: 7 xy^2z $7xy^2z$

A **polynomial** is a monomial or a sum of monomials. *Example*: $10r^3 - 8r^2s + 12rs - 9rs^2 + 3s^3$

A **binomial** is a polynomial consisting of two terms, while a **trinomial** consists of three terms.

Monomial and Polynomial Summary
Adding or Subtracting Polynomial Expressions

To add or subtract polynomials, only like terms can be combined. Like terms are terms that contain the same variables raised to the same power. Only the numerical coefficients of like terms can be different. To subtract a polynomial, add its additive inverse.

Example: $(4x^5 - 3x^3 + 2x^2 + x - 6) - (-2x^5 + 5x^4 - 6x^2 + 15) = ?$

- Change the subtraction sign to addition *and*
- Change the signs of all of the terms being subtracted:

$$(4x^5 - 3x^3 + 2x^2 + x - 6) + (2x^5 - 5x^4 + 6x^2 - 15)$$

- Students often find it easy to use a vertical format. Line up and add the like terms:

$$
\begin{array}{r}
4x^5 \quad\;\; - 3x^3 + 2x^2 + x - 6 \\
+ \quad 2x^5 - 5x^4 \quad\quad\; + 6x^2 \quad\;\; - 15 \\
\hline
6x^5 - 5x^4 - 3x^3 + 8x^2 + x - 21
\end{array}
$$

Multiplying a Polynomial by a Monomial

Multiply each term of the polynomial by the monomial (apply the distributive property).

Example

Multiply: $3x^2y(4x^2yz^4 + 9xy^2z^3 - 2x^3z^2)$

Multiply the coefficients separately from the variables. To multiply like variables, add their exponents.

$$12x^4y^2z^4 + 27x^3y^3z^3 - 6x^5yz^2$$

Multiplying Two Binomials

Multiply each term in the first binomial by each term in the second.

Example

Multiply: $(3x - 4)(x + 2)$

If the polynomials are both binomials, use the "FOIL" method:

Multiply the **F**irst elements in each set of parentheses: $3x \cdot x = 3x^2$

Multiply the **O**utside elements in each set of parentheses: $3x \cdot 2 = 6x$
Multiply the **I**nside elements in each set of parenthesis: $-4 \cdot x = \underline{-4x}$
Add together these like terms: $2x$

Multiply the **L**ast elements in each set of parenthesis: $-4 \cdot 2 = -8$

$$(3x - 4)(x + 2) = 3x^2 + 2x - 8$$

EVALUATING POLYNOMIAL EXPRESSIONS

To evaluate polynomial expressions at a specified value, replace the variable in each term with the number provided and perform the operations indicated.

Evaluating Polynomial Expressions: Example

If $x = 4$, what is the value of $x^3 + 2x^2 - 6x + 14$?

Solution:

Replace x with 4 and evaluate:

$$4^3 + 2(4)^2 - 6(4) + 14 =$$
$$64 + 32 - 24 + 14 = 86$$

SAT PRACTICE: MONOMIALS & POLYNOMIALS (MULTIPLYING BINOMIALS)

What is the value of *n* if $(n + 6)(n - 2) - (n + 3)(n - 7) = 5$?

(A) $-\dfrac{1}{2}$

(B)   0

(C) $-3\dfrac{1}{2}$

(D)   4

(E)   No real solution

Solution:

Multiply each pair of binomials using the *FOIL* method:

$$(n + 6)(n - 2) = n^2 + 4n - 12$$
$$(n + 3)(n - 7) = n^2 - 4n - 21$$

Subtract the second expression from the first:

$$
\begin{array}{r}
n^2 + 4n - 12 \\
(-)\ \underline{n^2 - 4n - 21} \\
8n\ +\ 9
\end{array}
$$

Set this result equal to 5 and solve for *n*:

$$8n + 9 = 5$$
$$8n\ =\ -4$$
$$n\ =\ -\dfrac{1}{2}$$

The answer is (A).

SAT PRACTICE: MONOMIALS & POLYNOMIALS (SOLVING FOR A COEFFICIENT IN A POLYNOMIAL EQUATION)

GRID-IN PROBLEM:

If $(3x^2 - nx + 1)(x + 2) = 3x^3 + 4x^2 - 3x + 2$, what is the value of *n*?

Solution:

* Begin by multiplying the two polynomials:

$$(3x^2 - nx + 1)(x + 2) = 3x^3 + 6x^2 - nx^2 - 2nx + x + 2$$

- Set this product equal to the expression stated in the problem and eliminate any identical terms occurring on both sides of the equation:

$$3x^3 + 6x^2 - nx^2 - 2nx + x + 2 = 3x^3 + 4x^2 - 3x + 2$$
$$6x^2 - nx^2 - 2nx + x = 4x^2 - 3x$$

- Group the "coefficients" of x^2 together and the "coefficients" of x together on the left side of the equation, factoring x^2 and x respectively:

$$(6 - n)x^2 - (2n - 1)x = 4x^2 - 3x$$

- Set each term or group of terms with the same exponents equal to each other:

$$(6 - n)x^2 = 4x^2$$

$$(6 - n)x^2 - (2n - 1)x = 4x^2 - 3x$$

$$-(2n - 1)x = -3x$$

- Set each coefficient group on the left side of the equation equal to its corresponding coefficient on the right side and solve for n:

$$(6 - n)x^2 = 4x^2 \qquad -(2n - 1)x = -3x$$
$$6 - n = 4 \qquad -(2n - 1) = -3$$
$$n = 2 \qquad n = 2$$

Grid-in 2.

ALGEBRA TOPIC #3:
ABSOLUTE VALUE
EQUATIONS AND INEQUALITIES

The word "absolute" is a variant of the word "absolve." One of the meanings of absolve is "to exempt or free from certain restrictions or conditions." The mathematical phrase absolute value and its symbol "| |" were first introduced in about 1841 by the German mathematician Karl Weierstrass, one of the founders of the modern theory of functions. Weierstrass applied the concept of absolute value to complex numbers, and the use of the term with respect to real values became common in the mid 1900s.

Absolute Value: Distance, Not Direction

The **absolute value** of x, denoted "$|x|$," signifies the distance of a number x from zero on a number line. Absolute value is never negative because it refers to *distance*, not *direction*.

A number line is frequently used to illustrate absolute value expressions.

$|3| = 3$, because the distance between 3 and 0 is 3.

$|-3| = 3$, because the distance between -3 and 0 is 3.

The solution to the equation $|x| = 3$ would be graphed as follows:

(Absolute value expressions can also be graphed in a coordinate plane; refer to the next chapter "Coordinate Geometry and Graphs in a Coordinate Plane").

Absolute Value Summary

$|x| = x$ if $x \geq 0$	$|x| = -x$ if $x < 0$	$|x| = 0$ if $x = 0$
$|16| = 16$	$|-16| = -(-16)$	$|0| = 0$
	$|-16| = 16$	

Absolute Value: Example 1

Solve: $|4x + 5| = 11$

Solution:

Because $|-11| = 11$ or $|11| = 11$, two distinct equations must be solved. Express the absolute value equation as an equivalent compound sentence (joined by the word "*or*") and then solve each part.

$$4x + 5 = 11 \quad \textit{or} \quad 4x + 5 = -11$$

Now solve for x in <u>each</u> of these equations:

$$4x = 6 \quad \textit{or} \quad 4x = -16$$
$$x = 1.5 \quad\quad\quad x = -4$$

$x = 1.5$ or -4

In the next example, first isolate the absolute value expression on one side of the equation before re-stating the equation as a compound sentence.

Absolute Value: Example 2

Solve: $2|4n| - 3 = 5$

Solution:

First, isolate $|4n|$ on one side of the equation:

$$2|4n| - 3 = 5$$
$$2|4n| = 8 \qquad \leftarrow \text{Add 3 to each side}$$
$$|4n| = 4 \qquad \leftarrow \text{Divide each side by 2}$$

Now create the corresponding compound sentence:

$$4n = 4 \qquad \textit{or} \qquad 4n = -4$$
$$n = 1 \qquad\qquad\qquad n = -1$$

$n = 1$ or -1

Absolute Value Inequalities

Solving absolute value inequalities also includes writing and then solving both parts of an equivalent compound sentence.

Examples:

$|x| > 6$

$|x| > 6$ means $x > 6$ **or** $x < -6$ (means x is **beyond** -6 or 6).
$|x| > 6$ is graphed as follows:

$|x| < 4$

$|x| < 4$ means $x > -4$ **and** $x < 4$ (means x is **between** -4 and 4), or $-4 < x < 4$.
$|x| < 4$ is graphed as follows:

Remember that if the signs are $\geq$ or $\leq$, solid dots are used when graphing the inequality.

Absolute Value: Example #3: "Greater Than" Inequality

Solve and graph: $|2x + 7| \geq 13$

Solution:

"Greater than" inequalities call for a compound sentence joined by the word "*or.*"

$$2x + 7 \geq 13 \qquad \textbf{\textit{or}} \qquad 2x + 7 \leq -13$$
$$2x \geq 6 \qquad\qquad\qquad 2x \leq -20$$
$$x \geq 3 \qquad\qquad\qquad x \leq -10$$

$x \leq -10$ or $x \geq 3$

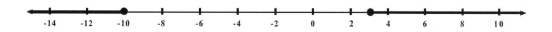

Absolute Value: Example #4: "Less Than" Inequality

Solve and graph: $|3x - 6| < 12$

Solution:

"Less than" inequalities call for a compound sentence joined by the word "*and.*"

$$3x - 6 < 12 \qquad \textbf{\textit{and}} \qquad 3x - 6 > -12$$
$$3x < 18 \qquad\qquad\qquad 3x > -6$$
$$x < 6 \qquad\qquad\qquad x > -2$$

$-2 < x < 6$

→SUCCESS STRATEGY←

A "less than" absolute value inequality can be written as a compound sentence in between a positive value and its additive inverse. It is usually faster to solve such inequalities in this format. The problem immediately above would be solved as follows:

$-12 < 3x - 6 < 12$
$-6 < 3x < 18$ ← Add 6 to each expression
$-2 < x < 6$ ← Divide each expression by 3

SAT PRACTICE: ABSOLUTE VALUE

If $|4x + 8| \leq 16$, which of the following is true?

(A) $x < 2$ or $x > 6$
(B) $x \leq -2$ or $x \geq 6$
(C) $-2 < x < 6$
(D) $-6 < x < 2$
(E) $-6 \leq x \leq 2$

Solution:

Write a compound sentence in between -16 and 16:

$$-16 \leq 4x + 8 \leq 16$$
$$-24 \leq 4x \leq 8 \qquad \leftarrow\text{Subtract 8 from each expression}$$
$$-6 \leq x \leq 2 \qquad \leftarrow\text{Divide each expression by 4}$$

The answer is (E).

ALGEBRA TOPIC #4:
RATIONAL EQUATIONS

A **rational expression** is a quotient of two polynomials.

$$Example: \quad \frac{2x+3}{5x-4}$$

A **rational equation or inequality** includes one or more rational expressions.

Steps for Solving Rational Equations

1. Multiply each side of the equation by the least common denominator (LCD) of all of its rational expressions. This clears the equation of all fractions.

2. Solve the resulting equation.

3. Check identified solutions in the original equation, making sure that they do not cause any of the denominators to equal zero (making the expression undefined). "Apparent solutions" that do not work in the original equation should be eliminated.

Rational Equations: Example

Solve: $\dfrac{2}{3x-9} = \dfrac{5}{12x-4x^2}$

First, factor each of the denominators to find the LCD:

$$\dfrac{2}{3(x-3)} = \dfrac{5}{-4x(x-3)}$$

The LCD is $(3) \cdot (-4x) \cdot (x-3)$

Multiply each side by the LCD:

$$[(3)(-4x)(x-3)] \cdot \dfrac{2}{3(x-3)} = [(3)(-4x)(x-3)] \cdot \dfrac{5}{-4x(x-3)}$$

Divide out common factors on each side: and simplify:

$$[\cancel{(3)}(-4x)\cancel{(x-3)}] \cdot \dfrac{2}{\cancel{3}\,\cancel{(x-3)}} = [(3)\cancel{(-4x)}\cancel{(x-3)}] \cdot \dfrac{5}{\cancel{-4x}\,\cancel{(x-3)}}$$

Simplify and solve:

$$-8x = 15 \qquad x = -\dfrac{15}{8}$$

Be sure to substitute the solution back into original the equation. This solution is correct, as it makes the equation true and does not cause either expression's denominator to equal zero.

ALGEBRA TOPIC #5:
RADICAL EQUATIONS

A radical equation includes at least one term containing a variable in a radicand (under the square root sign).

Examples: $3\sqrt{x} = 18$ *and* $\sqrt{5x-6} = 10$

Steps for Solving Equations with Radicals

1. When one term of a radical equation contains variables in the radicand (under the square root sign), isolate that term on one side of the equation.

2. If two terms of a radical equation contain variables in the radicand, the equation should be stated so that one of these terms is on each side of the equation.

3. Square both sides of the equation.

4. Because squaring both sides of the equation does not always produce equivalent equations, check all potential solutions. "Apparent solutions" that do not work in the original equation should be eliminated.

Radical Equations: Example #1

Solve: $\sqrt{3x+6} = 9$

Solution:

Square both sides of the equation:

$$\left(\sqrt{3x+6}\right)^2 = (9)^2$$

Solve:

$$3x + 6 = 9^2$$
$$3x + 6 = 81$$
$$3x = 75$$
$$x = 25$$

Check:

$$\overset{?}{\sqrt{3(25)+6} = 9} \qquad \sqrt{81} = 9 \qquad \checkmark$$

Radical Equations: Example #2

Solve: $2\sqrt{3x} - \sqrt{8x+16} = 0$

Solution:

First, add $\sqrt{8x+16}$ to both sides of the equation:

$$2\sqrt{3x} = \sqrt{8x+16}$$

Now square both sides of the equation:

$$\left(2\sqrt{3x}\right)^2 = \left(\sqrt{8x+16}\right)^2$$

Solve:

$$4 \bullet (3x) = 8x + 16$$
$$4x = 16$$
$$x = 4$$

Check:

$$2\sqrt{3(4)} - \sqrt{8(4)+16} \overset{?}{=} 0$$

$$4\sqrt{3} - 4\sqrt{3} = 0 \qquad \checkmark$$

SAT PRACTICE: RADICAL EQUATIONS

GRID-IN PROBLEM:

If $3 = \dfrac{15}{\sqrt{7a-10}}$, what is the value of a?

Solution:

Multiply both sides of the equation by $\sqrt{7a-10}$:

$$3\left(\sqrt{7a-10}\right) = 15$$

$$\sqrt{7a-10} = 5$$

Square both sides of the equation:

$$\left(\sqrt{7a-10}\right)^2 = 5^2$$

Solve:

$$7a - 10 = 25$$
$$7a = 35$$
$$a = 5$$

Check: $3 \overset{?}{=} \dfrac{15}{\sqrt{7(5)-10}}$ $3 \overset{?}{=} \dfrac{15}{\sqrt{25}}$ $3 = \dfrac{15}{5}$ ✓

Grid-in 5.

ALGEBRA TOPIC #6:
SIMPLIFYING RADICALS

No specific person is credited with having first invented the square root sign ($\sqrt{}$). In the 13th century, the word "radix" was first used to refer to square roots. Its symbol was a capital *R*, or the symbol R_x. The precursor of the modern symbol, $\sqrt{}$, originated during the 1500s in Germany. A long radical expression was put in parentheses and placed after the $\sqrt{}$. Descartes is recognized for having first placed a line over the parenthetical terms following the $\sqrt{}$ in his *La Geometrie* (1637). This led to the current modern square root symbol.

Definitions: Roots and Radicals

Square root: The number *b* is a **square root** of *a* if $b^2 = a$. A positive number *a* has two square roots denoted by $\sqrt{a}$ and $-\sqrt{a}$.

Example: Because $5^2 = 25$ and $(-5)^2 = 25$, the two square roots of 25 are as follows:
$$\sqrt{25} = 5 \text{ and } -\sqrt{25} = -5$$

The concept of square roots can be extended to other types of roots. For example, 2 is a cube root of 8 because $2^3 = 8$.

REAL NUMBER ROOTS: $\sqrt[n]{x}$

$$\left(\sqrt[n]{a}\right)^n \quad or \quad \sqrt[n]{a^n} = a \quad \text{(when } n \text{ is odd)}$$

$$\left(\sqrt[n]{a}\right)^n \quad or \quad \sqrt[n]{a^n} = |a| \quad \text{(when } n \text{ is even)}$$

$$\sqrt[n]{ab} = \sqrt[n]{a} \bullet \sqrt[n]{b}$$

n^{th} Root	Restrictions for Radicand "a" for Real Number Roots	Nature of Roots
n is an even integer	a must be a nonnegative real number	two real nth roots (one positive, one negative)
n is an odd integer	a can be either a positive or negative real number	only one real nth root (positive or negative)

Examples:

$\sqrt[4]{81} = 3$ Because $n = 4$ is even and $a = 81$ is positive, 81 has one positive and one negative real fourth root: $3^4 = 81$ and $(-3)^4 = 81$

$-\sqrt[4]{81} = -3$

$\sqrt[5]{32} = 2$ Because $n = 5$ is odd, 32 has one real fifth root: $2^5 = 32$

$\sqrt[3]{-64} = -4$ Because $n = 3$ is odd, -64 has one real cube root: $(-4)^3 = -64$

→SUCCESS STRATEGY←

$\sqrt{a}$ refers to the nonnegative square root of a. For any <u>even</u> root (square root, 4th root, 6th root, etc.) there is a principal square root – which is the nonnegative root. When a radical expression is <u>not</u> preceded by a (-) or (±) sign, you are being asked to find the principal, or nonnegative square root.

$$\sqrt{36} = 6 \text{ (the principal square root of 36)}$$
$$-\sqrt{36} = -6 \text{ (the negative square root of 36)}$$
$$\pm\sqrt{36} = \pm 6 \text{ (both square roots of 36)}$$

Simplifying Radicals

To simplify square roots, find any factors of the radicand (the quantity under the square root sign) that are perfect squares. *Examples:*

Simplify $\sqrt{72}$

$$\sqrt{72} = \sqrt{36 \bullet 2} = \sqrt{6^2} \bullet \sqrt{2} = 6\sqrt{2}$$

Simplify $\sqrt{x^4 y z^7}$ *(assuming x, y, z ≥ 0)*

$$\sqrt{x^4 y z^7} = \sqrt{(x^2)^2 (z^3)^2} \bullet \sqrt{yz} = x^2 z^3 \sqrt{yz}$$

$\uparrow$ $\uparrow$ $\uparrow$ These are the *y* and *z* factors that remain

Re-write as perfect $x^4 = (x^2)^2$ $z^6 = (z^3)^2$ once the perfect squares are extracted
squares

To simplify *n*th roots, find any factors that are *n*th powers. *Examples:*

Simplify $\sqrt[4]{96}$

$$\sqrt[4]{96} = \sqrt[4]{16 \bullet 6} = \sqrt[4]{(2^4)} \bullet \sqrt[4]{6} = 2\sqrt[4]{6}$$

Simplify $\sqrt[3]{r^{13} s^9 t^2}$

$$\sqrt[3]{r^{13} s^9 t^2} = \sqrt[3]{(r^4)^3 \bullet (s^3)^3} \bullet \sqrt[3]{rt^2} = r^4 s^3 \sqrt[3]{rt^2}$$

$\uparrow$ $\uparrow$ $\uparrow$ These are the *r* and *t* factors that remain

Re-write as perfect $r^{12} = (r^4)^3$ $s^9 = (s^3)^3$ once the perfect cubes are extracted
cubes

SAT PRACTICE: SIMPLIFYING RADICALS

Which of the following is equal to $-4ab^2$?

(A) $\sqrt{16ab^2}$

(B) $-\sqrt{4a^2 b^4}$

(C) $-a\sqrt{8b^2}$

(D) $\sqrt{-16a^2 b^4}$

(E) $-2b\sqrt{(2ab)^2}$

Solution:

Start by eliminating impossible answers:

- Eliminate choice (A), as it will yield a positive square root (the answer we are looking for is negative).
- Eliminate choice (D), as it will not yield a real number (there is a negative value in the radicand).

Simplify each remaining answer choice:

(B) $\quad -\sqrt{4a^2b^4} = -\sqrt{(2)^2 \bullet (a)^2 \bullet (b^2)^2} = -2ab^2$ $\qquad$ Rule out (B)

(C) $\quad -a\sqrt{8b^2} = -a\sqrt{(2)^2 \bullet (b)^2 \bullet 2} = -2ab\sqrt{2}$ $\qquad$ Rule out (C)

(E) $\quad -2b\sqrt{(2ab)^2}$ $\qquad$ By definition, $\sqrt{x^2} = x$, so $\sqrt{(2ab)^2} = 2ab$.

$\qquad\qquad\qquad\qquad$ Multiply this result by the quantity outside the radicand: $-2b \cdot 2ab = -4ab^2$

The answer is (E).

SAT PRACTICE: SIMPLIFYING RADICALS (CUBE ROOT APPLICATION)

GRID-IN PROBLEM:

If $18x$ represents the positive cube of an integer, what is the smallest integer that x could equal?

Solution:

Find the prime factors of 18: $\qquad\qquad\qquad 18 = 2 \bullet 3 \bullet 3$

This means: $\qquad\qquad\qquad\qquad\qquad \sqrt[3]{18x} = \sqrt[3]{2 \bullet 3^2 \bullet x}$

x will equal the product of the remaining factors of 2 and 3 that are needed to make $18x$ a perfect cube:

$$\sqrt[3]{18x} = \sqrt[3]{2 \bullet 3^2 \bullet x} = \sqrt[3]{2^3 \bullet 3^3}$$

Two more factors of 2 and one more factor of 3 are needed to make a perfect cube. Therefore:

$$x = 2 \bullet 2 \bullet 3 = 12$$

Grid-in 12.

ALGEBRA TOPIC #7:
INTEGER & RATIONAL EXPONENTS

Exponents in SAT math problems have historically been presented as positive integers, but expressions may

also include **negative exponents** (*example:* y^{-4}) and **fractional exponents** (*example:* $9^{\frac{1}{2}}$).

PROPERTIES OF EXPONENTS

$a^m \bullet a^n = a^{m+n}$ 　　　　　　　*Example:* $3^4 \bullet 3^5 = 3^9$

$(a^m)^n = a^{m \bullet n}$ 　　　　　　　　*Example:* $(r^2)^3 = r^6$

$(ab)^m = a^m b^m$ 　　　　　　　　*Example:* $(rs)^4 = r^4 s^4$

$a^{-m} = \dfrac{1}{a^m}$ 　　　　　　　*Example:* $2^{-5} = \dfrac{1}{32}$ **and** $\dfrac{1}{a^3 b^2} = a^{-3} b^{-2}$

$\dfrac{a^m}{a^m} = 1$ **and** $a^0 = 1, a \neq 0$

$\left(\dfrac{a}{b}\right)^m = \dfrac{a^m}{b^m}, b \neq 0$ 　　　*Example:* $\left(\dfrac{a^4 b^5 c}{x^2 yz^3}\right)^3 = \dfrac{a^{12} b^{15} c^3}{x^6 y^3 z^9}$

$\dfrac{a^m}{a^n} = a^{m-n}$, where $m > n$ **and** 　　*Example:* $\dfrac{a^2 b^4 c^7}{a^3 b^2 c} = \dfrac{b^2 c^6}{a}$

$\dfrac{a^m}{a^n} = \dfrac{1}{a^{n-m}}$, where $m < n$

Rational Exponent Theorem

If a is a real number $\neq 0$, m is an integer, and n is an integer > 0:

$a^{\frac{m}{n}} = (a^{\frac{1}{n}})^m = \left(\sqrt[n]{a}\right)^m$, or $a^{\frac{m}{n}} = (a^m)^{\frac{1}{n}} = \sqrt[n]{a^m}$ 　　*Example:* $27^{\frac{2}{3}} = \left(\sqrt[3]{27}\right)^2 = 3^2 = 9$

(except when n is even and a < 0)

Integer & Rational Exponents: Example #1

Solve: $x^{-3} = 64$

Solution:

$$x^{-3} = 64$$

$$\frac{1}{x^3} = 64 \qquad\qquad \leftarrow \text{Apply: } x^{-m} = \frac{1}{x^m}$$

$$64x^3 = 1 \qquad x^3 = \frac{1}{64} \qquad x = \sqrt[3]{\frac{1}{64}} = \frac{1}{4}$$

Integer & Rational Exponents: Example #2

If $r > 0$ and $5\,r^{\frac{2}{5}} = 20$, what is the value of r?

Solution:

$$5\,r^{\frac{2}{5}} = 20 \qquad\qquad\qquad r^{\frac{2}{5}} = 4$$

$$\sqrt[5]{r^2} = 4 \qquad\qquad\qquad \leftarrow \text{Apply: } r^{\frac{m}{n}} = \sqrt[n]{r^m}$$

$$r^2 = 4^5 = 1024 \qquad\qquad \leftarrow \text{Raise each side of the equation to the fifth power}$$

$$r = \sqrt{1024} = 32$$

SAT PRACTICE: INTEGER & RATIONAL EXPONENTS

If $27^{\frac{1}{x}} = y$, then $y^{\frac{2}{3}} =$

(A) $\qquad \dfrac{2}{3^x}$

(B) $\qquad \dfrac{9}{x}$

(C) $\qquad \dfrac{x^2}{81}$

(D) $\qquad 9^{\frac{1}{x}}$

(E) $\qquad \dfrac{2}{27^{3x}}$

Solution:

$$\left(27^{\frac{1}{x}}\right)^{\frac{2}{3}}$$ ←Replace y in the second expression with $27^{\frac{1}{x}}$

$$\left(27^{\frac{2}{3}}\right)^{\frac{1}{x}}$$ ←Interchange the exponents

$$\left(27^{\frac{2}{3}}\right)^{\frac{1}{x}} = 9^{\frac{1}{x}}$$ ←Evaluate

The answer is (D).

ALGEBRA TOPIC #8:
DIRECT AND INVERSE VARIATION

Sir Isaac Newton was born on Christmas Day in 1642, the same year that Galileo died. Newton arrived prematurely, and his mother reportedly said that he was so tiny that he could fit into a small pot.

In 1661, Newton enrolled in Cambridge's Trinity College. Unfortunately, the plague was spreading across Europe at that time. In the summer of 1665, the outbreak reached Cambridge and the university closed. Newton returned home where he spent two years in concentrated study of mathematics and physics. He later reported that it was during this time that he first understood the theory of gravitation. Newton hypothesized that the gravitational attraction between two bodies decreases with increasing distance between them as the inverse of the square of that distance.

Newton's inverse square law, $f = \dfrac{1}{d^2}$, is perhaps the most famous scientific application of inverse variation. The SAT includes problems covering both direct and inverse variation.

Definitions: Direct and Inverse Variation

- A **direct variation** occurs when the quantities represented by two variables always have the same ratio:

$$\frac{y}{x} = k$$

   y **is directly proportional to** x **if** $y = kx$, in which k is called the **"constant of variation"** or the **"constant of proportionality."**

   ➤ An example of a direct variation is the proportional relationship of the circumference of a circle to its diameter:

$$\frac{C}{d} = \pi \quad \text{or} \quad C = \pi d$$

   In this case, π is the constant of variation.

- An **inverse variation** occurs when the quantities represented by two variables always have the same product: $xy = k$

y **is inversely proportional to** *x* **if** $y = \dfrac{k}{x}$.

➤ An example of an inverse variation is the relationship between rate of speed and the time it takes to travel a certain distance:

$$\text{Distance} = \text{Rate} \bullet \text{Time}$$

As the rate increases, the time it takes to go a certain distance decreases, and vice versa.

Direct Variation	**Inverse Variation**
"*y* varies directly with *x*"	"*y* varies inversely with *x*"
$\dfrac{y}{x} = k$ or $y = kx$	$xy = k$ or $y = \dfrac{k}{x}$
For solutions (x_1, y_1) and (x_2, y_2),	For solutions (x_1, y_1) and (x_2, y_2),
$\dfrac{y_1}{x_1} = \dfrac{y_2}{x_2}$	$x_1 \bullet y_1 = x_2 \bullet y_2$

(*k* is the constant of variation)

When the variables are to the first degree, then the direct variation is linear. In these cases, the values for *x* and *y* are ordered pairs (*x*, *y*) that can be graphed in a coordinate plane, and *k*, the constant of variation, is actually the slope of the line.

Various adaptations of direct and inverse variation may be encountered on the SAT. For example, y^2 varies directly with *x* would be stated:

$$\frac{y^2}{x} = k \qquad \text{or}$$

$$y^2 = kx$$

SAT PRACTICE: DIRECT VARIATION

y^3 is directly proportional to *x*, and *y* = 3 when *x* = 81. When *y* = 2, *x* =

(A)   4
(B)   8
(C)   16
(D)   24
(E)   36

Solution:

In this direct variation, $\dfrac{y^3}{x} = k$, which leads to the following ratio:

$$\frac{(y_1)^3}{x_1} = \frac{(y_2)^3}{x_2} \qquad \frac{3^3}{81} = \frac{2^3}{x_2}$$

Solve for x_2 through cross multiplication:

$$81 \cdot 2^3 = 3^3 \cdot x_2$$
$$648 = 27 \cdot x_2$$
$$24 = x_2$$

The answer is (D).

SAT PRACTICE: INVERSE VARIATION

The price of commercial wiring made of a metal alloy is inversely proportional to the alloy's copper content. If a 100-foot spool of wire costs $27.00 when $\dfrac{1}{4}$ of the alloy's composition is copper, how much will a 100-foot spool of wire cost if $\dfrac{3}{4}$ of the alloy consists of copper?

(A) $3.00
(B) $9.00
(C) $20.25
(D) $81.00
(E) $243.00

Solution:

This is an inverse proportion; use the equation $x_1 \cdot y_1 = x_2 \cdot y_2$:

$$27 \cdot \frac{1}{4} = \frac{3}{4} \cdot y_2$$

Before you start pushing calculator buttons, look at this equation for a moment.
$\dfrac{3}{4}$ is three times as large as $\dfrac{1}{4}$, so 27 will be three times as large as y_2.
$27 \div 3 = 9$. The answer is (B).

ALGEBRA TOPIC #9:
FUNCTIONS

The 17th century German mathematician, philosopher and scientist Baron Gottfried Wilhelm von Leibniz is credited with having first applied the term "function" to mathematics. He used the term in describing a quantity related to a curve, such as its slope. Leibniz was a child prodigy. By the age of twelve he had taught himself how to read Latin and had begun to study Greek. As a teenager he mastered texts in mathematics, philosophy, theology, and law.

The Russian mathematician Leonhard Euler introduced modern function notation in the 18th century. The "function of x" was represented by $f(x)$. Read "f of x," this quantity represented the dependent variable associated with a given x-value (the independent variable). Euler was blind for the last 17 years of his life, but during that time he experienced an increase in mathematical productivity. Euler had tremendous powers of concentration and could perform extensive calculations mentally. Following his loss of vision he would dictate his mathematical findings to one of his sons or to his secretary.

Function Terms and Notation

A **relation** is any set of ordered pairs, (x, y).

A function is a special type of relation. A function is a set of ordered pairs (x, y), or $(x, f(x))$ in which every x-value is associated with exactly one $f(x)$ or y-value.

Function notation can include letters other than f; $g(x)$ and $h(x)$ are both commonly used. The notation $f(x)$ is read "f of x" or "f at x."

The **domain** of a function is the set of all of its x-values.

The **range** of a function is the set of all of its $f(x)$ or y-values.

Example:

$$f(x) = \frac{x^2}{x-3}$$

To find $f(6)$, replace x with 6 and evaluate:

$$f(6) = \frac{6^2}{6-3} = \frac{36}{3} = 12$$

So this particular ordered pair $(x, f(x))$ or (x, y) is $(6, 12)$.

The **domain** of a function consists of all x-values that produce real number $f(x)$ or y-values. A function cannot include any x-values that will cause the function to be "undefined" (such as having zero for the denominator). Set the denominator equal to zero to find any restrictions for the domain.

So, for $f(x) = \dfrac{x^2}{x-3}$, you would set $x - 3$ equal to 0 to find restrictions for the domain.

The domain for this function is, therefore, the set of all real numbers $\neq 3$.

Functions Summary

1. **A function** is a set of ordered pairs such that each element x corresponds with a unique element y; every element in the function's domain matches to exactly one element in the range.

2. **To determine whether a relation is also a function**, apply the "vertical line" test to its graph. If any vertical line crosses the graph of a relation at more than one point, the relation is not a function. (*Example*: a circle is a relation but not a function.)

(Functions can be graphed in a coordinate plane. Refer to the next chapter, "Coordinate Geometry and Graphs in a Coordinate Plane," regarding the graphs of various functions).

SAT PRACTICE: FUNCTIONS (EVALUATING A FUNCTION)

GRID-IN PROBLEM:

If the function f is defined by $f(x) = \dfrac{1}{2}x + 3^x$, what is the value of $f(2)$?

$$f(x) = \frac{1}{2}x + 3^x$$

$$\downarrow \qquad \downarrow \quad \downarrow$$

$$f(2) = \frac{1}{2}(2) + 3^2 = 1 + 9 = 10$$

Grid-in 10.

SAT PRACTICE: FUNCTIONS (BINARY OPERATIONS WITH STRANGE SYMBOLS – AN SAT CLASSIC)

(SAT writers like to use weird symbols in what are really relatively simple input/output problems or dressed up functions.)

GRID-IN PROBLEM:

If $s \ast t = t - \dfrac{1}{s}$, what is the value of $-2 \ast 9$?

Solution:

Substitute -2 for s and 9 for t: $-2 \ast 9 = 9 - \left(-\dfrac{1}{2} \right) = 9 + \dfrac{1}{2} = 9\dfrac{1}{2}$

Grid-in 9.5 or 19/2.

Algebra Topic #10:
Linear Equations

A **linear equation** has the following form:

$$ax + by + c = 0$$

a, b and c are real number constants. The graph of a linear equation is a line in a coordinate plane.

A linear equation is often written as follows:

$$y = mx + b$$

(x, y) are all coordinate pairs that are solutions for the equation, m is the slope of the line and b is the y-intercept for the line's graph. *(Linear equations are covered more extensively in the next chapter, "Coordinate Geometry and Graphs in a Coordinate Plane.")*

The following is an example of a linear equation:

Stated in "slope-intercept form": $y = 4x - 3$

Written in standard form: $4x - y - 3 = 0$

Solving a System of Linear Equations: Example

Find the solution set for the following system of equations:

$$3x + y = 5$$
$$5x - 2y = 1$$

Solution:

The solution set for a system of two intersecting lines is a point in a coordinate plane represented by an ordered pair (x, y).

Substitution Method

1. Solve one of the equations for one of the variables (get x in terms of y or y in terms of x). In this case, isolate y in the first equation:

$$y = 5 - 3x$$

2. Substitute the result of step #1 (state x in terms of y or state y in terms of x) in the other equation so that it now has only one variable. Solve for that variable. In this case, substitute $(5 - 3x)$ for y in the second equation:

$$5x - 2(5 - 3x) = 1$$
$$5x - 10 + 6x = 1$$
$$11x = 11$$
$$x = 1$$

3. Substitute the solution from step 2 back into one of the original equations to solve for the other variable. In this case, replace x with 1:

$$3(1) + y = 5$$
$$y = 2$$

The point of intersection is (1, 2). Solution set = {(1, 2)}

Addition/Multiplication Method

1. Multiply the first equation by a number that will make matching coefficients for the x or for the y variables in each equation:

$$2(3x + y) = 2 \cdot 5$$
$$6x + 2y = 10$$

2. Add or subtract the second equation from the modified first equation to eliminate one variable.

$$
\begin{array}{r}
6x + 2y = 10 \\
+ \quad 5x - 2y = 1 \\
\hline
11x \quad\quad = 11 \\
x = 1
\end{array}
$$

3. Substitute the solution from step back into one of the original equations to solve for the other variable (see step 3 of Substitution Method above.)

Graphing Calculator Method

An easy way to solve this problem is to enter the equations for the two lines into the equation editor **[Y =]** of a graphing calculator and then graph them. First, write each equation in $y = mx + b$ form:

$$3x + y = 5 \quad\quad \text{becomes} \quad\quad y = -3x + 5$$

$$5x - 2y = 1 \quad\quad \text{becomes} \quad\quad y = \frac{5}{2}x - \frac{1}{2}$$

To access the equation editor, press **[Y =]**.

After \Y$_1$ = , enter the first equation ($y = -3x + 5$) using the following key sequence:

[(-)] 3 [X, T, θ, *n*] + 5

After \Y$_2$ = , enter the second equation ($y = \frac{5}{2}x - \frac{1}{2}$) using the following key sequence:

5 ÷ 2 [X, T, θ, *n*] – 1 ÷ 2

Once the equations are entered, press **[GRAPH]** and the graph of the two equations (two intersecting lines) will appear in the screen. The goal now is to find the coordinates of the point of intersection. To accomplish this, access the yellow **[CALC]** menu by pressing **[2nd] [TRACE]**. Select **5:intersect**. The graph will reappear. Press **[ENTER]** three times. The following will appear at the bottom of the screen:

Intersection

$x = 1$ $y = 2$

The point of intersection is (1, 2). Solution set = {(1, 2)}

Graphing Calculator Screen:

$y = -3x + 5$ and $y = \dfrac{5}{2}x - \dfrac{1}{2}$

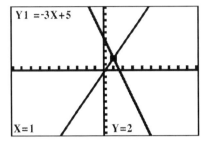

SAT PRACTICE: LINEAR EQUATIONS (SOLVING A SYSTEM OF LINEAR EQUATIONS)

GRID-IN PROBLEM:

If $5x - 2y = 16$ and $2x + y = 10$, then what is the value of $x - y$?

Solution:

For actual SAT problems, do not begin by going through multiple steps to solve for x and then y; simply adding or subtracting the two equations directly often leads to the answer. Try adding the equations and see what happens. If this fails to produce a workable result, then try subtracting one equation from the other.

Add the two equations:

$$\begin{array}{r} 5x - 2y = 16 \\ +\quad \underline{2x + y = 10} \\ 7x - y = 26 \end{array}$$

This result is not a multiple of $x - y$. Try subtraction:

$$\begin{array}{r} 5x - 2y = 16 \\ (-)\quad \underline{2x + y = 10} \\ 3x - 3y = 6 \end{array}$$

Dividing through by 3 reveals the actual answer:

$$\frac{3x}{3} - \frac{3y}{3} = \frac{6}{3}$$

$$x - y = 2$$

Grid-in 2.

ALGEBRA TOPIC #11:
QUADRATIC EXPRESSIONS & EQUATIONS

Al-Khwarizmi, a 9th century A.D. Islamic astronomer and mathematician, wrote several math texts, including a book about linear and quadratic equations. He was born in Baghdad and worked in the House of Wisdom, an important center of research and study that operated under the patronage of the Caliph Al-Mamun. Al-Khwarizmi and his colleagues' tasks included translating Greek scientific manuscripts and studying algebra, geometry and astronomy. Al-Khwarizmi used both algebraic and geometric methods of solution, and he provided a geometric proof of the approach to solve quadratic equations known as "completing the square." Al-Khwarizmi is considered the father of algebra. The English word "algorithm" is derived from the Latin form of al-Khwarizmi's name.

Quadratics

A **quadratic equation** has the following form:

$$ax^2 + bx + c = 0$$

a, b and c are real number constants, and $a \neq 0$. The graph of a quadratic equation is a parabola (*refer to the next chapter, "Coordinate Geometry and Graphs in a Coordinate Plane"*).

The following is an example of a quadratic equation:

$$3x^2 + 2x - 8 = 0$$

Factored Forms of Quadratic Expressions

$(a + b)^2 = a^2 + 2ab + b^2$

Example: $(3x + 4)^2 = 9x^2 + 24x + 16$

$(a - b)^2 = a^2 - 2ab + b^2$

Example: $(2x - 5)^2 = 4x^2 - 20x + 25$

The difference of squares:

$(a + b)(a - b) = a^2 - b^2$

Example: $(4x + 6)(4x - 6) = 16x^2 - 36$

Quadratic Formula

For any quadratic equation in the form $ax^2 + bx + c = 0$:

$$x = \frac{-b \pm \sqrt{b^2 - 4ac}}{2a}$$

Factoring Quadratic Expressions

Example: Factor $x^2 + 5x - 24$

Solve this riddle: Find two numbers a and b whose product is -24 and whose sum is 5.

$a \cdot b = -24$	$a + b = 5$
$-3 \cdot 8$	$-3 + 8$

The pair of numbers that works is -3 and 8, so $x^2 + 5x - 24$ factors into $(x - 3)(x + 8)$.

Example: Factor $4x^2 + 8x - 5$

This problem is more complex because the coefficient for the x^2 term is not 1.

•   The product of the first terms in each set of parentheses must equal the squared term ($4x^2$).

•   The product of the second term in each set of parentheses must equal the constant term (-5).

•   Experiment with the possibilities until you find one that produces the middle term of $8x$:
     $(4x + 1)(x - 5)$: Middle term would be $(4x \cdot -5) + (1 \cdot x)$, or $-19x$ NO
     $(4x + 5)(x - 1)$: Middle term would be $(4x \cdot -1) + (5 \cdot x)$, or x NO
     $(2x + 5)(2x - 1)$: Middle term would be $(2x \cdot -1) + (5 \cdot 2x)$, or $8x$ YES
          $4x^2 + 8x - 5 = (2x + 5)(2x - 1)$

Factoring quadratics to divide polynomial fractions:

Example: Simplify $\dfrac{x^2 + 4x - 21}{x^2 - 49}$

Factor both the numerator and the denominator. Divide out any common binomial factors.

$$\frac{\cancel{(x+7)}(x - 3)}{\cancel{(x+7)}(x - 7)} = \frac{x - 3}{x - 7}$$

Quadratic Equations: Example #1

Solve for x: $3x^2 - 4x = 7$

Solution:

Factoring Method

1. Write the equation in the standard form:

   $$ax^2 + bx + c = 0 \qquad\qquad 3x^2 - 4x - 7 = 0$$

2. Factor the equation:

   $$(3x - 7)(x + 1) = 0$$

3. Set each binomial term equal to zero and solve for x:

$3x - 7 = 0$	$x + 1 = 0$
$3x = 7$	$x = -1$
$x = \dfrac{7}{3}$	

$x = \dfrac{7}{3}$ or -1

Quadratic Formula Method

Quadratic formula: $x = \dfrac{-b \pm \sqrt{b^2 - 4ac}}{2a}$

$$3x^2 \;-\; 4x \;-\; 7 \;\;= 0$$
$$\uparrow \qquad \uparrow \qquad \uparrow$$
$$a = 3 \quad b = -4 \quad c = -7$$

$$x = \frac{-(-4) \pm \sqrt{(-4)^2 - 4(3)(-7)}}{2(3)} = \frac{4 \pm \sqrt{16 + 84}}{6}$$

Simplify further:

$$x = \frac{4 \pm \sqrt{100}}{6} \qquad So:$$

$$x = \frac{4 + 10}{6} = \frac{14}{6} = \frac{7}{3} \qquad \textbf{or} \qquad x = \frac{4 - 10}{6} = \frac{-6}{6} = -1$$

$x = \dfrac{7}{3}$ or -1

Graphing Calculator Method

This problem can be quickly solved with a graphing calculator. Some calculators are programmed with the quadratic formula, which is the easiest graphing calculator method of solution for quadratic equations. But you can also enter the equation into the equation editor of a graphing calculator, graph the function and then find the solution(s), or "zeroes" (x-values at which $y = 0$) for the equation.

First, rewrite the equation in the form $ax^2 + bx + c = 0$:

$$3x^2 - 4x = 7 \text{ becomes } 3x^2 - 4x - 7 = 0$$

Press **[Y =]** to access the equation editor. After \Y_1 = , enter the equation:

$$\textbf{3 [X, T, θ, } n\textbf{] [}x^2\textbf{] – 4 [X, T, θ, } n\textbf{] – 7}$$

Next press **[GRAPH]** and the graph of the equation (a parabola) will appear in the screen.

To find the values at which $y = 0$, access the yellow **[CALC]** menu by pressing **[2ⁿᵈ] [TRACE]**. Select **2:zero.**

The graph will reappear and the question "Left bound" will appear at the bottom of the screen. Press the **[<]** key to move the blinking cursor to the *left* of one of the x-intercepts and then press **[ENTER]**.

The question "Right bound" will then appear at the bottom of the screen. Press **[>]** to move the blinking cursor to the *right* of this x-intercept and press **[ENTER]**. The boundaries for this particular zero have now been established. When the question "Guess?" appears at the bottom of the screen, place the blinking cursor between the established boundaries and press **[ENTER]**. The following will appear at the bottom of the screen:

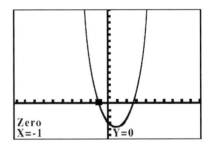

Zero

X = -1   Y = 0

Graphing Calculator Screen:
Identifying the zeroes for
$y = 3x^2 - 4x - 7$

Repeat this process to establish left and right bounds for the other x-intercept. The following will appear at the bottom of the screen:

Zero
X = 2.3333333   Y = 0

$x = $ -1 or $2.\overline{3}$ ($2.\overline{3}$ = $\dfrac{7}{3}$).

SAT PRACTICE: QUADRATIC EXPRESSIONS AND EQUATIONS

GRID-IN QUESTION:

If $(x + y)^2 = 64$ and $x^2 + y^2 = 34$, then what is the value of xy?

Solution:

Variations of this problem have appeared on several past SATs. The key is to recognize the relationship between the two equations.

Start by expanding $(x + y)^2 \rightarrow$

Subtract the second equation $\rightarrow$

$$x^2 + 2xy + y^2 = 64$$
$$(-) \quad x^2 \qquad + y^2 = 34$$
$$\overline{\qquad 2xy \qquad = 30}$$

$xy = 15$

Grid-in 15.

SAT PRACTICE: QUADRATIC EXPRESSIONS AND EQUATIONS (DOMAIN & RANGE)

Let the function f be defined by $f(x) = x^2 - 4$. Which of the following is true?

(A)   The domain of the function is the set of all real numbers ≥ 4.

(B)   The domain of the function is the set of all real numbers ≥ -4.

(C)   The range of the function is the set of all real numbers.

(D)   The range of the function is the set of all real numbers ≥ 4.

(E)   The range of the function is the set of all real numbers ≥ -4.

Solution:

Inspection Method

Many students will be able to inspect the equation and realize that because x^2 will always be nonnegative, the smallest possible value of x^2 will be 0. Therefore, all $f(x)$ values for this function (the function's range) will be greater than or equal to $0 - 4$, or -4, making (E) the correct answer.

Process of Elimination and Graphing Calculator Method

The domain for any equation that does not contain a radical or rational expression is the set of all real numbers. Because this function meets these criteria, its domain is the set of all real numbers. Therefore, answer choices (A) and (B) can be eliminated.

The graph of a function will reveal the function's minimum or maximum value, which will dictate its range. The range of the function will include all values greater than or equal to its minimum y-value or less than or equal to its maximum y-value. Begin by pressing **[Y =]** to access your graphing calculator's equation editor. After $\backslash Y_1 =$, enter the equation:

$$[X, T, \theta, n] \ [x^2] - 4$$

Press **[GRAPH]** and the graph of the equation (a parabola) will appear in the screen. It is clear that the vertex of the parabola is a minimum point, as the curve opens upward. If you cannot visually identify the coordinates of the minimum point, access the yellow **[CALC]** menu by pressing **[2nd] [TRACE]**. Select **3:minimum**. (*If the parabola opened downward, we would have selected* **4:maximum**.)

The graph will reappear with a blinking cursor over the minimum point. Establish bounds as explained on page 90 (next to graphing calculator screen). The following will appear at the bottom of the screen:

Minimum

X = 0   Y = -4

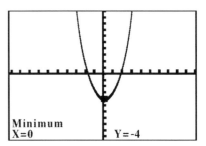

Graphing Calculator Screen:
Minimum point for $f(x) = x^2 - 4$

The minimum point of the graph is at the vertex (0, -4), and all other $f(x)$ or y-values (the range of the function) will be greater than or equal to -4.

The answer is (E).

ALGEBRA TOPIC #12:
GEOMETRIC (EXPONENTIAL GROWTH) SEQUENCES

In a **geometric or exponential sequence**, the ratio of successive terms is the same constant number, often referred to as k:

Term #1 • k = Term #2
Term #2 • k = Term #3
Term #3 • k = Term #4

…and so on.

The following is an example of a geometric or exponential growth sequence:

2, 8, 32, 128…

The constant ratio in this sequence is 4, as each successive term is obtained by multiplying the preceding term by 4. The expression for finding the nth term would be $2 \cdot 4^{n-1}$.

Geometric or Exponential Sequences

General rule for finding a term in a geometric sequence:

$$n\text{th term} = 1^{st}\text{ term} \bullet (\text{Constant Ratio})^{n-1}$$

$a_n = a_1(r)^{n-1}$, where a_1 is the first term of the sequence and a_n is the nth term

PRACTICE: GEOMETRIC (EXPONENTIAL GROWTH) SEQUENCES

Which of the following is the 7th term of the following geometric sequence?

$$3, 15, 75\ldots$$

(A)   300
(B)   450
(C)   1,875
(D)   9,375
(E)   46,875

Solution:

First, find the constant ratio:

$$15 \div 3 = 5$$
$$75 \div 15 = 5$$

The constant ratio is 5.

Now multiply successive terms by 5 to find the 7th term:

$$3, 15, 75, \underline{}, \underline{}, \underline{}, \underline{}$$

$$4^{th}\text{ term} = 75 \bullet 5 = 375$$
$$5^{th}\text{ term} = 375 \bullet 5 = 1,875$$
$$6^{th}\text{ term} = 1,875 \bullet 5 = 9,375$$
$$7^{th}\text{ term} = 9,375 \bullet 5 = 46,875$$

The following method is faster:

$$a_7 = 3(5)^{7-1}$$
$$= 3(5)^6$$
$$= 46,875$$

The answer is (E).

PRACTICE: GEOMETRIC (EXPONENTIAL GROWTH) SEQUENCES

GRID-IN PROBLEM

The expression $x \cdot 2^{\frac{h}{5}}$ can be used to calculate the growth of a bacteria culture in which h represents time in hours and x represents the initial bacteria population. If there are 1,200 bacteria present after 15 hours, what is the value of x?

Solution:

Set the expression equal to 1,200. Substitute 15 for h and solve for x:

$$1{,}200 = x \cdot 2^{\frac{15}{5}}$$
$$1{,}200 = x \cdot 2^{3}$$
$$1{,}200 = 8x$$

$x = 150$

Grid-in 150.

Mathematics
Chapter 4

Coordinate Geometry & Graphs in a Coordinate Plane

Coordinate plane geometry topics on the SAT include slope and equation of a line, slopes of parallel and perpendicular lines, finding the midpoint of a line segment, and finding the distance between two points in a coordinate plane. Students are also expected to identify and compare the graphs of functions and to have a working knowledge of the characteristics of graphs. Other test questions feature real life applications of graphs, including functions as models and scatterplots.

COORDINATE PLANE GEOMETRY & GRAPHS TOPIC #1:
COORDINATE GEOMETRY BASICS

When he was eight years old, the famous 17th century French philosopher and mathematician Rene Descartes was sent to Jesuit College, a boarding school in La Fleche. Because the young Descartes was a frail and sickly boy, the headmaster allowed him to stay in bed every morning for as long as he wished. Descartes became accustomed to this habit, and later claimed that his greatest ideas in philosophy and mathematics occurred during hours spent lying in bed.

Legend has it that one morning as he lay resting in bed, Descartes observed a fly crawling on the ceiling. Descartes contemplated how he could mathematically report the fly's position. All of a sudden he realized that the fly's position could be described in terms of its distance from two adjacent walls. Coordinate geometry was born, and the coordinate plane is also referred to as the Cartesian plane in Descartes' honor.

Coordinate Geometry Terms

The **coordinate plane** is a system based upon two perpendicular number lines.

The **x-axis** is the horizontal axis or line.

The **y-axis** is the vertical axis or line.

The **origin** is the intersection point of the x- and y-axes.

The coordinates of every point in the plane are specified by an ordered pair of real numbers, (x, y). The coordinates of the origin are $(0, 0)$.

Example:

In the coordinate plane shown, point *R* has the coordinates (4, -2) and point *S* has the coordinates (-6, 3).

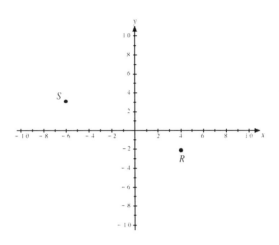

Slope is the measurement of the steepness of a line segment. The numerical value for slope can be positive, negative, or zero; the slope of a vertical line is "undefined." If the segment of a line rises from left to right, the line will have a positive slope. If it falls from left to right, it will have a negative slope. *Example:* In the coordinate plane shown, $\overleftrightarrow{RT}$ has a positive slope and $\overleftrightarrow{RS}$ has a negative slope.

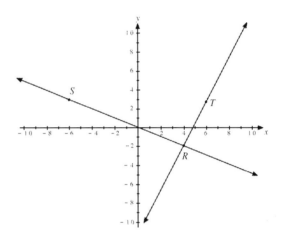

Slope of a Line

Equation to find slope *m* of a non-vertical line that contains segment $\overline{AB}$ with endpoints $A(x_1, y_1)$ and $B(x_2, y_2)$, $x_1 \neq x_2$:

$$m = \frac{rise}{run} = \frac{y_2 - y_1}{x_2 - x_1}$$

Slope of a Line: Example

Find the slope m of $\overline{AB}$ for A (5, 4) and B (-3, 1).

Solution:

Substitute the coordinates for A and B into the slope formula. (*Be sure to start with the same point for both the numerator and the denominator.*)

$$m = \frac{y_2 - y_1}{x_2 - x_1} = \frac{1 - 4}{-3 - 5} = \frac{-3}{-8} = \frac{3}{8}$$

The slope of $\overline{AB}$ is $\frac{3}{8}$.

SAT PRACTICE: SLOPE

GRID-IN PROBLEM:

In the figure shown, if the slope of line l is $-\frac{1}{5}$, what is the value of r?

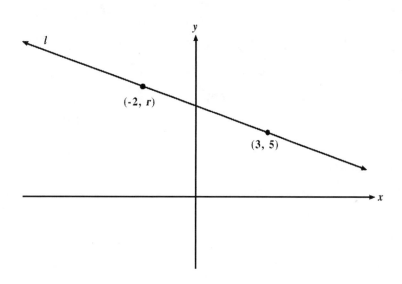

Solution:

$$m = \frac{y_2 - y_1}{x_2 - x_1} \qquad -\frac{1}{5} = \frac{r - 5}{(-2 - 3)} \qquad \leftarrow \text{Insert the known coordinates of the two points}$$

Cross multiply to solve for r:

$$-1(-5) = 5(r - 5)$$
$$5 = 5r - 25$$
$$30 = 5r$$
$$6 = r$$

Grid-in 6.

COORDINATE PLANE GEOMETRY & GRAPHS TOPIC #2:
EQUATION OF A LINE AND
SLOPES OF PARALLEL AND PERPENDICULAR LINES

As presented in the previous chapter, a **linear equation** has the following form:

$$ax + by + c = 0$$

a, b and c are real number constants.   *Example:* $3x - 4y + 6 = 0$

The graph of a linear equation is a line in a coordinate plane.

Linear Equation Summary

Standard form: $ax + by + c = 0$

Point-slope equation of a line with slope m containing the point (x_1, y_1):
$$y - y_1 = m(x - x_1)$$

Slope-intercept form of the equation of a line with slope m and y-intercept b:
$$y = mx + b$$

Equation of a Line: Example

What is the equation of a line (in slope-intercept form) having slope $\dfrac{3}{4}$ and passing through the point P (6, 2)?

Solution:

Start with the point-slope form of the equation: $y - y_1 = m(x - x_1)$

$$y - 2 = \frac{3}{4}(x - 6) \quad \leftarrow \text{Substitute the slope and the coordinates of the point given}$$

$$y - 2 = \frac{3}{4}x - \frac{18}{4}$$

$$y = \frac{3}{4}x - \frac{5}{2} \quad \leftarrow \text{This is the equation of the line in slope-intercept form.}$$

The y-intercept (the point at which the line crosses the y-axis) would be the point $(0, -\dfrac{5}{2})$.

SLOPE

Parallel, Perpendicular, Horizontal & Vertical Lines

A **horizontal line** is a line parallel to the *x*-axis. Its equation is in the form $y = b$ where *b* is the *y*-coordinate of all of the points on the line. Because all of the *y*-coordinates are equal, the value of the slope fraction's numerator is zero. Thus, the slope of any horizontal line is zero.

Example: $y = 5$ *(This is the line in which all ordered pairs have a y-coordinate of 5)*

The equation of the *x*-axis is $y = 0$.

A **vertical line** is any line parallel to the *y*-axis. Its equation is in the form $x = a$ where *a* is the *x*-coordinate of all of the points on the line. Because all of the *x*-coordinates are equal, the value of the slope fraction's denominator is zero. Thus, the slope of any vertical line is undefined.

Example: $x = -2$ *(This is the line in which all ordered pairs have an x-coordinate of -2)*

The equation of the *y*-axis is $x = 0$.

If two lines have equal slopes and different *y*-intercepts, the lines are **parallel**.

Example: The equations $y = \dfrac{2}{3}x + 6$ and $y = \dfrac{2}{3}x - 7$

represent parallel lines.

If the product of the slopes of two lines is -1 (the slopes are negative reciprocals), then the lines are **perpendicular.**

Example: The equations $y = \dfrac{2}{5}x - 3$ and $y = -\dfrac{5}{2}x + 8$

represent perpendicular lines because $\left(\dfrac{2}{5}\right) \bullet \left(-\dfrac{5}{2}\right) = -1$

Slope Summary		
Line	**Slope**	**Equation**
Horizontal	0	$y = b$, in which the *y*-coordinate for every point on the line equals *b*
Vertical	undefined	$x = a$, in which the *x*-coordinate for every point on the line equals *a*
Pair of Lines	**Slopes**	**Slope of Each Line**
Parallel	Equal	m, m
Perpendicular	Negative Reciprocals (Their product is -1)	$m, -\dfrac{1}{m}$

SAT PRACTICE: LINEAR EQUATIONS (SLOPE)

The slope of line p is $\frac{a}{b}$. Which of the following are true?

I.   The slope of a line parallel to line p is $\frac{a}{b}$.

II.   The slope of a line perpendicular to line p is $\frac{b}{a}$.

III. If p has a positive slope, the value of a must be greater than the value of b.

(A)   I only
(B)   II only
(C)   III only
(D)   I and II
(E)   None are true

Solution:

Consider each statement (I, II and III).

I.   Parallel lines have the same slope, so statement I is TRUE.

II.   Perpendicular lines have negative reciprocal slopes, so any line perpendicular to line p would have a slope of $-\frac{b}{a}$. Statement II is FALSE.

III. A line has a positive slope if both a and b values are positive or if both values are negative. It does not matter whether or not the value of a is greater than the value of b. Statement III is FALSE.

Because only statement I is true, the answer is (A).

COORDINATE PLANE GEOMETRY & GRAPHS TOPIC #3:
GRAPHING LINEAR EQUATIONS & INEQUALITIES

Questions on the SAT may ask you to identify the graph of a linear equation or of a linear inequality. These test questions may have different formats. You may be asked to select the correct graph among the answer choices, or you may be asked to choose the answer that best describes the graph. In either event, the key is to understand how a line or linear equation is represented in a coordinate plane.

SAT PRACTICE: IDENTIFYING THE GRAPH OF A LINEAR EQUATION

Which of the following represents the graph of $4x + 3y = 6$?

(A)

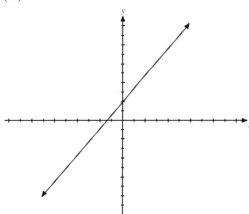

(D)

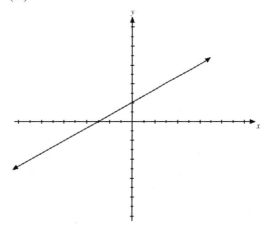

(B)

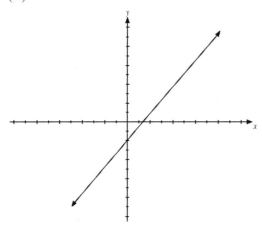

(E)

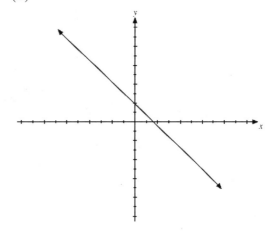

(C)

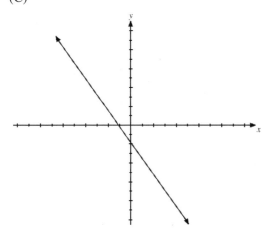

Solution:

Mental Math & Inspection Method

Place the equation in $y = mx + b$ form:

$$4x + 3y = 6 \qquad \text{becomes} \qquad y = -\frac{4}{3}x + 2$$

The line has a negative slope, so reject choices (A), (B) and (D). The line's y-intercept is 2, so choose (E).

Graphing Calculator Method

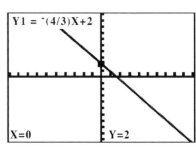

You can identify the graph by inputting the equation of the line into your graphing calculator's equation editor and then graphing the line. *(Refer to pages 85 – 86 in the Algebra chapter for more specific instructions regarding inputting and graphing a linear equation.)* Match your calculator-created graph with the correct answer choice. The answer is (E).

Graphing Calculator Screen:
$$y = -\frac{4}{3}x + 2$$

Linear Inequalities in Two Variables

The graph of a linear inequality (in two variables) is a half-plane that is bordered by the graph of the corresponding linear equation.

Graph of a Linear Inequality: Example

Identify the graph of $5x - 3y > 12$.

Solution:

State the inequality in slope-intercept form:

$$5x - 3y > 12$$
$$-3y > -5x + 12$$
$$y < \frac{5}{3}x - 4 \qquad \textit{(Remember to invert the inequality sign when you divide by}$$
$$\textit{a negative number)}$$

The graph of $5x - 3y > 12$ is an open half plane.

A dotted line (used for < or > inequalities) passes through the y-intercept (0, -4) and has a slope of $\frac{5}{3}$. The half plane to be shaded is below the dotted line.

Graphing Calculator Screen:

$$y < \frac{5}{3}x - 4$$

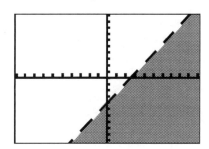

COORDINATE PLANE GEOMETRY & GRAPHS TOPIC #4:
DISTANCE & MIDPOINT

One of the most important applications of the coordinate plane is the global system of latitude and longitude. The "origin" of the earth's coordinate plane is the point at which the Prime Meridian (0° E or W longitude) meets the Equator (0° N or S latitude); this point is actually located in the Atlantic Ocean near West Africa's Gold Coast region. The latitude-longitude system can be used to quickly locate places on maps. Geographical coordinates can be used to determine the distance between two points.

Certain questions on the SAT require students to find the midpoint of a line segment or to determine the distance between two points in a coordinate plane. A line segment in a coordinate plane is divided into two congruent segments by its **midpoint**. The **distance** between two points in a coordinate plane is found through an application of the Pythagorean Theorem.

Midpoint Formula

Given A (x_1, y_1) and B (x_2, y_2), the coordinates of the midpoint, M, of $\overline{AB}$ are as follows:

$$M = \left(\frac{x_1 + x_2}{2}, \frac{y_1 + y_2}{2} \right)$$

Distance Formula

The distance, d, between A (x_1, y_1) and B (x_2, y_2) is given by the following formula:

$$d = \sqrt{(x_2 - x_1)^2 + (y_2 - y_1)^2}$$

Midpoint Formula: Example

Find the midpoint of $\overline{RS}$ if R has the coordinates (3, 5) and S has the coordinates (-7, 12).

Solution:

First, sketch $\overline{RS}$ with midpoint M for visual reference.

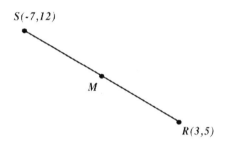

Now apply the Midpoint Formula. Substitute the coordinates for R and S:

$$M = \left(\frac{x_1 + x_2}{2}, \frac{y_1 + y_2}{2} \right) = \left(\frac{3 + (-7)}{2}, \frac{5 + 12}{2} \right) = \left(\frac{-4}{2}, \frac{17}{2} \right) = \left(-2, 8\frac{1}{2} \right)$$

The coordinates of the midpoint of $\overline{RS}$ are $\left(-2, 8\frac{1}{2} \right)$.

Distance Formula: Example

Find the distance between points R and S if R has the coordinates (3, 5) and S has the coordinates (-7, 12).

Solution:

$(x_1, y_1) = (3, 5)$ $(x_2, y_2) = (-7, 12)$

Substitute the coordinates of R and S into the distance formula: $d = \sqrt{(x_2 - x_1)^2 + (y_2 - y_1)^2}$

$$d = \sqrt{((-7) - 3)^2 + (12 - 5)^2} = \sqrt{(-10)^2 + (7)^2} = \sqrt{100 + 49} = \sqrt{149}$$

The distance between points R and S is $\sqrt{149}$, or approximately 12.2.

Note: Assigning the specific points to (x_1, y_1) and (x_2, y_2) is arbitrary. The order of subtraction does not matter because the difference between the two coordinates is squared, always producing a positive number.

SAT PRACTICE: MIDPOINT OF A LINE SEGMENT

The midpoint M of $\overline{JK}$ has the coordinates $\left(-\dfrac{7}{2}, 6\right)$. If the coordinates of J are $\left(8, -\dfrac{3}{2}\right)$, what are the coordinates of K?

(A) $\left(\dfrac{5}{2}, \dfrac{13}{2}\right)$

(B) $(2, 27)$

(C) $\left(\dfrac{11}{2}, \dfrac{9}{2}\right)$

(D) $\left(-1, \dfrac{21}{2}\right)$

(E) $\left(-15, \dfrac{27}{2}\right)$

Solution:

First, draw a simple sketch for visual reference depicting $\overline{JK}$ with midpoint M.

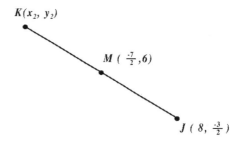

Let K have the coordinates (x_2, y_2). Apply the midpoint formula to find the x-coordinate of K:

$$-\frac{7}{2} = \left(\frac{8 + x_2}{2}\right) \qquad 2 \bullet \left(-\frac{7}{2}\right) = \left(\frac{8 + x_2}{2}\right) \bullet 2 \;\leftarrow \text{Multiply each side of the equation by 2}$$

Solve for x_2:

$$-7 = 8 + x_2$$
$$-15 = x_2 \qquad \text{The } x\text{-coordinate of } K \text{ is -15.}$$

Now apply the midpoint formula to find the y-coordinate of K:

$$6 = \left(\frac{-\dfrac{3}{2} + y_2}{2}\right) \qquad 2 \bullet 6 = \left(\frac{-\dfrac{3}{2} + y_2}{2}\right) \bullet 2 \leftarrow \text{Multiply each side of the equation by 2}$$

Solve for y_2:

$$12 = -\frac{3}{2} + y_2$$

$$13\frac{1}{2} = y_2 \qquad \text{The } y\text{-coordinate of } K \text{ is } 13\frac{1}{2}.$$

The coordinates of K are $(-15, 13\frac{1}{2})$

$13\frac{1}{2} = \frac{27}{2}$, so the answer is (E).

SAT PRACTICE: DISTANCE BETWEEN TWO POINTS

The distance between points A and B is 10. If the coordinates of A are $(3, c)$ and the coordinates of B are $(9, -c)$, what is the value of c?

(A)   4 or -4
(B)   5 or -5
(C)   6 or -6
(D)   7 or -7
(E)   8 or -8

Solution:

Substitute the coordinates of A and B into the distance formula: $d = \sqrt{(x_2 - x_1)^2 + (y_2 - y_1)^2}$

$$10 = \sqrt{(3-9)^2 + (c-(-c))^2} = \sqrt{(-6)^2 + (2c)^2} = \sqrt{36 + 4c^2}$$

$$10^2 = \left(\sqrt{36 + 4c^2}\right)^2 \qquad \leftarrow \text{Square both sides of the equation}$$

Now solve for c:

$$100 = 36 + 4c^2$$
$$64 = 4c^2$$
$$16 = c^2$$
$$\pm 4 = c \qquad \text{(Because there are two coordinates, } c \text{ and } -c\text{, both } +4 \text{ and } -4 \text{ are solutions)}$$

The answer is (A).

COORDINATE PLANE GEOMETRY & GRAPHS TOPIC #5:
GRAPHS OF IMPORTANT NON-LINEAR FUNCTIONS

A parabola is a conic section in which all points are equidistant from a specific point (known as the "focus") and a line (the "directrix"). If a plane intersects a cone so that the plane is parallel to the cone's slanted edge, the result is a parabola. This important mathematical curve has many interesting physical properties. The cross section of a dish antenna is a parabola. Incoming signals that are parallel to the axis of symmetry reflect off the dish and pass through the receiver, which is placed at the focus. Automobile headlights also have a parabolic shape with the bulb placed at the focus; light rays reflect off the parabolic surface and are emitted as parallel rays. The cables of a suspension bridge take the shape of a parabola because the weight of the bridge is equally distributed along the curve. Water spouting out of a fountain takes the shape of a parabola. The trajectory of a baseball thrown into the air and then pulled back to ground by gravity follows the arc of a parabola.

In a coordinate plane, a parabola represents the graph of the quadratic function $f(x) = ax^2 + bx + c = 0$ in which $a \neq 0$.

You can expect to see graphs of both quadratic functions and absolute value functions on the SAT. The algebra chapter covered the equations for these expressions. Here we will review the graphs of these functions.

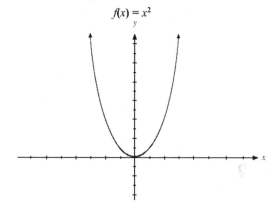

QUADRATIC FUNCTION

$f(x) = ax^2 + bx + c = 0$ in which $a \neq 0$.

The SAT frequently refers to the following basic quadratic function:

$$f(x) = x^2$$

ABSOLUTE VALUE FUNCTION

$$f(x) = |x|$$

For both of the functions
$f(x) = x^2$ and $f(x) = |x|$:

Vertex: (0, 0)
Domain: the set of all real numbers
Range: the set of all real numbers ≥ 0

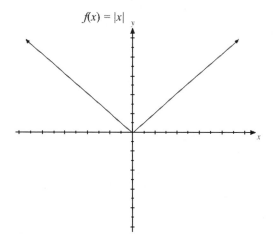

COORDINATE PLANE GEOMETRY & GRAPHS TOPIC #6:
TRANSFORMATIONS AND THEIR EFFECTS ON GRAPHS OF FUNCTIONS

A function's equation can be transformed, or altered, causing its graph to change in appearance or location in the coordinate plane. A transformation may have the following effects on the graph of a function:

- A vertical or horizontal shift
- A change in orientation (opens downward instead of upward or vice versa)
- A dilation, making the graph wider or narrower (stretched or compressed)

The coefficients and numerical terms within the equation affect its graph.

VARIOUS TRANSFORMATIONS
(Given a graph $y = f(x)$ and $c > 0$)

Function	Transformation	Description
$f(x) + c$	Shift $f(x)$ c units up	Vertical Translation
$f(x) - c$	Shift $f(x)$ c units down	Vertical Translation
$f(x + c)$	Shift $f(x)$ c units to the left	Horizontal Translation
$f(x - c)$	Shift $f(x)$ c units to the right	Horizontal Translation
$-f(x)$	Reflected across x-axis	Reflection
$f(-x)$	Reflected across y-axis	Reflection
$c \cdot f(x)$	If $0 < |c| < 1$, the graph is vertically compressed by a factor of c If $|c| > 1$, the graph is vertically stretched by a factor of c	Dilation

You can compare graph transformations with your graphing calculator. Input $y = x^2$ into the **[Y =]** equation editor along with the following variations of this function. Press **[GRAPH]** after the equations are entered.

$y = 5x^2 - 3$

$y = (x + 1)^2$

$y = -\frac{1}{2}x^2 + 3$

$y = (x - 2)^2$

$y = x^2 - 4$

Graphing Calculator Screen:
$\downarrow y = x^2$ $\downarrow y = (x - 2)^2$

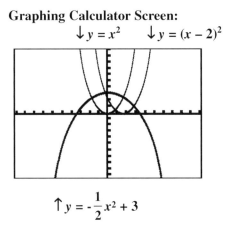

$\uparrow y = -\frac{1}{2}x^2 + 3$

What did you discover about the various functions with respect to vertical and horizontal shifts, reflections or dilations?

Note: If you ever have a graph that does not appear in your calculator's graph screen, go back to the home screen and press [WINDOW]. Set the minimum, maximum and scale values for the x- and y-axes so that they fit the data points for the graph.

After you have completed the preceding graphing calculator exercise, compare your results with the graphs below.

Examples of Graph Transformations

Inner curve: $f(x) = x^2$

Outer curve: $f(x) = \dfrac{1}{2}x^2$

$f(x) = \frac{1}{2}x^2 \quad f(x) = x^2$

Inner curve: $f(x) = -5x^2$

Outer curve: $f(x) = -x^2$

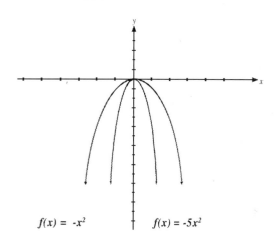

$f(x) = -x^2 \qquad f(x) = -5x^2$

Graphing Calculator Screen:
$f(x) = (x + 1)^2$ and $f(x) = (x - 3)^2$

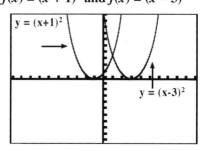

$y = (x+1)^2$

$y = (x-3)^2$

Graphing Calculator Screen:
$f(x) = x^2 + 1$ and $f(x) = x^2 - 3$

$y = x^2-3$

$y = x^2+1$

Summary for Comparing Graphs

$$f(x) = x^2 \qquad \text{versus} \qquad g(x) = a(x \pm b)^2 \pm c$$

a: If $|a| > 1$, the graph of $g(x)$ vertically stretched by a factor of a.
   If $-1 < a < 0 \; or \; 0 < a < 1$, the graph of $g(x)$ is vertically compressed by a factor of a.
   If a is negative, the graph of $g(x)$ is reflected over the x-axis.

b: If b is added, the graph of $g(x)$ will shift b units to the left of the graph of $f(x)$.
   If b is subtracted, the graph of $g(x)$ will shift b units to the right of the graph of $f(x)$.

c: If c is added, the graph of $g(x)$ will shift c units up from the graph of $f(x)$.
   If c is subtracted, the graph of $g(x)$ will shift c units down from the graph of $f(x)$.

Graph Transformations: Example

Compare the graph of $f(x) = x^2$ with the graph of $g(x) = 4(x + 5)^2 - 3$

Solution:

Graphing Calculator Method

Use your graphing calculator to compare the two functions. Press **[Y =]** to access the equation editor. Enter the two equations as follows:

   After $\backslash Y_1 =$ press **[X, T, θ, *n*] [*x²*]**
   After $\backslash Y_2 =$ press **4 ([X, T, θ, *n*] + 5) [*x²*] – 3**

Press **[GRAPH]** and the two parabolas will appear in the window. One of the keys in comparing the two graphs is to contrast the respective locations of their vertices. It is clear that the vertex of $f(x) = x^2$ is the minimum point $(0, 0)$. The vertex of $g(x)$ is also a minimum point, as its curve opens upward.

If you cannot visually identify the coordinates of the minimum point for $g(x)$, access the yellow **[CALC]** menu by pressing **[2ⁿᵈ] [TRACE]**. Select **3:minimum**.

After the graphs reappear, press the cursor keys so that the blinking cursor is on the curve for $g(x)$ with $Y_2 = 4(x + 5)^2 - 3$ appearing in the top left corner of the screen. Use the cursor keys to establish the left and right bounds to determine the minimum point of $g(x)$ (*see pages 91 – 92 in the Algebra chapter for details in this regard*). When the question "Guess?" appears at the bottom of the screen, press **[ENTER]**. The following will appear at the bottom of the screen:

   Minimum
   X = -5   Y = -3

(*Again, if the parabola opened downward, we would have selected* **4:maximum.**)

The graph of $g(x) = 4(x + 5)^2 - 3$ is shifted 3 units down and 5 units to the left of the graph of $f(x) = x^2$. By inspection, it is fairly easy to see that $g(x)$ is also a dilation (vertical stretch) of $f(x)$.

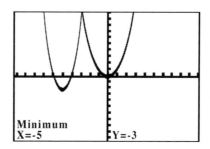

Graphing Calculator Screen:
$g(x) = 4(x + 5)^2 - 3$ and $f(x) = x^2$

Numerical Evaluation Method

If you do not wish to use a graphing calculator for this problem, you can evaluate the role of each numerical term in $g(x)$ with respect to the role of a, b and c in $g(x) = a(x \pm b)^2 \pm c$.

a: The coefficient "4" in front of the first parenthesis indicates that the graph of $g(x)$ is a dilation (vertical stretch) of $f(x)$.

b: The "+5" inside the parentheses indicates that graph of $g(x)$ will shift five units to the left of the graph of $f(x)$.

c: The "-3" outside the parentheses indicates that the graph of $g(x)$ will shift three units down from the graph of $f(x)$.

SAT PRACTICE: GRAPH TRANSFORMATIONS

If the graph shown here represents $f(x) = |x|$, which of the following is the graph of $f(x) = -|x + 2|$?

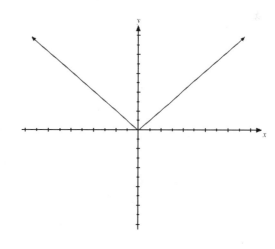

(A)

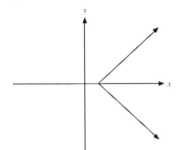

(D)

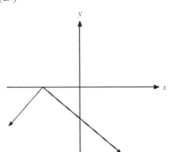

(B)

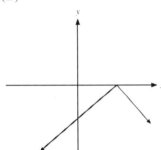

(E)

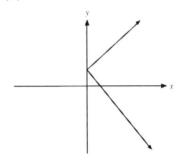

(C)

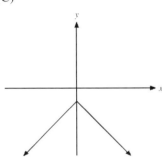

Graphing Calculator Method

Solution:

Use your graphing calculator to show the graph of
-|x + 2|. Press **[Y =]** to access the equation editor.
After \Y₁ = press **[(-)] [MATH] [>] 1 [X, T, θ, *n*] + 2)**

Press **[GRAPH]**. The graph in answer choice (D) is correct.

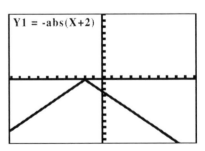

Graphing Calculator Screen:
$f(x) = -|x + 2|$

Establish Data Points & Match to Graph Method

x	$f(x) = -\lvert x + 2 \rvert$
-1	-1
0	-2
1	-3

Only the graph in answer choice (D) contains all three of these points.

COORDINATE PLANE GEOMETRY & GRAPHS TOPIC #7:
CHARACTERISTICS OF GRAPHS OF FUNCTIONS

The SAT includes questions in which you will be asked to interpret different aspects of graphs of functions. In this regard, you should be able to do the following:

➢ Identify the *x*- and/or *y*-coordinates of specified points.

➢ Identify the *x*- and/or *y*-intercepts of the graph (where the graph crosses the *x*- or *y*-axes).

➢ Know where certain points are with respect to the coordinate plane's origin (0, 0).

Example:

In the section of the graph shown:

• There are two values for which $f(x) = 1$.

• The graph's *y*-intercept is located at $(0, -\dfrac{1}{2})$.

• The graph has two *x*-intercepts.

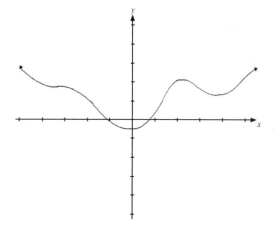

SAT PRACTICE: QUALITATIVE BEHAVIOR OF GRAPHS & FUNCTIONS

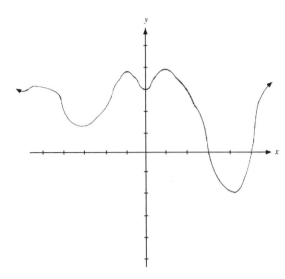

In the section of graph shown above, which of the following are true:

      I.   There are exactly three values for which $f(x) = 2$.

      II.   The graph's y-intercept is $(3, 0)$.

      III.   There are no points (x, y) such that both coordinates are negative.

(A)   I only

(B)   II only

(C)   III only

(D)   II and III

(E)   I, II and III

Solution:

Inspect the graph and determine which statements (I, II or III) are true.

I. $f(x) = 2$ means the same thing as $y = 2$. If you trace your finger across the line where $y = 2$, you will see that there are four x-values for which $y = 2$. Statement I is FALSE.

II. The y-intercept of the graph is the point at which it crosses the y-axis. The y-intercept shown has the coordinates $(0, 3)$, not $(3, 0)$. Another SAT trick! Statement II is also FALSE.

III. Any points for which x and y would both have negative values would be in the third quadrant of the coordinate plane (lower left). Since the graph does not enter the third quadrant, this statement is TRUE.

Because only statement III is true, the answer is (C).

COORDINATE PLANE GEOMETRY & GRAPHS TOPIC #8:
FUNCTIONS AS MODELS

Linear, quadratic, exponential and other functions can provide models for many real-life scenarios. The graph of a function serves as a visual "model" for a given situation. The model can then be used to predict the function's other values.

SAT PRACTICE: FUNCTIONS AS MODELS

A colony of ants grows in population by 40% every week. The colony started with 1,000 ants. Which of the following best describes the mathematical model for the weekly growth of the ant colony?

(A)   A linear function in which $y = x + .40$

(B)   A linear function in which $y = .40x + 1000$

(C)   An absolute value function in which $y = |x| + .40$

(D)   A quadratic function in which $y = 1.4(x^2)$

(E)   An exponential function in which $y = 1000 \cdot (1.4)^x$

Solution:

This problem is asking you to identify the equation that fits a certain data pattern. Only one of the equations in the answer choices will generate this same data set.

Graphing Calculator Method

Begin by establishing a few (x, y) values reflecting the growth of the ant colony. Let x equal the number of weeks that have passed and y equal the number of ants in the colony:

x	y	
0	1000	← beginning ant population
1	1400	← 40% more ants than the week before: $1000 + (.40 \cdot 1000)$
2	1960	← 40% more ants than the week before: $1400 + (.40 \cdot 1400)$

Now enter the equations in the answer choices into the equation into the equation editor of your graphing calculator. Press **[Y =]**:

After \\Y_1 = press **[X, T, θ, *n*] + .40**	← *equation in choice* (A)
After \\Y_2 = press **.4 [X, T, θ, *n*] + 1000**	← *equation in choice* (B)
After \\Y_3 = press **[MATH] [>] 1 [X, T, θ, *n*]) + .40**	← *equation in choice* (C)
After \\Y_4 = press **1.4 [X, T, θ, *n*] [x^2]**	← *equation in choice* (D)
After \\Y_5 = press **1000 (1.4) [^] [X, T, θ, *n*]**	← *equation in choice* (E)

The table feature will allow us to compare the y-values for each of these equations at specified x-values. To access the yellow **[TABLE]** screen, press **[2nd] [GRAPH]**. The first column of the table will exhibit increasing values for x, and each successive column will reflect the corresponding values for Y_1, Y_2, Y_3, Y_4, and Y_5. Cursor across the table and you will see that the values under Y_5 match the values we established in the chart shown above; y-values displayed of 1000, 1400 and 1960 correspond with x-values of 0, 1 and 2 respectively. The answer is (E).

X	Y₁	Y₂
0	.4	1000
1	1.4	1000.4
2	2.4	1000.8
3	3.4	1001.2
4	4.4	1001.6
5	5.4	1002
6	6.4	1002.4

$Y_1 = X + .4$

Graphing Calculator Screen: Columns Y_1 and Y_2 reflect the data values for answer choices (A) and (B).

Data Substitution Method

If you do not wish to use a graphing calculator, you can substitute data values into each of the equations to see which is a match. Begin by establishing the same (x, y) values as described for the graphing calculator method. Substitute this data into each equation to find the one that works. The equation $y = 1000 \cdot (1.4)^x$ is the only one that fits all of the data:

At the beginning: $1,000 = 1000 \cdot (1.4)^0$

At the end of the second week: $1,400 = 1000 \cdot (1.4)^1$

At the end of the second week: $1,960 = 1000 \cdot (1.4)^2$

→SUCCESS STRATEGY←

Matching an Equation to Certain Data

If you are asked to select an equation that matches a certain set of data, eliminate by inspection any answer choices containing equations that could not possibly work. For example, in the question above, the ant population's rate of growth is increasing as time passes. Neither a linear function nor an absolute value function could represent a compounding increase. Choices (A), (B), and (C) can be eliminated.

BECAUSE POPULATION GROWTH IS ALWAYS EXPONENTIAL, CHOICE (E) BECOMES THE OBVIOUS ANSWER FOR THE PROBLEM ABOVE!

SAT PRACTICE: FUNCTIONS AS MODELS

A computer manufacturer has fixed operating costs of $50,000 per month. It costs $500 to make each computer and the computers are sold for $1,500 each. Which graph below illustrates the company's monthly profit or loss based on the number of computers sold?

(A)

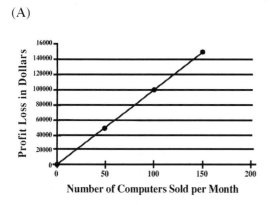

(D)

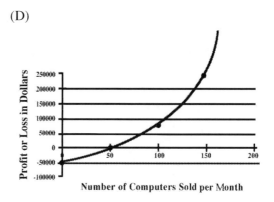

(B)

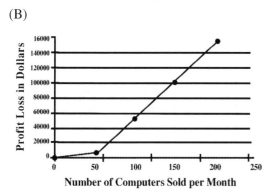

(E)

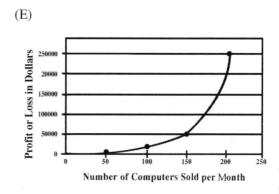

(C)

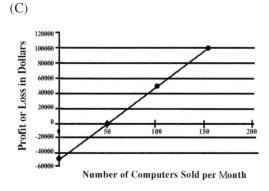

Solution:

This problem is asking you to match a mathematical model to its correct graph.

Graphing Calculator Method

Begin by establishing a few (x, y) values reflecting the scenario presented. The graphs among the answer choices reflect the number of computers sold (along the x-axis) and the profit or loss in dollars (along the y-axis). The net profit for each computer sold is $1,000 ($1,500 sale price minus $500 manufacturing cost). Additionally, $50,000 must be subtracted from the computer sales profit for each y-value to account for the fixed overhead:

x	y
0	-50,000
50	0
100	50,000
150	100,000

The next step is to enter and plot the above-listed data points in order to match the resulting graph with the correct answer choice. To enter the data points, press **[STAT]** to access the data editor and select **1:Edit**. The spreadsheet format arranges data in columns. Input the x-values listed above in the L1 column and the corresponding y-values in the L2 column. Press the **[ENTER]** key or use the cursor keys to move up and down or across the columns in the data editor.

Now plot the data points. Once the above data is entered, press **[2nd] [Y =]** to access the yellow **[STAT PLOTS]** screen. Press **1** to select **1:Plot1...On**. On the next screen, make sure that the blinking cursor highlights **On** in the first row and that the first graph type is highlighted after **Type**: in the second row.

To view the data points in the screen, press **[ZOOM]** and then press **9** or cursor down to select **9:ZoomStat**. The data entered will now appear as points in a coordinate plane.

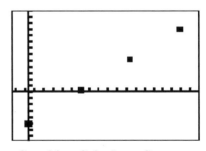

Graphing Calculator Screen: Plotted Data Points

A line drawn through the plotted data points matches the graph in answer choice (C).

Establish Data Points/Sketch Method

If you do not wish to use a graphing calculator for this problem, you can sketch a graph to represent the data. On exam day, use the margin of your test booklet to sketch figures. Begin by establishing the same (x, y) values as described for the graphing calculator method. Sketch a graph representing this data. The graph in answer choice (C) is the best match.

COORDINATE PLANE GEOMETRY & GRAPHS TOPIC #9:
SCATTERPLOTS

On January 28, 1986 the space shuttle Challenger exploded and seven astronauts died. The cause of the explosion was traced to two failed rubber O-rings during takeoff. The O-rings leaked because of the low temperature outside. The night before the launch, a telephone conference call took place among rocket engineers and NASA officials to determine whether or not to proceed with the launch. The engineers reviewed data for 23 previous shuttle launches; the data set correlated the temperature at launch time with the number of O-rings damaged during that particular launch. The engineers felt that the data suggested a link between O-ring damage and low outdoor temperature at launch time, so they recommended that the flight be delayed. NASA decided to proceed with the flight anyways. During the investigation that followed, it was suggested that the engineers could have made a clearer, more persuasive argument if they had presented a simple scatterplot of the data they had studied.

A **scatterplot** presents various points in a coordinate plane. A "**line of best fit**," also known as a "**trend line**," is drawn through a scatterplot to illustrate the pattern of association between two variables.

This table and accompanying scatterplot presents data regarding the 1987 Chicago Bulls players' total points scored versus total minutes played. The line of best fit with an approximate slope of .9 has been included; its equation is at the top of the scatterplot. Can you see from his data point that Michael Jordan was already a rising star?

Chicago Bulls Basketball Data
1987-1988 Season
(Total Minutes Played Versus Total Points Scored)

PLAYER	MINUTES	POINTS
Corzine	2328	804
Grant	1827	622
Jordan	3311	2868
Oakley	2816	1014
Paxson	1888	640
Pippen	1650	625
Sparrow	1044	260
Sellers	2212	777
Vincent	1501	573

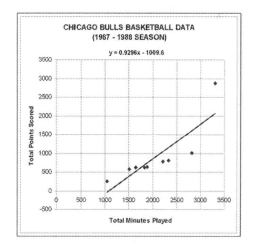

The **line of best fit** may pass through some of the data points, none of the points, or all of the points presented in a scatterplot. It is a straight line that best represents the scatterplot data.

SAT PRACTICE: SCATTERPLOTS

Which of the following best describes the line of best fit for the scatterplot shown?

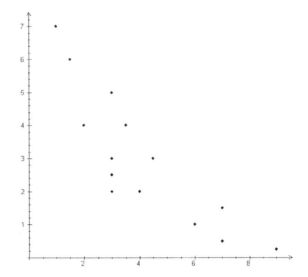

(A)   The slope of the line of best fit is between 0 and 1.

(B)   The slope of the line of best fit is between 1 and 2.

(C)   The slope of the line of best fit is negative.

(D)   The y-intercept of the line of best fit is at approximately (0, 5).

(E)   A line of best fit cannot be drawn for this scatterplot.

Solution:

Draw an approximated line of best fit with points represented equally and equidistantly on both sides of the line:

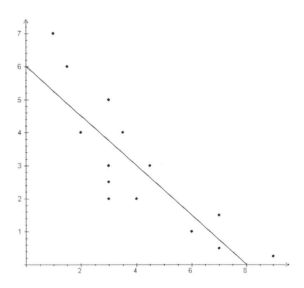

The slope of this line is negative, so the answer is (C).

Mathematics
Chapter 5
Plane & Solid Geometry

1. Geometric Notation

2. Basic Concepts: Lines, Line Segments, Angles & Degrees

3. Triangles

4. Special Right Triangles & Trigonometry

5. Quadrilaterals

6. Circles

7. Tangent Lines

8. Multiple & Overlapping Geometric Shapes

9. Solid Figures

10. Geometric Probability

The ancient Greek astronomer Ptolemy once asked Euclid, the father of geometry, if there was any shorter way to learn the subject than that presented by Euclid's the *Elements*, a geometry text including definitions, postulates, and proofs. Euclid replied that there was "no royal road to geometry."

There may not be a "royal road" to geometry, but hopefully this chapter will be your road to success on the geometry section of the SAT!

GEOMETRY TOPIC #1:
RECOGNIZE AND UNDERSTAND GEOMETRIC NOTATION

The representation of points, lines, and planes by an alphabetical letter or letters was begun by Hippocrates of Chios, a Greek geometer who lived in the 5th century B.C. He was reportedly a brilliant mathematician but absent-minded and lackadaisical in his daily affairs. Apparently Hippocrates was not much of a businessman. One of his colleagues reported that Hippocrates had once been a merchant, but he was defrauded and lost all of his money and property when a pirate vessel captured him. Hippocrates then went to Athens to pursue the offenders. While in Athens, he attended math lectures. Hippocrates became proficient in geometry and was allowed to make some money by teaching. He became the first person to write a book regarding the elements of geometry, paving the way for Euclid's future work.

The SAT requires students to have a working knowledge of the geometric notation commonly used in a high school geometry course.

Make sure that you fully understand the use and meaning of the following basic geometric terms and symbols:

NOTATION	ITEM	DEFINITION/DESCRIPTION
Represented by a dot: • Referred to by a single capital letter: R	**Point R**	A **point** indicates a position in space; it has no actual size. All geometric figures consist of points.
$\overleftrightarrow{RS}$	**Line RS** (the **line** through points R and S)	A **line** is an infinite number of points (represented by a straight line and two arrowheads) extending in two directions.
$\overline{RS}$	**Line segment RS** (the segment connecting points R and S; the same line segment can also be referred to as SR)	A **line segment** consists of two endpoints and all of the points between those two endpoints.
$\overrightarrow{RS}$	**Ray RS** (the ray with endpoint R extending through and infinitely beyond point S)	A **ray** is part of a line; it has an endpoint and extends infinitely in one direction only.
$\angle RST$	**Angle RST** (the angle formed by rays $\overrightarrow{SR}$ and $\overrightarrow{ST}$ with point S as the vertex)	An **angle** is the union of two rays at a common endpoint. The rays are the *sides* of the angle while the endpoint is known as the angle's *vertex*.
	Plane M	A **plane** is a flat surface that has infinite length and width but no thickness. A plane contains an infinite number of points and lines.
	Collinear	Points lying in the same line.
	Coplanar	Points or lines lying in the same plane.
	Intersection	The place where two geometric figures meet or cross. • Two lines intersect in a point. • The intersection of two planes is a line. • A line not lying in a plane intersects a plane in a point. (A line parallel to a plane will not intersect it.)
//	**Parallel**	Parallel lines run like railroad tracks; they are coplanar and do not intersect.
⊥	**Perpendicular**	Perpendicular lines form a right angle at their intersection point.
≅	**Congruent**	• Congruent angles and arcs have the same measure. • Congruent segments have the same length. • Congruent polygons have congruent, corresponding sides and angles. • Congruent circles have congruent radii.
	Midpoint	The point at which a line segment is divided into two congruent segments.

SAT PRACTICE: GEOMETRIC NOTATION

If $\overline{RS} \cong \overline{ST}$ and $\overrightarrow{RT}$ contains point S, which of the following is true?

(A) S is the midpoint of $\overline{RT}$

(B) T is the midpoint of $\overline{RS}$

(C) $\overline{RS} \perp \overline{ST}$

(D) $\overrightarrow{RS}$ does not contain point T

(E) $\overrightarrow{TS}$ does not contain point R

Solution:

Draw a sketch of the information presented.

Because $\overrightarrow{RT}$ contains point S, points, R, S
and T lie in the same line (are collinear). The
problem also states that $\overline{RS} \cong \overline{ST}$; because
the three points are collinear, S must be
situated as the midpoint of $\overline{RT}$.

S is the midpoint of $\overline{RT}$, so the answer is (A).

GEOMETRY TOPIC #2:
BASIC CONCEPTS:
LINES, LINE SEGMENTS, ANGLES & DEGREES

We are accustomed to a base-10 number system. But the ancient Babylonians used a base-60 mathematical system, and the Babylonian calendar consisted of 360 days (6 • 60). Babylonian astronomers believed that a full orbital period of the earth around the sun (although they actually believed that it was the sun that orbited the earth) consisted of precisely 360 days. In about 700 B.C., the Babylonians decided that circles should comprise 360 equal parts or degrees. The idea stuck, and circles have been divided into 360 equal degrees ever since that time.

A line drawn down through the center of a circle (a diameter), divides a circle into two semi-circles of 180 degrees each. Thus, **a straight line (or straight angle) has 180 degrees.**

Angles

Adjacent angles share a common internal ray or side.

An **acute angle** measures less than 90°.

Two perpendicular lines form four right angles, each of which measures 90 degrees. In the figure shown, angles 1, 2, 3 and 4 are all right angles.

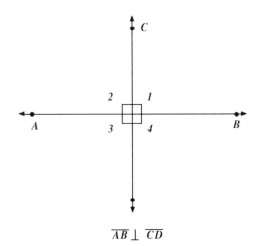

$$\overline{AB} \perp \overline{CD}$$

The measure of an **obtuse angle** is greater than 90°.

Complementary angles add up to 90°. Any right angle can be divided into two adjacent complementary angles.

Straight angles equal 180°.

Supplementary angles add up to 180°. Adjacent angles that lie in the same line are supplementary.

Vertical angles are angles formed by two intersecting lines. They share the same vertex and are opposite each other. Vertical angles are always congruent.

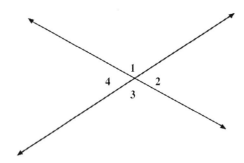

Angles 1 and 3 are vertical angles.
Angles 2 and 4 are also vertical angles.

Angles in Polygons

The sum of the measures of the interior angles in any polygon of *n* sides =

$$(n - 2) \cdot 180°$$

# of Sides	Polygon	Sum of the Measures of the Interior Angles
3	Triangle	180°
4	Quadrilateral	360°
5	Pentagon	540°

If you cannot recall the formula stated above, sketch the polygon and then draw all diagonals from one particular vertex. This will divide the polygon into triangles. Simply multiply the number of resultant triangles by 180.

Example:

In the hexagon shown, the three diagonals shown create a total of four triangles within the hexagon. 4 • 180 = 720, so the sum of the measures of the interior angles in a hexagon is 720.

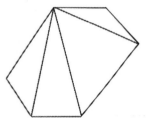

Parallel Lines Crossed by a Transversal

When two parallel lines are crossed by another line called a "transversal," all of the pairs of angles formed are either equal or supplementary.

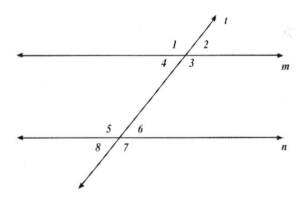

In the diagram above, line *m* is parallel to line *n*, and these lines are crossed by a transversal, *t*. All of the even-numbered angles are equal, and all of the odd-numbered angles are equal. Any even-numbered angle plus any odd-numbered angle equals 180 degrees (they are supplementary).

The following chart summarizes the relationships of the angles in the diagram shown:

Description	Angle Pairs	Pairs Equal or Supplementary?
Corresponding angles	$\angle 1$ & $\angle 5$; $\angle 2$ & $\angle 6$; $\angle 3$ & $\angle 7$; $\angle 4$ & $\angle 8$	Equal
Vertical angles	$\angle 1$ & $\angle 3$; $\angle 2$ & $\angle 4$; $\angle 5$ & $\angle 7$; $\angle 6$ & $\angle 8$	Equal
Alternate interior angles	$\angle 3$ & $\angle 5$; $\angle 4$ & $\angle 6$	Equal
Alternate exterior angles	$\angle 1$ & $\angle 7$; $\angle 2$ & $\angle 8$	Equal
Same side interior angles	$\angle 3$ & $\angle 6$; $\angle 4$ & $\angle 5$	Supplementary
Same side exterior angles	$\angle 1$ & $\angle 8$; $\angle 2$ & $\angle 7$	Supplementary

SAT PRACTICE: LINES & ANGLES (PARALLEL LINES CROSSED BY A TRANSVERSAL)

In the figure shown, line l // line m.
$m\angle ABC =$

(A) $46°$
(B) $52°$
(C) $76°$
(D) $82°$
(E) $88°$

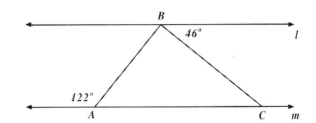

Solution:

$m\angle BAC = 180° - 122°$ *(Adjacent supplementary $\angle$s; exterior rays form a straight line)*
$m\angle BAC = 58°$

Because lines l and m are parallel, $m\angle BCA = 46°$ *(Alternate interior angles are congruent)*

$m\angle ABC + m\angle BAC + m\angle BCA = 180°$ *(Sum of the measures of the interior angles of a triangle)*
          $\downarrow$ $\downarrow$
$m\angle ABC + 58°$ $+$ $46° = 180°$

$m\angle ABC = 76°$

The answer is (C).

SAT PRACTICE: LINES & ANGLES (ANGLES IN A TRIANGLE)

In the figure shown, which of the following is true?

(A) $a° = 2c° - b°$

(B) $a° = b° + c° - 180$

(C) $2a° + b° + c° = 360$

(D) $2(c° - a°) = b°$

(E) $\dfrac{a° + b° + c°}{3} = 90$

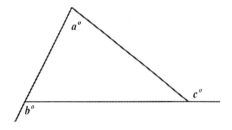

Solution:

Let the measures of the remaining interior angles of the triangle equal $d°$ and $e°$ respectively. Label the triangle as shown:

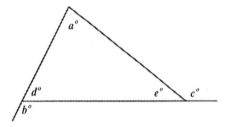

Establish equations expressing the known relationships among the angles:

$a° + d° + e° = 180°$ *(Sum of the measures of the interior angles of a triangle)*
$d° + b° = 180°$ *(Adjacent supplementary ∠s; exterior rays form a straight line)*
$c° + e° = 180°$ *(Adjacent supplementary ∠s; exterior rays form a straight line)*

Now, "Paint by Numbers."

Assign values for *a*, *d* and *e* such that their sum will equal 180:

> Let $a = 45°$, $d = 65°$, and $e = 70°$
> In this case, $b = 115°$ and $c = 110°$

Substitute these values into the answer choices to see which one is true:

(A) $45 \neq 2(110) - 115$

(B) $45 = 115 + 110 - 180$

(C) $2(45) + 115 + 110 \neq 360$

(D) $2(110 - 45) \neq 115$

(E) $\dfrac{45 + 115 + 110}{3} = 90$

In this case, both answers (B) and (E) appear to be true. Thus, we need to try new numbers and substitute them into answer choices (B) and (E):

Let $a = 25°$, $d = 75°$, and $e = 80°$

In this case, $b = 105°$ and $c = 100°$

(B) $25 = 105 + 100 - 180$

(E) $\dfrac{25 + 105 + 100}{3} \neq 90$

The answer is (B).

SAT PRACTICE: LINES & ANGLES (SUPPLEMENTARY ANGLES)

In the figure shown, $a° = \dfrac{3}{4} b°$

$b° =$

(A) $39°$
(B) $46°$
(C) $48°$
(D) $52°$
(E) $56°$

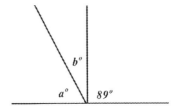

Note: Figure not drawn to scale.

Solution:

The three angles lie in a straight line, so:

$$a° + b° + 89° = 180°$$
$$\downarrow$$
$$\frac{3}{4} b° + b° + 89° = 180°$$
$$\frac{7}{4} b° = 180° - 89° = 91°$$
$$b° = 52°$$

The answer is (D).

SAT PRACTICE: LINES & ANGLES (LINE SEGMENTS)

$$BC = \frac{3}{2}AB \quad CD = \frac{4}{3}BC \quad DE = \frac{5}{4}CD$$

If $AB = x$, then $AE =$

Note: Figure not drawn to scale.

(A) $\frac{5}{2}x$

(B) $\frac{61}{12}x$

(C) $6x$

(D) $7x$

(E) $\frac{15}{2}x$

Solution:

Determine the length of each segment in terms of x:

$$BC = \frac{3}{2}AB \text{ or } \frac{3}{2}x \qquad CD = \frac{4}{3}BC = \frac{4}{3} \cdot \frac{3}{2}x = 2x \qquad DE = \frac{5}{4}CD = \frac{5}{4} \cdot 2x = \frac{5}{2}x$$

Now add up all of the individual segments (in terms of x):

$$AB + BC + CD + DE = AE$$
$$\downarrow \quad \downarrow \quad \downarrow \quad \downarrow \quad \downarrow$$
$$x + \frac{3}{2}x + 2x + \frac{5}{2}x = 7x \qquad \text{The answer is (D).}$$

Geometry Topic #3:
Triangles

Pythagoras, the famous Greek mathematician, philosopher and mystic, founded his Pythagorean Brotherhood in a small seaport in Southern Italy in around 525 B.C. This unique aristocratic fraternity was devoted to the study of mathematics, philosophy and religion. Its inner circle lived communally and practiced vegetarianism. Women were allowed to join the society, and many female Pythagoreans became famous philosophers.

Pythagoras' most famous mathematical contribution, the Pythagorean Theorem, states the mathematical relationship between the legs and hypotenuse of a right triangle. The proof of this theorem was considered so momentous by the Pythagoreans that they are said to have offered a sacrifice of 100 oxen to the gods.

Types of Triangles

Acute: Each angle measures less than 90°.

Obtuse: One angle measures more than 90°.

Right: One angle measures exactly 90°.

Scalene: All three sides have different lengths.

Isosceles: Two legs of the triangle are congruent, and the base angles are congruent.

Equilateral: All three sides are congruent and each angle has a measure of 60°.

Examples:

Obtuse, Scalene Triangle   **Acute, Isosceles Triangle**   **Equilateral Triangle**

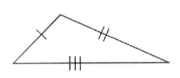   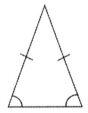   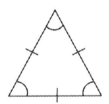

Triangle Properties

Interior angles are found inside a triangle. The sum of the measures of the three interior angles equals 180°.

Exterior angles are found outside of a triangle and are adjacent and supplementary to the interior angles. The measure of an exterior angle of a triangle equals the sum of the remote interior angles.

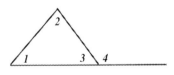

In this triangle, angles 1 and 2 are "remote interior" angles to exterior angle 4.

$m\angle 1 + m\angle 2 + m\angle 3 = 180°$ ← Sum of the measures of the interior angles of a triangle

$m\angle 3 + m\angle 4 = 180°$ ← Supplementary angles

Therefore, $m\angle 1 + m\angle 2 = m\angle 4$

Area of a triangle = $\frac{1}{2}$ (base • height)

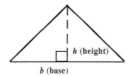

Similar triangles have congruent corresponding angles and their corresponding sides are proportional. The ratio of the areas of two similar triangles is equal to the ratio of the squares of the corresponding sides.

Right Triangles

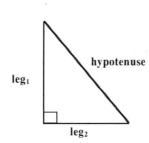

A **right triangle** has one 90° angle and two acute angles.

The two acute angles in a right triangle are always complementary (add up to 90°).

The side opposite the 90° angle is known as the **hypotenuse**.

The **legs** are the two sides that meet to form the 90° angle.

The **area of a right triangle** equals one-half the product of the two legs:

$$\frac{1}{2}(\text{leg}_1 \cdot \text{leg}_2)$$

The **Pythagorean Theorem** states that the sum of the squares of the two legs of a right triangle equals the square of its hypotenuse:

$$(\text{leg}_1)^2 + (\text{leg}_2)^2 = (\text{hypotenuse})^2$$

or

$$a^2 + b^2 = c^2$$

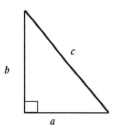

The following are some well-known "Pythagorean Triples" (values for the legs and corresponding hypotenuse of certain right triangles):

"a"	"b"	"c"
leg₁	**leg₂**	**hypotenuse**

"a" leg₁	"b" leg₂	"c" hypotenuse
3	4	5

(Multiples of 3-4-5):

6	8	10
9	12	15
12	16	20
15	20	25

(Other Pythagorean Triple favorites on the SAT):

5	12	13
8	15	17
7	24	25

SAT PRACTICE: TRIANGLES (FINDING MISSING ANGLE)

In the figure shown, $m\angle B =$

(A)   34°
(B)   44°
(C)   102°
(D)   132°
(E)   138°

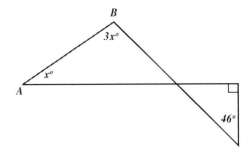

Note: Figure not drawn to scale.

Solution:

Label points C, D and E as shown:

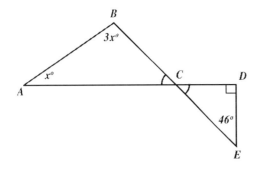

$\angle BCA \cong \angle DCE$ because they are vertical angles. This means that the sum of the two remaining angles in $\triangle BCA$ equals the sum of the two remaining angles in $\triangle DCE$:

$$m\angle A + m\angle B = m\angle D + m\angle E$$
$$\downarrow \quad\quad \downarrow \quad\quad \downarrow \quad\quad \downarrow$$
$$x° + 3x° = 90° + 46°$$
$$4x° = 136°$$
$$x° = 34°$$
$$m\angle B = 3x° = 102°$$

The answer is (C).

SAT PRACTICE: TRIANGLES (FINDING MISSING SIDE FROM AREA)

In the figure shown, C is the midpoint of

$\overline{AB}$, B is the midpoint of $\overline{CD}$, and

$FD = \dfrac{1}{2}AC$. If the area of $\triangle FDC$ is 32,

then $AD =$

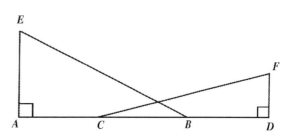

(A)   9
(B)   12
(C)   15
(D)   18
(E)   24

Note: Figure not drawn to scale.

Solution:

Because C is the midpoint of $\overline{AB}$ and B is

the midpoint of $\overline{CD}$, $\overline{AC} \cong \overline{CB} \cong \overline{BD}$.

Mark the figure accordingly, identifying

each segment as equal to "x" and FD

equal to $\dfrac{1}{2}x$:

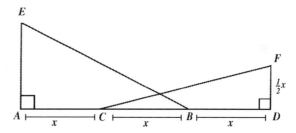

$$\text{Area } \triangle FDC = \frac{1}{2}(FD \bullet DC), \text{ or } \frac{1}{2}(\frac{1}{2}x \bullet 2x)$$

$$32 = \frac{1}{2}(x^2)$$
$$64 = x^2$$
$$\sqrt{64} = 8 = x$$
$$AD = 3x = 24$$

The answer is (E).

Note: There is no value whatsoever to the existence of point E or of $\triangle EBA$. But that is how some SAT math problems are – filled with extraneous information.

SAT PRACTICE: TRIANGLES (EQUILATERAL TRIANGLE)

If the area of equilateral ΔABC is 60 and $\overline{AE} \cong \overline{DC}$, what is the area of equilateral ΔEDC?

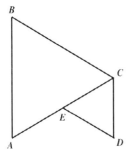

(A)   6
(B)   8
(C)   10
(D)   12
(E)   15

Solution:

Because ΔEDC is equilateral and $\overline{AE} \cong \overline{DC}$, $\overline{AE}$ is also $\cong \overline{EC}$ and E is the midpoint of $\overline{AC}$.

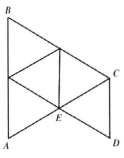

Knowing this makes it possible to draw in auxiliary line segments to divide equilateral ΔABC into several smaller equilateral triangles congruent to ΔEDC:

Because the area of ΔABC is 60, the area of each of the four smaller triangles equals 15, and the area of ΔEDC also equals 15. The answer is (E).

SAT PRACTICE: TRIANGLES (SIMILAR TRIANGLES)

In the figure shown, $\overline{AB} \, / \! / \, \overline{CD}$. Which of the following statements are true?

I. $CD = DE$

II $\dfrac{CD}{AB} = \dfrac{ED}{BD}$

III. $\dfrac{Area \ \Delta ABE}{Area \ \Delta CDE} = \dfrac{(EB)^2}{(ED)^2}$

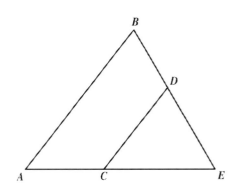

Note: Figure not drawn to scale.

(A)   I only
(B)   II only
(C)   III only
(D)   I and III
(E)   I, II and III

Solution:

Because $\overline{AB} \, /\! / \, \overline{CD}$, ΔABE is similar ($\sim$) to ΔCDE.

Consider each statement (I, II and III) with respect to the properties of similar triangles.

I.   The diagram shown makes it look as if $CD = DE$, but the disclaimer indicates that figure is not drawn to scale. Further, the properties of similar triangles do not support this notion. Statement I is FALSE.

II.   Corresponding sides of similar triangles are proportional, but these are not corresponding sides! *ED* does not correspond to *BD*; it corresponds to and is proportional to *EB*. The following is the correct similarity proportion: $\dfrac{CD}{AB} = \dfrac{ED}{EB}$. Statement II is FALSE.

III.   The ratio of the areas of two similar triangles is equal to the ratio of the squares of the corresponding sides. Statement III is TRUE.

Because only statement III is true, the answer is (C).

SAT PRACTICE: TRIANGLES (ISOSCELES TRIANGLE WITH PYTHAGOREAN THEOREM APPLICATION)

If the area of isosceles ΔABC is 60, what is the perimeter of ΔABC?

(A)   27
(B)   32
(C)   36
(D)   39
(E)   48

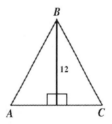

Note: Figure not drawn to scale.

Solution:

Label point X as shown below and mark congruent parts:

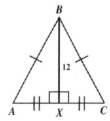

$\overline{AB} \cong \overline{BC}$ $\leftarrow$ congruent legs

$\overline{AX} \cong \overline{XC}$ $\leftarrow$ congruent segments

Solve for the base of the triangle using the area:

Area of $\triangle ABC = \dfrac{1}{2}\ (b \bullet h)$

$$60 = \dfrac{1}{2}(12 \bullet AC)$$

$$AC = 10, \text{ and } AX = XC = 5$$

Now apply the Pythagorean Theorem to find one of the legs of the triangle:

$$(AX)^2 + (BX)^2 = (AB)^2$$
$$5^2 + 12^2 = (AB)^2$$

$AB = 13$, and because $\triangle ABC$ is isosceles, BC also $= 13$.
Perimeter $\triangle ABC = 13 + 13 + 10 = 36$. The answer is (C).

┌─────────────────────────────────────┐

→SUCCESS STRATEGY←

The altitude of an isosceles triangle (drawn from the vertex angle) is perpendicular to the base at its midpoint.

└─────────────────────────────────────┘

SAT PRACTICE: TRIANGLES (EXPANDED AREA & PERIMETER)

If the area of a right triangle is increased by a factor of four, then its perimeter will be:

(A)   quadrupled
(B)   tripled
(C)   doubled
(D)   it cannot be determined
(E)   none of the above

Solution:

Look for a contradiction in cases to prove that the answer is (D), "it cannot be determined." Draw a right triangle and assign values for the lengths of its legs and hypotenuse (use numbers that form a "Pythagorean triple"):

Area of triangle $= \dfrac{1}{2}\ (9 \bullet 12) = 54$

Perimeter of triangle $= 9 + 12 + 15 = 36$

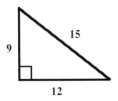

Now draw another triangle to represent one that is four times as large as the previous triangle by doubling both the base and the height of the original:

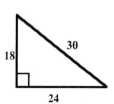

Area = $\dfrac{1}{2}(18 \bullet 24) = 216$, which is four times 54.

Use the Pythagorean Theorem to find the hypotenuse of this triangle:

$$(18)^2 + (24)^2 = 900$$
$$\text{Hypotenuse} = \sqrt{900} = 30$$
$$\text{Perimeter} = 18 + 24 + 30 = 72$$

In this case, the perimeter has DOUBLED.

Next draw a third triangle – again to represent one that is four times as large as the original triangle – that has different dimensions than the second triangle. This time use the same height as the original triangle but multiply the base by 4:

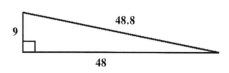

Area = $\dfrac{1}{2}(48 \bullet 9) = 216$

(same as for the second Δ)

Use the Pythagorean Theorem to find the hypotenuse of the triangle:

$$9^2 + 48^2 = 2{,}385$$
$$\text{Hypotenuse} = \sqrt{2{,}385} = 48.8$$
$$\text{Perimeter} = 9 + 48 + 48.8 = 105.8$$

Because 105.8 (the perimeter of the third triangle) $\neq$ 72 (the perimeter of the second triangle), results for the expanded triangles vary, and a relationship cannot be determined. The answer is (D).

GEOMETRY TOPIC #4:
SPECIAL RIGHT TRIANGLES & TRIGONOMETRY AS AN
ALTERNATIVE METHOD IN SOLVING GEOMETRY PROBLEMS

Pythagoras believed that the elegance of mathematics was based upon the idea that all natural phenomena could be explained by ratios of integers, or rational numbers. The concept of irrational numbers was abhorrent to Pythagoras.

Trouble brewed when Pythagoras' young student Hippasus demonstrated that the square root of 2 was not a rational number. The new knowledge that the square root of 2 is irrational was probably particularly upsetting to Pythagoras because the ratio of leg: hypotenuse in an isosceles right triangle turned out to be $1: \sqrt{2}$.

Pythagoras remained devout in his belief that the measures of lengths were always integral multiples of one another. When Pythagoras could not logically refute Hippasus' argument, he reportedly sentenced him to death by drowning. Not the best day at the math brotherhood.

Special Right Triangles

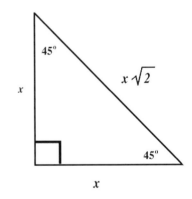

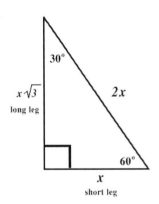

45°-45°-90° Right Triangle

- Legs have equal length
- Hypotenuse = (leg) • $\sqrt{2}$

30°-60°-90° Right Triangle

- The "short leg" is opposite the 30° angle
- The "long leg" is opposite the 60° angle
- Hypotenuse = (Short leg) • 2
- Long leg = (Short leg) • $\sqrt{3}$

Trigonometry and Right Triangles

Simple trigonometric ratios for **sine, cosine** and **tangent** can also be used to find the side lengths and angle measures of right triangles. In right triangle *ABC*:

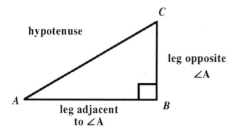

$$\sin \angle A = \frac{\text{leg opposite } \angle A}{\text{hypotenuse}}$$

$$\cos \angle A = \frac{\text{leg adjacent to } \angle A}{\text{hypotenuse}}$$

$$\tan \angle A = \frac{\text{leg opposite } \angle A}{\text{leg adjacent to } \angle A}$$

Trigonometry students memorize these relationships by reciting "SOH-CAH-TOA" (pronounced *so-kuh-tow-a):
Sine equals Opposite over Hypotenuse, Cosine equals Adjacent over Hypotenuse, Tangent equals Opposite over Adjacent*

SAT PRACTICE: SPECIAL RIGHT TRIANGLES

In $\triangle RST$, $ST =$

(A)   8

(B) $4\sqrt{2}$

(C)   10

(D) $6\sqrt{2}$

(E) $8\sqrt{2}$

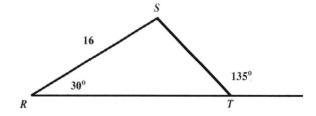

Note: Figure not drawn to scale.

You should quickly see that there are no right triangles in the figure. Draw an altitude from point *S* to point *X* on $\overline{RT}$, creating two right triangles within $\triangle RST$:

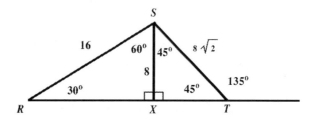

┌───┐

→**SUCCESS STRATEGY**←

If a problem presents a triangle that does not contain a right angle, draw an altitude
("drop a perpendicular") to create two right triangles.
You can then use the Pythagorean Theorem to solve for missing sides or angles.

└───┘

The original triangle is now divided into two right Δs. The following characteristics become apparent:

*   ΔSRX is a 30°-60°-90° right triangle, so the "short leg" SX must equal 8 ($\frac{1}{2}$ of the hypotenuse, which is 16).

*   m ∠XTS= 45°, because it is supplementary to the adjacent 135° angle.

*   m ∠XST must therefore also equal 45°, making ΔXST a 45°-45°-90° right triangle.

*   The hypotenuse of ΔXST, which is ST, = $\sqrt{2}$ • SX.   SX = 8, so ST = $8\sqrt{2}$

The answer is (E).

SAT PRACTICE: SPECIAL RIGHT TRIANGLES (USING TRIGONOMETRY AS AN ALTERNATIVE METHOD OF SOLUTION)

In right ΔXYZ as shown, which of the following is the approximate length of XY?

(A)   6.1
(B)   9.8
(C)   12.1
(D)   13.4
(E)   14.0

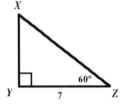

Note: Figure not drawn to scale.

Solution:

This problem can be solved by applying the relationships found in a 30°-60°-90° right triangle or by using trigonometry. To solve using trigonometry, set up the tangent ratio:

$$\tan \angle Z(60°) = \frac{\text{length of leg } XY, \text{ which is OPPOSITE } \angle Z}{7, \text{ which is length of the leg ADJACENT to } \angle Z}$$

$$1.732 = \frac{XY}{7} \qquad XY = 7 • 1.732 = \text{approximately } 12.1$$

The answer is (C).

GEOMETRY TOPIC #5:
QUADRILATERALS

Pat Ballew, a high school math teacher whose hobby is exploring the origins and history of the terms we use in mathematics, explains the origin of the word "rhombus":

> *If you have ever been to a rodeo, you have probably been impressed with the agility and courage of the rodeo clowns as they distract the bull after the rider departs from the bull. You may even think it was a sport created by cowboys of the old American west. The truth, however, is that playing tag with a bull may date back to the ancient Greek civilizations around 2000 BC. Archeologists working on Minoan ruins found pots with illustrations that seemed to show that taunting a bull was a popular pastime for young males of that culture. It seems that sometimes, however, the bull was bored by the whole routine. It is hard to be macho if the bull is doing his "Ferdinand" routine and smelling the daisies, so, to prod the animal into more ferocious activity, the young men began twirling an object on a string around their heads that made a roaring noise.*
>
> *...The ancient Minoan object that twisted as it twirled and made the roaring sound was called a rhomb. The root began to be used in words that suggested rotation or twisting motions, such as spinning tops, but none of the others seem to have made it into modern language. The use that did prevail was for shapes that looked like the four-sided object that they swung on the end of the string. This is how we came to call the equilateral quadrilateral a rhombus.*

The rhombus does not receive much attention on the SAT. In fact, quadrilaterals are entirely overshadowed on the exam by triangles and circles. Nonetheless, you must be familiar with their features.

Quadrilateral Facts and Definitions

A **quadrilateral** is any four-sided figure.

A **parallelogram** is a quadrilateral with two pairs of parallel, congruent sides.

$\overline{CB} \cong$ and // to $\overline{AD}$ and

$\overline{AB} \cong$ and // to $\overline{CD}$.

Parallelogram *ABCD*

Opposite angles of a parallelogram are congruent. $\angle A \cong \angle C$ and $\angle B \cong \angle D$.

Consecutive angles of a parallelogram are supplementary.

$m\angle A + m\angle B = 180°$ $m\angle B + m\angle C = 180°$
$m\angle C + m\angle D = 180°$ $m\angle D + m\angle A = 180°$

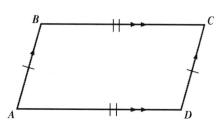

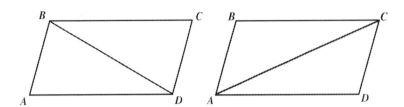

Parallelograms can always be divided into two congruent triangles by drawing a diagonal.
In these parallelograms,
$\triangle ABD \cong \triangle CDB$ and $\triangle ABC \cong \triangle CDA$.

Features of Special Parallelograms

Parallelogram	Figure	Sides	Angles	Diagonals
Rectangle	$\overline{BD} \cong \overline{AC}$	Opposite sides congruent and parallel	All angles are congruent and equal 90°	Congruent
Rhombus	$\overline{BD} \perp \overline{AC}$	All sides congruent	Opposite angles congruent	Perpendicular
Square (has all of the properties of both a rectangle and a rhombus)	$\overline{BD} \cong \overline{AC}$ $\overline{BD} \perp \overline{AC}$	All sides congruent	All angles are congruent and equal 90°	Congruent and perpendicular

A **trapezoid** is a special quadrilateral that is not a parallelogram. It has two parallel sides. The parallel sides are called bases. The nonparallel sides are called legs.

An **isosceles trapezoid** has two congruent legs:

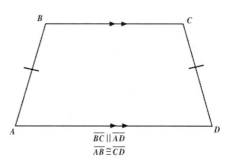

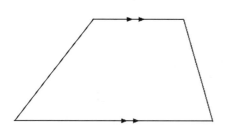

$$\overline{BC} \parallel \overline{AD}$$
$$\overline{AB} \cong \overline{CD}$$

Area and Perimeter of Quadrilaterals
s = side b = base h = height

Parallelogram

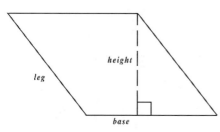

Area = $b \cdot h$
Perimeter = 2 (*leg* + *base*)

Rectangle

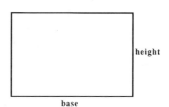

Area = $b \cdot h$
Perimeter = $2(b + h)$

Square

Area = s^2
Perimeter = $4s$

Trapezoid

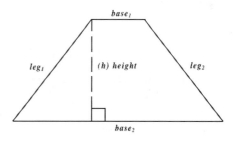

Area = $\dfrac{1}{2} \, h(b_1 + b_2)$

Perimeter = $b_1 + b_2 + leg_1 + leg_2$

SAT PRACTICE: QUADRILATERALS (AREA)

In the figure shown, E is the midpoint of $\overline{DB}$ and F is the midpoint of $\overline{DC}$. If the area of square $ABCD$ is 144, what is the area of quadrilateral $BCFE$?

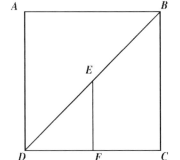

(A)   24
(B)   36
(C)   54
(D)   66
(E)   72

Solution:

Draw auxiliary line segment $\overline{EC}$, add point X as the midpoint of $\overline{BC}$, and draw auxiliary line segment $\overline{EX}$:

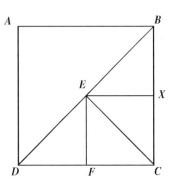

• Diagonal $\overline{DB}$ divides the square in half, so the area of ΔBAD equals the area of ΔBCD. The area of each of these triangles is $\dfrac{1}{2} \cdot 144$, or 72.

• The four smaller triangles within ΔBCD (ΔDEF, ΔEFC, ΔECX, & ΔBEX) are congruent, as they all have equal heights and bases.

• [Area of each of the smaller triangles (ΔDEF, ΔEFC, ΔECX, & ΔBEX)] = $\dfrac{1}{4} \cdot 72 = 18$. Quadrilateral $BCFE$ contains 3 of these smaller triangles, so its area equals $18 \cdot 3 = 54$.

The answer is (C).

SAT PRACTICE: QUADRILATERALS (AREA OF A PARALLELOGRAM – PYTHAGOREAN THEOREM APPLICATON)

Area parallelogram *GHIJ* =

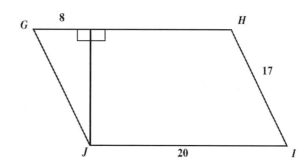

(A)   120
(B)   200
(C)   240
(D)   300
(E)   320

Solution:

GJ = HI = 17
Use the Pythagorean Theorem to find the height *(h)* of the parallelogram.

$$(\text{leg}_1)^2 + (\text{leg}_2)^2 = (\text{hypotenuse})^2$$
$$\downarrow \qquad \downarrow \qquad \qquad \downarrow$$
$$8^2 + h^2 = 17^2$$
$$h^2 = 17^2 - 8^2 = 225$$
$$h = \sqrt{225} = 15$$

Now find the area of *GHIJ*: $b \cdot h = 15 \cdot 20 = 300$

The answer is (D).

SAT PRACTICE: QUADRILATERALS (AREA AND PERIMETER OF A RECTANGLE WITH ALGEBRAIC EXPRESSIONS)

The base of a rectangle equals $x - 4$ and the height equals $2x + 5$. If the area of the rectangle equals 150, then its perimeter equals:

(A)   50
(B)   55
(C)   62
(D)   70
(E)   106

Solution:

Use the information provided to set an equation for area of the rectangle.

$$\text{Area} = (base \cdot height) \qquad 150 = (2x + 5)(x - 4)$$

Multiply the binomials *("FOIL")*:

$$(2x + 5)(x - 4) = 150$$
$$2x^2 - 3x - 20 = 150$$
$$2x^2 - 3x - 170 = 0$$

The above equation is somewhat difficult to factor. You may wish to use your graphing calculator or apply the quadratic formula. *(See pages 87 – 90 in the Algebra chapter for instructions regarding quadratic equations.)*

The equation actually factors as follows:

$$(2x + 17)(x - 10) = 0$$

$x = 10$ or -8.5, but in this case x can only equal 10, because negative solutions cannot be used for the length of the side of a figure.

Now solve for the base and height of the rectangle substituting 10 for x:

$$\text{Base} = 2x + 5 = 2(10) + 5 = 25$$
$$\text{Height} = x - 4 = 10 - 4 = 6$$

Perimeter = 2(*base* + *height*) = 2(25 + 6) = 62
The answer is (C).

SAT PRACTICE: QUADRILATERALS (BORDER AROUND A RECTANGLE)

GRID-IN PROBLEM:

Stan plans to pour a concrete walkway around his rectangular swimming pool. The length of the pool is 26 feet and the width is 14 feet. If the walkway is to be uniformly 3 feet wide, what is the area of the walkway?

First, draw a figure to represent the pool and the walkway

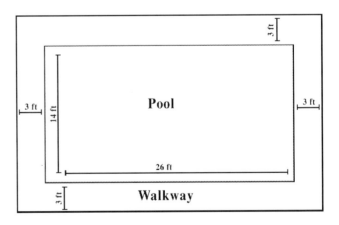

To find the area of just the walkway, subtract the area of the pool itself from the area of the pool plus the walkway:

Area of pool and walkway:

   length   width
    ↓   ↓

$(26 + 3 + 3)(14 + 3 + 3) =$
$32 \cdot 20 = 640$ square feet

Area of pool alone:
$26 \cdot 14 = 364$ square feet

Area of walkway:
$640 - 364 = 276$ square feet

Grid-in 276.

> **→SUCCESS STRATEGY←**
>
> To find the area of the "border" around a rectangle or of the "ring" around a circle, subtract the interior area from the total area:
>
> Area of Larger Shape *minus*
> Area of Smaller Shape =
> Area of "Border" or
> Area of "Ring"

SAT PRACTICE: QUADRILATERALS (EXPANDED PERIMETER AND AREA OF A SQUARE)

If the perimeter of a square is tripled, its area is increased by:

(A)   300%

(B)   600%

(C)   800%

(D)   900%

(E)   1200%

Solution:

Arbitrarily choose the length of a side of a square and calculate its perimeter and area. Let the side of the square = 2

$$\text{Area of square} = 2^2 = 4$$
$$\text{Perimeter of square} = 4 \cdot 2 = 8$$

Now triple the perimeter of this square and calculate this new square's area.

$$\text{Perimeter of expanded square: } 8 \cdot 3 = 24$$

$$\text{Side of expanded square: } \frac{1}{4} \cdot 24 = 6$$

$$\text{Area of expanded square: } 6^2 = 36$$

Percent increase in area $= \dfrac{\text{Area of Larger Square} - \text{Area of Smaller Square}}{\text{Area of Smaller Square}} \cdot 100\%$

$\dfrac{36-4}{4} = \dfrac{32}{4} = 8 \cdot 100\% = 800\%$ The answer is (C).

GEOMETRY TOPIC #6:
CIRCLES

The constant *pi* (π) has intrigued mathematicians since ancient times. It is not known exactly who first discovered that the ratio of the circumference to the diameter of a circle is a constant value. The earliest references to π include a biblical passage regarding King Solomon's temple. Its great basin measured approximately 15 feet in diameter and 45 feet in circumference, yielding a crude estimate of π equaling approximately 3. The Greek mathematician Archimedes performed the first known theoretical calculation of π during the 3rd century B.C.

In September 2002 computer scientist Yasumasa Kanada and his associates at the University of Tokyo computed 1,241,100,000,000 decimal digits of π, surpassing their own previous 1999 world record of 206,158,430,000 digits. The new 2002 calculation took approximately 500 hours using a Hitachi super computer. Hiroyuki Goto of Tokyo, Japan recited the value of π from memory to 42,195 decimal places on February 18, 1995. He is the world record holder for this event on the Pi World Ranking List.

Circles: Definitions and Important Facts

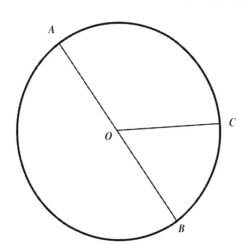

A **circle** is the set of all points in a plane that are a given distance from a fixed point in that plane. The fixed point is the **center** of the circle. A circle is named by its center point preceded by the symbol ⊙. The circle to the left would be referred to as circle ⊙*O*.

All circles are comprised of 360 degrees. The degree measure of a circle was established by the ancient Babylonians (*see the introduction to the "Basic Concepts" section in this chapter*).

The constant **π**, an irrational number, is the value by which the diameter of any circle is multiplied to find its circumference.

$$\pi = \text{approximately } \frac{22}{7} \text{ or } 3.141592654\ldots$$

Radius: A segment from the circle's center to any point on the circle. In ⊙*O* above, $\overline{OC}$ is a radius.

Chord: A line segment with endpoints on a circle.

Diameter: A chord running through the center of the circle. A diameter is the longest chord in a circle. In ⊙*O* above, $\overline{AB}$ is a diameter.

Central Angle: An angle whose vertex is the center of the circle. In ⊙*O* above, ∠*COA* is a central angle.

Semi-Circle: Half of a circle. A diameter divides a circle into two semi-circles, each of which contains 180°. **Any triangle inscribed in a semi-circle is a right triangle.**

Circumference: The perimeter of a circle.

Arc: An unbroken section of the circle's circumference.

Area of a Circle: The region inside of a circle.

Sector: A portion of the circle's area that is bounded by an arc and two radii whose endpoints are also the endpoints of that arc. A sector has the shape of a wedge or a piece of pie.

<u>**Formulas for Circles**</u>

<u>**Area and Circumference**</u>

Circumference $= 2\pi r$ or πd

Area $= \pi r^2$

r = radius d = diameter

Examples:

Radius	Diameter	Circumference	Area
3	6	6π	9π
5	10	10π	25π

<u>**Length of Arc and Area of Sector**</u>

Let n = degree measure of the arc or its central angle. Then:

Length of arc $= \dfrac{n°}{360°} \cdot 2\pi r$ **Area of sector** $= \dfrac{n°}{360°} \cdot \pi r^2$

Example:

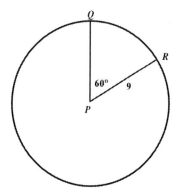

Radius of $\odot P = 9$

Measure of central angle $(\angle QPR) = 60°$

Length of arc $\overarc{QR} = \dfrac{60}{360} \cdot 2 \cdot \pi \cdot 9 = 3\pi$

Area of sector formed by $\angle PQR =$
$$\dfrac{60}{360} \cdot \pi \cdot 9^2 = 13.5\pi$$

SAT PRACTICE: CIRCLES (CIRCUMFERENCE)

GRID-IN PROBLEM:

In the diagram shown, it takes gear B $1\frac{1}{2}$ revolutions to go completely around the circumference of gear A. If gear A has a circumference of 27π, what is the radius of gear B?

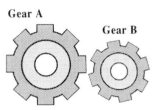

Solution:

Solve for circumference of gear B: Circumference of $A = 1\frac{1}{2}$ • Circumference of B

$$27\pi = 1\frac{1}{2} \text{ • Circumference of } B \quad 18\pi = \text{Circumference of } B$$

Use the circumference of gear B to solve for its radius:

$$\text{Circumference of } B = 18\pi = 2\pi r \quad \text{Radius} = \frac{18\pi}{2\pi} = 9$$

Grid-in 9.

SAT PRACTICE: CIRCLES (DEGREES)

A clock shows that it is 3:40 p.m. What is the angle measure between the hour and minute hands?

(A)   100°
(B)   105°
(C)   120°
(D)   130°
(E)   150°

Solution:

There are 60 minutes on the clock. 360° in a circle ÷ 60 minutes = 6° per minute. This means that every 5 minute section of the clock = 30°.

Draw a picture representing the time on the clock.

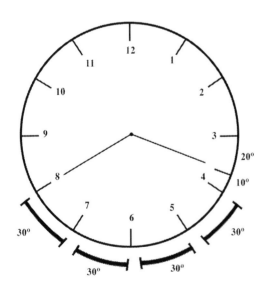

Calculate the angle measure of the clock hands as follows:

- At 3:40, the hour hand ("little hand") has moved $\dfrac{(40\ \text{minutes})}{(60\ \text{minutes})}$ or $\dfrac{2}{3}$ of the way from the numeral $\underline{3}$ on the clock to the numeral $\underline{4}$, or $20°$ out of $30°$. It is $10°$ from reaching the numeral $\underline{4}$.

- From the $\underline{4}$ on the clock to the $\underline{8}$ on the clock (where the minute hand or "big hand" is pointed) are four 5-minute segments of $30°$ each.

<u>degrees between hour hand & numeral 4</u>   <u>degrees between numeral 4 & minute hand</u>
$\downarrow$ $\downarrow$
$10°$ $+$ $4 \cdot (30°)$ $= 130°$

The answer is (D).

SAT PRACTICE: CIRCLES (RADIUS/AUXILIARY LINE)

If the area of $\triangle ABC$ is 50, the radius of circle A equals:

(A)   5

(B) $5\sqrt{2}$

(C) $\dfrac{25}{2}$

(D)   10

(E) $10\sqrt{2}$

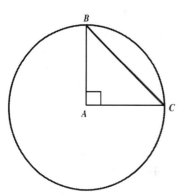

Solution:

Because both $\overline{AB}$ and $\overline{AC}$ are radii of the circle, they are congruent legs of right triangle ABC. $AB = AC = \text{radius}\ (r)$. Then:

$$\text{Area } \triangle ABC = \frac{1}{2}r^2 = 50$$
$$r^2 = 100 \qquad r = 10$$

The answer is (D).

Alternative Method:

Draw auxiliary line segments to create square *ABDC*.

The area of the square *ABDC* will be twice that of $\triangle ABC$:

$$50 \cdot 2 = 100.$$

The length of radius *AB* or radius *AC* is the square root of the area of square *ABCD*:

$$\text{Radius } AB = \sqrt{100} = 10$$

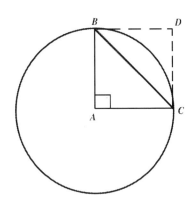

The answer is (D).

SAT PRACTICE: CIRCLES (AREA OF "RING")

In the figure shown, $OX = \dfrac{1}{3} OY$. If the area of the smaller $\odot O$ is 4π, what is the area of the shaded region?

(A) 8π
(B) 12π
(C) 32π
(D) 60π
(E) 140π

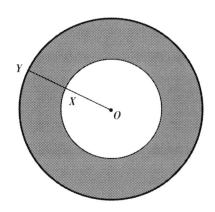

Solution:

Find radius *OX* of smaller $\odot O$ from the area given:

Note: Figure not drawn to scale.

$$\text{Area of small } \odot O \text{ is } 4\pi$$
$$r = \sqrt{4} = 2 \qquad (OX = 2)$$

Now find radius *OY* and then determine the area of the larger $\odot O$.

$$2 = \frac{1}{3} OY \qquad 6 = OY$$

$$[\text{Area of the larger } \odot O] = 6^2 \cdot \pi = 36\pi$$

<u>area of large circle</u> – <u>area of small circle</u> = <u>area of ring</u>
        ↓   ↓   ↓
       36π – 4π = 32π

The answer is (C).

SAT PRACTICE: CIRCLES (AREA OF "CRESCENT")

In $\odot O$, $m\angle BOC = 90°$ and $BO = 12$. The area of
the shaded region equals:

(A) 12π

(B) $24\pi - 60$

(C) $36(2 - \pi)$

(D) $36(\pi - 2)$

(E) $36\pi - 144$

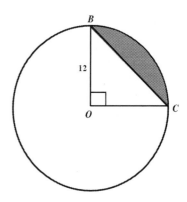

Use the formula for area of a sector to determine the area of the sector formed by $\angle BOC$.

$$\text{Area of sector} = \frac{m\angle BOC}{360°} \cdot \pi r^2 = \frac{90}{360} \cdot \pi \cdot 12^2 = 36\pi$$

Find the area of ΔBOC: Area of triangle $= \dfrac{1}{2} b \cdot h = \dfrac{1}{2} \cdot 12 \cdot 12 = 72$

<u>Area of sector</u> – <u>Area of ΔBOC</u> = <u>Area of shaded region ("crescent")</u>
   ↓   ↓   ↓
 36π – 72 = $36(\pi - 2)$

The answer is (D).

GEOMETRY TOPIC #7:
TANGENT LINES

The concept of a line tangent to a circle dates back at least 2,500 years to the beginnings of Greek geometry. A **tangent** to a circle is a line that is coplanar with the circle and intersects the circle in exactly one point, which is called the point of tangency.

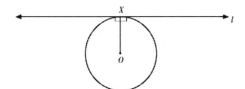

In this figure, line l is a tangent to circle O at point X.

A tangent line is perpendicular to the radius of a circle at the point of tangency. In the figure shown, radius $\overline{XO}$ is $\perp$ line l.

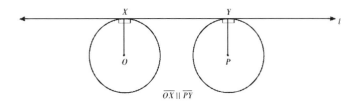

$$\overline{OX} \parallel \overline{PY}$$

If a tangent line is tangent to two or more circles as shown, the radii to the points of tangency are parallel.

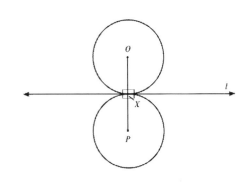

If two circles touch at one point as shown, the tangent line through that point is tangent to both circles, and the radii of the circles to the points of tangency are collinear. In this figure, line l is tangent to circles O and P at point X. Points O, X and P are collinear.

SAT PRACTICE: TANGENT LINES

In the figure shown, $\overleftrightarrow{AB}$ is tangent to $\odot O$ at point A and to $\odot P$ at point B. If $\odot O \cong \odot P$ and the diameter of $\odot O$ is 12, what is the area of $\triangle ABP$?

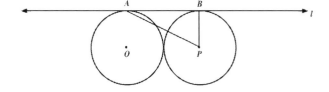

(A)   18
(B)   36
(C)   54
(D)   72
(E)   96

Solution:

Begin by applying the properties of tangent lines:

The problem indicates that $\odot O \cong \odot P$, and that the diameter of $\odot O$ is 12. Diameter = 2 • Radius, so the radius of each circle is 6.

Because $\overleftrightarrow{AB}$ is tangent to $\odot O$ at point A and to $\odot P$ at point B:

$\overleftrightarrow{AB} \perp$ radius $\overline{AO}$ of $\odot O$

$\overleftrightarrow{AB} \perp$ radius $\overline{BP}$ of $\odot P$

Label the lengths of all radii and mark right angles formed at points of tangency:

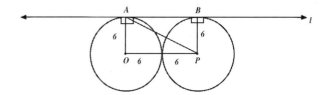

$\triangle ABP$ is a right triangle.

$BP = 6$ (height of $\triangle ABP$)

$AB = OP = 6 + 6 = 12$
(base of $\triangle ABP$)

Because the two circles are congruent, the radii of each circle equals 6 (half of circle O's stated diameter).

Because *ABPO* has two consecutive right angles, it is a rectangle, and $AB = OP$.

Area of $\triangle ABP =$

$\dfrac{1}{2}$ (*base • height*) =

$\dfrac{1}{2}$ • 12 • 6 = 36.

The answer is (B).

GEOMETRY TOPIC #8:
MULTIPLE & OVERLAPPING GEOMETRIC SHAPES

SAT math problems sometimes combine two or more circles or polygons in one problem. The shapes may be treated separately, may overlap, or one may be inscribed inside the other.

There are no set procedures for these problems, but it is usually best to treat each geometric figure separately (even if the shapes overlap) and determine the perimeter and/or area of each individual part.

SAT PRACTICE: MULTIPLE & OVERLAPPING GEOMETRIC SHAPES (INSCRIBED SQUARE/CIRCLES)

In the figure shown, the smaller square is inscribed inside a circle that is in turn inscribed in the larger square. If the radius of the circle is r, what is the ratio of the area of the smaller square to the area of the larger square?

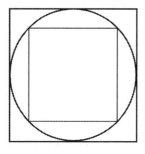

(A) $\sqrt{2} : r$

(B) $r : \sqrt{2}$

(C)   1:r

(D)   1:2

(E) r:2

Solution:

Draw in radii of the circle as indicated. The radius of the circle is $\frac{1}{2}$ of the length of the diameter, which equals the length of the diagonal of the small square.

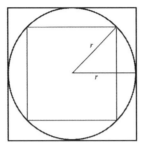

Both added segments are radii (r) of the circle.
Diagonal of smaller square = $2r$
Side of larger square = $2r$

Area of a square $= \dfrac{(diagonal)^2}{2}$

Area of small square: $\dfrac{(2r)^2}{2} = \dfrac{4r^2}{2} = 2r^2$

Area of large square: $2r \cdot 2r = 4r^2$

$\dfrac{\text{Area of small square}}{\text{Area of large square}} = \dfrac{2r^2}{4r^2} = \dfrac{1}{2}$

The answer is (D).

→**SUCCESS STRATEGY**←

Important Ratios

Circle Inscribed in Square: **Square Inscribed in Circle:**

$\dfrac{\text{Area of Circle}}{\text{Area of Square}} = \dfrac{\pi}{4}$ $\dfrac{\text{Area of Square}}{\text{Area of Circle}} = \dfrac{2}{\pi}$

SAT PRACTICE: MULTIPLE & OVERLAPPING GEOMETRIC SHAPES (OVERLAPPING FIGURES)

ONLY FOR THE VERY BRAVE. YOU WON'T SEE ONE HARDER THAN THIS.

$\odot A$ and $\odot B$ overlap as shown. Each circle has a radius of 6. What is the area of the overlapping (shaded) region?

(A) 18π

(B) $24\pi + 9\sqrt{3}$

(C) $24\pi + 18\sqrt{3}$

(D) $4(6\pi - 4\sqrt{3})$

(E) $6(4\pi - 3\sqrt{3})$

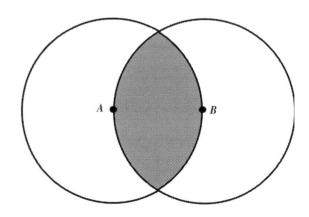

Solution:

Add auxiliary points C and D. Draw radii as shown.

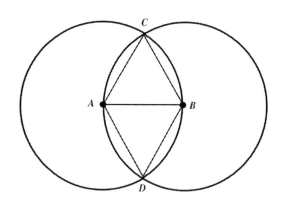

$\overline{AC} \cong \overline{AB} \cong \overline{AD} \cong \overline{BC} \cong \overline{BD}$ because each of these segments is a radius of one or both of the circles. Therefore, equilateral $\triangle ACB \cong$ equilateral $\triangle ADB$ (each side of these $\triangle$s = 6).

There are 6 "component parts" of the overlapping (shaded) region:

(1) Two identical equilateral triangles
(2) Four identical segments of the circles (crescent shapes)

(1) Area of equilateral $\triangle ACB$ or $\triangle ABD = \dfrac{s^2\sqrt{3}}{4} = \dfrac{6^2\sqrt{3}}{4} = \dfrac{36\sqrt{3}}{4} = 9\sqrt{3}$

(2) The four central angles ($\angle CAB$, $\angle CBA$, $\angle DAB$ and $\angle DBA$) each measure $60°$ (because each angle is an interior angle in an equilateral triangle).

Area of sector formed by each central $\angle = \dfrac{n°}{360°} \bullet \pi r^2 = \dfrac{60°}{360°} \bullet 6^2\pi = 6\pi$

Area of each segment of the four segments = $\underline{\text{Area of Sector}}$ – $\underline{\text{Area of Equilateral } \triangle}$

$\qquad\qquad\qquad\qquad\qquad\qquad\quad \downarrow \qquad\qquad\qquad \downarrow$

$\qquad\qquad\qquad\qquad\qquad\qquad\quad 6\pi \qquad - \qquad 9\sqrt{3}$

Calculate the total area of the 6 "component parts" of the shaded region:

Area of two equilateral triangles $\triangle ACB$ and $\triangle ABD = 2 \bullet 9\sqrt{3} = 18\sqrt{3}$

Area of four segments = $4(6\pi - 9\sqrt{3}) = 24\pi - 36\sqrt{3}$

$18\sqrt{3} + 24\pi - 36\sqrt{3} = 24\pi - 18\sqrt{3} = 6(4\pi - 3\sqrt{3})$

The answer is (E).

GEOMETRY TOPIC #9:
SOLID FIGURES

Archimedes of Syracuse, the great 3rd century Greek mathematician and thinker, contributed a myriad of discoveries that advanced science and mathematics in the ancient world. In addition to deriving the value of π, he discovered the concept of specific gravity, demonstrated the mechanical advantage of a lever, and conducted experiments about density and buoyancy. However, Archimedes himself was apparently the most proud of his discovery about the relationships among the volumes of a cone, sphere, and cylinder. He so favored this discovery that he requested that it be inscribed on his tombstone. Archimedes got his wish. His tombstone depicts a cylinder enclosing a sphere, as well as an expression stating the ratio of their volumes.

The SAT has traditionally included a few problems about solid figures. These problems usually involve volume, surface area, or both.

The SAT most frequently features these solid figures:

- Rectangular solids, including cubes

- Cylinders

- Cones

SOLID FIGURES

b = base w = width h = height s = side l = slant height

Rectangular Solid (Box)

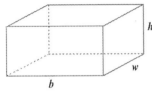

b

All angles are right angles

Cube

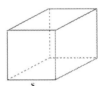

s

All angles are right angles

Volume = $b \cdot w \cdot h$
Surface area = $2(b \cdot w) + 2(w \cdot h) + 2(b \cdot h)$

Volume = s^3
Surface area = $6s^2$

Cylinder

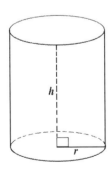

Volume = $\pi r^2 \cdot h$
Surface area = $2\pi r \cdot h + 2\pi r^2$

Cone

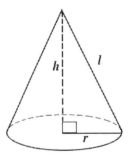

Volume = $\dfrac{1}{3}\pi r^2 \cdot h$

SAT PRACTICE: SOLID FIGURES (SURFACE AREA AND VOLUME OF A CUBE)

GRID-IN PROBLEM:

The surface area of a cube is 150 square inches. What is the cube's volume in cubic inches?

Determine the length of the side from the surface area:

$$\text{Surface area of a cube} = 6 \cdot (\text{side})^2$$
$$150 = 6s^2$$
$$25 = s^2$$
$$s = \sqrt{25} = 5$$

Determine the volume:

$$\text{Volume of a cube} = (\text{side})^3$$
$$5^3 = 125$$

Grid-in 125.

SAT PRACTICE: SOLID FIGURES (VOLUME OF A CYLINDER)

The volumes of a cube and a cylinder are equal. The cube's side length is 2π and the height of the cylinder is 4. What is the radius of the cylinder's base area?

(A) $2\sqrt{h}$

(B) $\pi\sqrt{2}$

(C) $2\sqrt{\pi}$

(D) $2h\sqrt{2\pi}$

(E) $\dfrac{\pi}{2}$

Solution:

Volume of the cube = $(\text{side})^3 = (2\pi)^3 = 8\pi^3$
Volume of the cylinder = $\pi r^2 \cdot h = 8\pi^3$
$$\downarrow$$
$$\pi r^2 \cdot 4 = 8\pi^3$$
$$r^2 = 2\pi^2 \qquad \leftarrow \text{Divide both sides of the equation by } 4\pi$$
$$r = \sqrt{2\pi^2} = \pi\sqrt{2}$$

The answer is (B).

GEOMETRY TOPIC #10:
GEOMETRIC PROBABILITY

Geometric probability involves the study of the distributions of points, length, area, and volume within an identified geometric object under certain conditions. It is the likelihood that a set of specified points, segments, sectors, or partial volumes will be found within a particular region or solid figure.

Questions may ask about the probability that a certain point will be found in a particular region of a plane figure. Many geometric probability questions can be solved by applying the following ratios:

Probability that a certain point will be found in a specified region in a plane figure (quadrilateral, circle, etc.) =

Probability that a certain point will be found in a specified portion of a solid figure (rectangular solid, cylinder, cone) =

$$\frac{\text{area of specified region}}{\text{total area}}$$

$$\frac{\text{specified partial volume}}{\text{total volume}}$$

Example: Geometric Probability

A cube measuring 4 inches on each side is painted and then cut into one-inch cubes. If the cubes are then placed in a bag, what is the probability that a cube randomly drawn from the bag will be painted on exactly 3 faces?

First, calculate the number of 1-inch cubes that are created from the larger 4" cube:

Volume of cube = 4^3 = 64 cubic inches
There are 64 one-inch cubes.

The cubes that will be painted on three faces will have been on the corners of the original 4" x 4" x 4" cube. There are eight corner cubes painted on three faces each. One corner cube is highlighted in the figure shown:

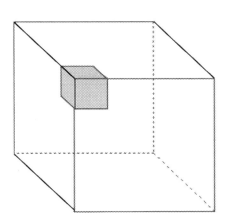

Probability cube is painted on three faces = $\dfrac{8 \text{ cubes painted on three sides}}{64 \text{ total cubes}} = \dfrac{1}{8}$

The probability that a cube painted on three faces will be randomly drawn from the bag is $\dfrac{1}{8}$.

SAT PRACTICE: GEOMETRIC PROBABILITY

GRID-IN PROBLEM:

In the special dartboard shown, the point value for each sector varies directly with the size of the sector (the low score wins). What is the probability of throwing a dart and hitting the 5-point sector?

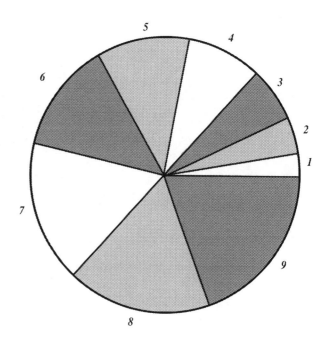

Determine the total area of the dartboard based on the representation of the dartboard's sectors.

There are nine sectors in the circle with area ratios corresponding to their point values. The total area of the circle in terms of 1-point sectors would be the sum of the point values of all of the sectors:

$$1 + 2 + 3 + 4 + 5 + 6 + 7 + 8 + 9 = 45$$

If the circle consisted only of 1-point sectors, there would be 45 such sectors.

Now find the probability that a dart will hit the sector labeled "5":

$$\text{Probability of hitting 5-point sector} = \frac{\text{Area of 5-point sector}}{\text{Total area of dartboard}} = \frac{5}{45} = \frac{1}{9}$$

Grid-in $\frac{1}{9}$.

Mathematics
Chapter 6

Data Charts, Miscellaneous Math Topics & Classic Word Problems

1. Data Charts & Tables

2. Probability & Combinations

3. Brainteasers

4. Word Problems

MISCELLANEOUS MATH TOPIC #1:
INTERPRETING A CHART, GRAPH OR DATA TABLE

➤ **Carefully inspect the chart, graph or data table before reading the accompanying questions.** Read the legend and any labels above it, below it or on its sides. Form a general idea about what the diagram represents. Study the table below to understand the units of measure that may be used.

CHARTS AND TABLES

Unit of Measure	Possible Units	Examples
Distance, Length or Height	millimeters, centimeters, meters, kilometers, inches, feet, yards, miles	Inches of rainfall
Numeric	ones, tens, hundreds, thousands, ten thousands, hundred thousands, millions	Population Money
Percent	percentage points (Total = 100%)	Any amount broken down into fractional parts

➤ **Line graphs** are drawn in a coordinate plane within x- and y-axes. Line segments connect various data points. The slopes of these various line segments can be compared to quickly determine relative increases or decreases. Line graphs can also be used to predict trends or data not shown.

➤ A **pie graph** is a circle comprised of various sized wedges. The "pie" represents a whole quantity broken down into component parts. Each wedge or slice of the pie is proportional in size to the fraction of the whole it represents.

➤ In **bar graphs,** the length of each bar is proportional to the magnitude of the quantity it represents. Bar graphs are situated within x- and y-axes.

➤ **Be very careful when reading questions about charts, graphs and data tables.** Be certain that you know what the question is asking. Errors that students make in answering these problems typically stem from misreading or misinterpreting the questions.

SAT PRACTICE: DATA INTERPRETATION (BAR GRAPH)

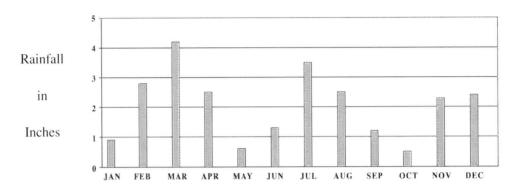

AVERAGE MONTHLY RAINFALL IN BILLROTH JUNCTION

In Billroth Junction, a "high precipitation" month is considered one in which rainfall is over 2 inches. According to the bar graph above, which of the following is the closest approximation of the average monthly rainfall in Billroth Junction during the "high precipitation" months?

(A)   2.6 inches
(B)   2.9 inches
(C)   3.3 inches
(D)   3.6 inches
(E)   3.8 inches

Solution:

- Draw a bold line horizontally across the graph at the point on the *y*-axis where rainfall equals 2 inches. The months with rainfall bars that reach above this line are "high precipitation" months.

- Approximate the rainfall for each "high precipitation" month:

    February: $\approx$ 2.8 inches
    March: $\approx$ 4.2 inches
    April: $\approx$ 2.5 inches
    July: $\approx$ 3.5 inches
    August: $\approx$ 2.5 inches
    November: $\approx$ 2.3 inches
    December: $\approx$ 2.4 inches

- Find the average monthly rainfall during the "high precipitation" using the above approximations:

$$\frac{2.8 + 4.2 + 2.5 + 3.5 + 2.5 + 2.3 + 2.4}{7} = 2.89$$

The closest answer choice is (B).

SAT PRACTICE: DATA INTERPRETATION (PIE GRAPH)

Based on the information in the graph shown, if 2,205 students major in either mathematics or in business at Newton University, how many total students are enrolled at the university?

(A)   5,250
(B)   5,485
(C)   5,780
(D)   6,300
(E)   6,500

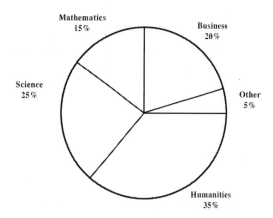

Newton University: Percentage of Students per Major

Solution:

According to the graph's legend:

Business majors ↓		Math majors ↓		
20%	+	15%	=	35% of the total number of students enrolled.

35% • *n* total students = 2,205

$$n = \frac{2,205}{.35} = 6,300$$

The answer is (D).

SAT PRACTICE: DATA INTERPRETATION (LINE GRAPH)

According to the graph shown, which of the following is the closest approximation of the average increase per year in Donner Creek's population between 1960 and 1990?

(A)   1,050
(B)   1,500
(C)   4,500
(D)   15,000
(E)   45,000

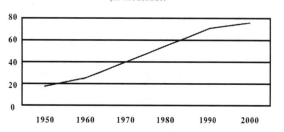

POPULATION OF DONNER CREEK
(in thousands)

Solution:

• Study the graph and estimate the population in 1960 and in 1990. Subtract 1960's population from 1990's.

$$70,000 \text{ 1990 population}$$
$$- \underline{\text{ }25,000 \text{ 1960 population}}$$
$$45,000 \text{ (population increase for 30 year period)}$$

• Divide this change in population by 30 to determine the average increase per year:

$$45,000 \div 30 = 1,500.$$

The answer is (B).

SAT PRACTICE: DATA INTERPRETATION (PICTOGRAPH)

If the national park service closes $\frac{1}{5}$ of the campsites in the eastern region of Walter Island and opens a total of 645 new campsites in the other three regions, what will be the percentage increase of campsites on the island?

CAMPSITES ON WALTER ISLAND

Eastern Region	▲▲▲
Southern Region	▲▲▲▲▲▲
Western Region	▲▲▲▲▲▲▲▲
Northern Region	▲▲⌐

▲ = 100 campsites

(A)   20
(B)   25
(C)   30
(D)   35
(E)   40

Solution:

• Determine from the pictograph how many campsites exist in each region:

Eastern: 3 triangles •100 = 300 campsites
Southern: 6 triangles • 100 = 600 campsites
Western: 8 triangles • 100 = 800 campsites
Northern: 2.5 triangles • 100 = 250 campsites

• Find the total number of campsites on Walter Island before any are opened or closed:

Total: 300 + 600 + 800 + 250 = 1950

• Determine the number of campsites that will be closed in the eastern region:

$$300 \cdot \frac{1}{5} = 60 \text{ campsites}$$

- Calculate the total change (from closings and openings) there will be in the number of campsites:

$$1,950 - 60 + 645 = 2,535$$

- Calculate the percent increase in the number of campsites:

$$2,535 - 1,950 = 585$$

$$\frac{585}{1,950} = .3, \text{ or } 30\%$$

There will be a 30% increase in the total number of campsites. The answer is (C).

SAT PRACTICE: DATA INTERPRETATION (COMPLETING A TABLE)

Ticket Summary	Matinee	Evening	Both Performances
Adult Tickets	212		549
Child Tickets		54	
All Tickets			765

The incomplete table above reflects ticket sales for the matinee and evening performances of a play. If the table is correctly completed, which of the following is true?

(A)   More adult tickets were sold for the matinee than for the evening performance.

(B)   Child ticket sales exceeded adult ticket sales for the matinee.

(C)   Child ticket sales accounted for more than 50% of the total tickets sold.

(D)   More total tickets were sold for the evening performance than for the matinee.

(E)   Adult ticket sales for the matinee exceeded the sales of all child tickets.

Solution:

Systematically solve for one missing item at a time until the table is complete:

- (765 total tickets) – (549 total adult tickets) = 216 total child tickets
- (549 total adult tickets) – (212 adult matinee tickets) = 337 adult evening tickets
- (337 adult evening tickets) + (54 child evening tickets) = 391 total evening tickets
- (216 total child tickets) – (54 child evening tickets) = 162 child matinee tickets
- (212 adult matinee tickets) + (162 child matinee tickets) = 374 total matinee tickets

Ticket Summary	Matinee	Evening	Both Performances
Adult Tickets	212	337	549
Child Tickets	162	54	216
All Tickets	374	391	765

Evaluate each answer choice:

(A)   FALSE, because 337 adult tickets were sold for the evening performance while only 212 adult tickets
        were sold for the matinee.
(B)   FALSE, because 212 adult matinee tickets were sold while only 162 child matinee tickets were sold.
(C)   FALSE, because the 216 child tickets sold represent less than 50% of the 765 total tickets sold.
(D)   TRUE, because 391 tickets were sold for the evening performance and 374 tickets were sold for the matinee.
(E)   FALSE, because 216 total child tickets were sold while 212 adult matinee tickets were sold.

The answer is (D).

MISCELLANEOUS MATH TOPIC #2:
PROBABILITY AND COMBINATIONS

The **probability** that a certain event will occur is expressed as a fraction between 0 and 1 or its equivalent as
a decimal or percent. If there is no possibility that the event will occur, the probability is 0. If a specified outcome
is a certainty, the probability is 1 or 100%.

FINDING PROBABILITY

$$\text{Probability} = \frac{\text{Number of ways to get desired outcome}}{\text{Total number of possible outcomes}}$$

SAT PRACTICE: PROBABILITY AND COMBINATIONS (PROBABILITY)

A bag contains twice as many blue marbles as white marbles and three times as many green marbles as blue
marbles. If one marble is drawn from the bag, what is the probability that it will be blue?

(A) $\dfrac{1}{9}$

(B) $\dfrac{1}{6}$

(C) $\dfrac{2}{9}$

(D) $\dfrac{1}{3}$

(E) $\dfrac{4}{9}$

Solution:

- Let x equal the number of white marbles. Determine the number of blue and green marbles relative to the number of white marbles.

Marble Color	Number in Bag
White	x
Blue	$2x$
Green	$3(2x) = 6x$

- Create a probability ratio expressing the number of blue marbles and the total number of marbles.

$$\frac{\text{Number of blue marbles}}{\text{Total number of marbles}} = \frac{2x}{x + 2x + 6x} = \frac{2x}{9x} = \frac{2}{9}$$

The answer is (C).

Combinations

SAT "combination" problems involve counting the number of possible arrangements or combinations that can create a specified result.

Fundamental Principle of Counting

If one event can occur m different ways and another event can occur n different ways, the events can occur together in $m \cdot n$ different ways.

Example: If Batman's wardrobe includes 3 different capes, 5 different masks, and 2 different pairs of boots, he would have a total of $3 \cdot 5 \cdot 2$, or 30 different costume options (Bat-suits with Bat-boots) available.

SAT PRACTICE: PROBABILITY AND COMBINATIONS (COMBINATIONS)

GRID-IN PROBLEM:

A manufacturer assigns a three-digit identification code to each of its products. The first digit of the code is always an odd number, the second digit is always an even number, and the third digit is any number other than those used as the first or second digits of the code. How many such codes can be made?

Solution:

The first digit can be one of 5 odd numbers: 1, 3, 5, 7 or 9
The second digit can be one of 5 even numbers: 2, 4, 6, 8 or 0
The third number can be any one of ten digits other than those previously used: $10 - 2 = 8$

$$5 \cdot 5 \cdot 8 = 200 \text{ codes}$$

Grid-in 200.

SAT PRACTICE: PROBABILITY AND COMBINATIONS (COMBINATIONS)

At a movie theatre, the "snack combination special" consists of any three of the following five items: a hot dog, a candy bar, popcorn, ice cream, and a soda. How many different snack combinations could be purchased? (Assume that only one of each item may be included in the order; e.g., one hot dog, not two.)

(A)   8
(B)   10
(C)   12
(D)   15
(E)   20

Solution:

Let H = hot dog, C = candy bar, P = popcorn, I = ice cream, S = soda

Systematically write out the different combinations available.

Because there are three items per combination, the two remaining items, soda and ice cream, have been covered in all of the other combinations shown in this table.

Description	Combinations			Number
Combinations that include a hot dog	HCP HPS	HCI HPI	HCS HIS	6
Combinations that include a candy bar but not a hot dog	CPI	CPS	CIS	3
Combinations that include popcorn but no hot dog or candy bar	PIS			1

6 + 3 + 1 = 10 different combinations.

The answer is (B).

SAT PRACTICE: PROBABILITY AND COMBINATIONS (COMBINATION – ROUTES)

Mrs. Quigley wants to drive from Dana Point to Newport Coast, stopping at Aliso Creek on the way. According to the map, how many different routes can Mrs. Quigley take if she does not visit any city more than once and she does not travel on any section of road more than once?

(A)   5
(B)   6
(C)   7
(D)   8
(E)   9

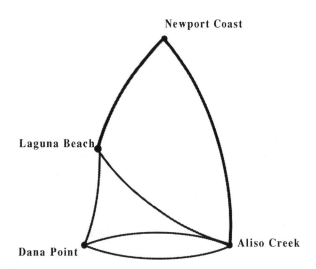

Solution:

• Label each section of road with a number.

• Using the numbers assigned to refer to the various sections of the road, systematically list all of the ways to go from Dana Point to Newport Coast through Aliso Creek not traveling any section of the road more than once and not visiting any city more than once.

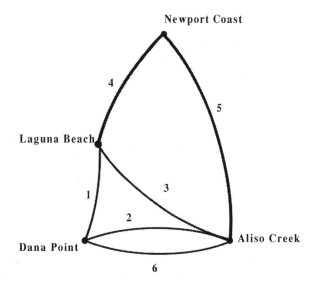

Description	Combinations	Total Routes
Starting with Section 1	1 - 3 - 5	1
Starting with Section 2	2 - 5 2 - 3 - 4	2
Starting with Section 6	6 - 5 6 - 3 - 4	2

1 + 2 + 2 = 5 total routes available.

The answer is (A).

MISCELLANEOUS MATH TOPIC #3:
BRAINTEASERS

The SAT always includes a few perplexing problems, or "**brainteasers**," that cannot always be solved via traditional or systematic methods of solution. Here are a few tips for solving SAT brainteasers:

1. **Read the problem carefully and underline what you are being asked to find.** Make sure that you understand exactly what the question is asking.

2. **Break the problem down into components.** Sort out what the problem tells you and what it doesn't. How can the stated information lead to the answer?

3. **Identify the first step that should be taken.**
   - Is there a particular strategy, formula or equation that might work?
   - Would it help to form a pictorial representation (draw a sketch or make a chart)?
   - Should you try to "translate" the problem into easier-to-understand terminology?
   - Would it help to "Throw it in Reverse" and work backwards?

4. **Work progressively forward, one step at a time, toward a solution.** If your methodology runs into a dead end, try a different approach.

5. **Be careful not to become too absorbed in these problem types,** as they can become a real time drain. If you are still stumped after a few minutes, quit doing the problem and move on.

SAT PRACTICE: BRAINTEASERS (NUMBERS THAT FIT CERTAIN CRITERIA)

How many three-digit numbers exist in which the hundreds digit is three times the tens digit?

(A)   10
(B)   30
(C)   50
(D)   90
(E)   100

Solution:

- Make "number skeletons" for the possible three digit numbers that fit the criteria specified, using a question mark for the one's digit. There are three possible configurations for three digit numbers in which the hundreds digit is three times the tens digit:

$$\underline{9} \quad \underline{3} \quad \underline{?} \qquad \underline{6} \quad \underline{2} \quad \underline{?} \qquad \underline{3} \quad \underline{1} \quad \underline{?}$$

- Multiply the number of "number skeletons" by the ten possibilities (0 – 9) that can go into the one's place:

$$3 \text{ number skeletons} \cdot 10 \text{ possible digits for the one's place} = 30.$$

There are 30 three-digit numbers that fit the criteria. The answer is (B).

SAT PRACTICE: BRAINTEASERS (EXCHANGED QUANTITIES)

Heidi gave $10.00 to Charlynn and $5.00 to Allison. Charlynn then gave $20.00 to Allison and $5.00 back to Heidi. Which of the following transactions would restore each individual to her original amount of money?

(A)   Allison should give $10 to Heidi and $5 to Charlynn
(B)   Allison should give $15 to Heidi and $10 to Charlynn
(C)   Allison should give $10 to Heidi and $15 to Charlynn
(D)   Allison should give $20 to Heidi and $5 to Charlynn
(E)   Allison should give $20 to Heidi and $15 to Charlynn

Solution:

Make a table itemizing the transactions.

	Heidi	Charlynn	Allison
Heidi gave $10.00 to Charlynn and $5.00 to Allison	-15	+10	+ 5
Charlynn then gave $20.00 to Allison and $5.00 back to Heidi	+ 5	-25	+20
	-10	-15	+25

In order to square the accounts, Allison should give $10 to Heidi and $15 to Charlynn.

The answer is (C).

SAT PRACTICE: BRAINTEASERS (NO REMAINDER)

Mr. Shapiro has a jar containing red, green and blue pencils in his classroom. He has two more blue pencils than red pencils and four times as many green pencils as blue pencils. Which of the following could be the total number of pencils in the jar?

(A)   25
(B)   31
(C)   37
(D)   46
(E)   53

Solution:

- Let r represent the number of red pencils. Determine the number of blue and green pencils with respect to the number of red pencils.

- The total number of pencils is represented by the expression:

Color	*Number*
Red	r
Blue	$r + 2$
Green	$4(r + 2)$

$$\underset{\downarrow}{Red} \quad \underset{\downarrow}{Blue} \qquad \underset{\downarrow}{Green}$$

$$r + (r + 2) + [4(r + 2)] = r + r + 2 + 4r + 8 = 6r + 10$$

- The total number of pencils is $6r + 10$ in which r must be a whole number. Set $6r + 10$ equal to each answer choice and solve for r. The equation in which r turns out to be a whole number is the answer:

(A)	$6r + 10 = 25$	$6r = 15$	r is not a whole number
(B)	$6r + 10 = 31$	$6r = 21$	r is not a whole number
(C)	$6r + 10 = 37$	$6r = 27$	r is not a whole number
(D)	$6r + 10 = 46$	$6r = 36$	$r = 6$ THE ANSWER!
(E)	$6r + 10 = 53$	$6r = 43$	r is not a whole number

The answer is (D).

MISCELLANEOUS MATH TOPIC #4:
WORD PROBLEMS

The SAT typically includes a few of the following classic word problems:

- "Cash Register" Math
- Consecutive Integers
- Distance, Rate & Time (Motion)
- Mixture
- Work

With the exception of "cash register" math problems, these problems are solved by implementing specific equations. It is very important to be able to implement all of the specific word problem equations that are presented in this section.

SAT PRACTICE: WORD PROBLEMS (CASH REGISTER MATH)

Willa and Ted had lunch at the county fair. Willa was charged $3.10 for two hot dogs and a cookie. Ted paid $4.35 for three hot dogs and a cookie. What was the price of two cookies?

(A) $0.50
(B) $0.60
(C) $1.20
(D) $1.25
(E) $2.50

Solution:

- Subtract the less expensive lunch (Willa's) from the more expensive lunch (Ted's) to determine the cost of one hot dog:

$4.35 = 3 hot dogs + 1 cookie (Ted's)

(−) $3.10 = 2 hot dogs + 1 cookie (Willa's)

$1.25 = 1 hot dog + 0 cookies   One hot dog costs $1.25.

- Calculate the cost of one cookie:

Willa's lunch total		Cost of two hot dogs		Cost of one cookie
↓		↓		↓
$3.10	–	2($1.25)	=	$0.60

- Calculate the cost of two cookies: $0.60 • 2 cookies = $1.20

The answer is (C).

SAT PRACTICE: WORD PROBLEMS (CONSECUTIVE INTEGERS)

The lengths of the sides of a triangle are represented by three consecutive integers. Which of the following could not be its perimeter?

(A)   36
(B)   49
(C)   51
(D)   63
(E)   78

- Using x, $x + 1$, and $x + 2$ to represent the three consecutive integers, the perimeter can be written as:

  $x + x + 1 + x + 2 = 3x + 3$

- $3x + 3$ represents a number that must be divisible by 3. This means that one of the answer choices will contain a number that is not divisible by 3.

- Check each answer choice for divisibility by 3. A number is divisible by 3 if the sum of its digits is divisible by 3:

  (A)   36: 3 + 6 = 9 (divisible by 3)
  (B)   49: 4 + 9 = 13 (not divisible by 3)
  (C)   51: 5 + 1 = 6 (divisible by 3)
  (D)   63: 6 + 3 = 9 (divisible by 3)
  (E)   78: 7 + 8 = 15 (divisible by 3)

The answer is (B).

→SUCCESS STRATEGY←

- Consecutive integers include positive numbers, negative numbers and zero.
- Consecutive odd integers skip the even integers between them. *Examples:*

  77, 79, 81, 83

  -3, -1, 1, 3
- Consecutive even integers skip the odd integers between them. *Examples:*

  78, 80, 82, 84

  -4, -2, 0, 2, 4
- Consecutive integers can be algebraically expressed as follows:

  n, $n + 1$, $n + 2$, $n + 3$, $n + 4$...
- Consecutive odd or consecutive even integers can be algebraically expressed as follows:

  n, $n + 2$, $n + 4$, $n + 6$, $n + 8$...

SAT PRACTICE: WORD PROBLEMS (DISTANCE, RATE & TIME)

GRID-IN PROBLEM

Patricia drove from her home to Lake Maurice at an average speed of 50 miles per hour and returned home at an average speed of 40 miles per hour. If it took her 3 hours to drive from her home to Lake Maurice, how many hours did the return trip take (from Lake Maurice to her home)?

Solution:

Set up two distance, rate & time equations:

DEPARTURE: Distance = 50 • 3

RETURN: Distance = 40 • t

Because both distances are equal, the products of the rate and time in each equation are also equal:

$$50 • 3 = 40 • t$$
$$150 = 40t$$
$$3.75 = t$$

Grid-in 3.75.

→SUCCESS STRATEGY←

- The following is the general equation for solving motion problems:

    Distance = Rate • Time

- *Distance* is usually expressed in miles, feet, or kilometers.

- *Rate* is usually expressed in miles per hour, kilometers per hour, or meters per second.

- *Time* is usually expressed in hours, minutes, or seconds.

- To find "average rate," use the following definition:

$$\text{Average Rate} = \frac{\text{Total Distance}}{\text{Total Time}}$$

SAT PRACTICE: WORD PROBLEMS (DISTANCE, RATE & TIME – AVERAGE RATE)

Jacob rode his bicycle from his dormitory building to his college campus at an average speed of 20 miles per hour and then immediately returned back the same distance at an average speed of 30 miles per hour. What was Jacob's average speed for the round-trip?

(A)   22 miles per hour
(B)   24 miles per hour
(C)   25 miles per hour
(D)   26 miles per hour
(E)   28 miles per hour

Solution:

•   Choose a hypothetical distance between the two points that is a multiple of the average speeds indicated for each direction of the trip. Do not be concerned if this number does not match the situation suggested by the problem. 20 and 30 both divide evenly into 60. Assume that the distance from Jacob's dormitory to the college campus is 60 miles.

•   Based on the hypothetical distance specified in the previous step, calculate the time it took to travel each direction.

$$\text{Distance} = \text{Rate} \cdot \text{Time}$$

To college campus: 60 miles = 20 miles per hour • time

$60 \div 20 = 3$ hours to travel to the college campus

From college campus: 60 miles = 30 miles per hour • time

$60 \div 30 = 2$ hours to travel back from the college campus

•   Use the equation for finding "average rate":

$$\text{Average Rate} = \frac{\text{Total Distance}}{\text{Total Time}} = \frac{120 \text{ miles round-trip distance} (60 \text{ miles} \bullet 2)}{5 \text{ total hours} (3+2)}$$

Average Rate = 24 miles per hour.

The answer is (B).

Note: **This is a variation of a "weighted average" problem. You cannot simply average the two rates of speed – the answer is not** $\dfrac{20+30}{2}$ **= 25 miles per hour. Because it takes a little longer to drive one direction than the other, the average speed is always a little less than half of the average of the two rates.**

SAT PRACTICE: WORD PROBLEMS (MIXTURE PROBLEMS)

GRID-IN PROBLEM:

Mrs. Pretzel purchased 2 pounds of almonds at $5.50 per pound, 3 pounds of pecans at $4.25 per pound, and 5 pounds of walnuts for $6.75 per pound. If Mrs. Pretzel mixes all of these nuts together to serve at a party, what is the price of the mixture in dollars per pound?

→SUCCESS STRATEGY←

· Mixture problems involve combining items that have different values.

· The "value" of an item is determined by the product of its quantity and its cost per unit. *Example:* Value = (number of pounds A · cost per pound A)

· The equation for mixture problems follows the same format as the equation for weighted averages:

$$\frac{(\text{\# Pounds A} \cdot \text{Cost per pound A}) + (\text{\# Pounds B} \cdot \text{Cost per pound B})}{\text{Total Pounds (A + B)}} = \text{Value of Mixture}$$

Solution:

Set up the mixture equation with the information provided:

Almonds   Pecans   Walnuts
↓   ↓   ↓

$$\frac{(2 \cdot \$5.50) + (3 \cdot \$4.25) + (5 \cdot \$6.75)}{10} = \text{Dollar amount of mixture (per pound)}$$

↑

Total number
of pounds of all nuts
(2 + 3 + 5)

Simplify and solve the equation: $\dfrac{11.00 + 12.75 + 33.75}{10} = \$5.75$ per pound

Grid-in 5.75.

SAT PRACTICE: WORD PROBLEMS (MIXTURE)

How many liters of water should be added to 3 liters of pure sulfuric acid to make a 60% solution?

(A)   1.2
(B)   1.5
(C)   1.75
(D)   2
(E)   2.25

- This is another variety of a mixture problem. In this case:
  Value = (strength of solution • quantity)

- In chemical solutions, "pure" substances such as alcohol or acid always have a strength of 100%. Water is used to dilute pure substances; it always has a strength of 0%.

It is easy to use the following chart when solving mixture problems in which a pure substance is diluted:

	Water		Pure Acid		Solution
Strength of solution	0%		100%		60%
Quantity (in liters)	x		3		$x + 3$
Value (strength of solution • quantity in liters)	**0**	**+**	**300**	**=**	**60(x + 3)**

The final equation is found in the bottom row of the chart:

$$300 = 60(3 + x)$$
$$300 = 180 + 60x$$
$$120 = 60x$$
$$x = 2$$

The answer is (D).

SAT PRACTICE: WORD PROBLEMS (WORK)

It takes Jewel 4 hours working alone to paint a fence, and it takes Alexis 3 hours working alone to paint the same fence. How long will it take Jewel and Alexis to paint the fence if they work together?

→SUCCESS STRATEGY←

- "Work" problems usually involve calculating how long it takes two individuals to perform a certain job or complete a project based on how long it takes each individual to do the job alone. Other variations of this theme also show up on the SAT.

- The following is the basic equation for "work" problems:

$$\frac{\text{Time it takes two indivuals to complete job}}{\text{Time it takes individual A to do the job alone}} + \frac{\text{Time it takes two individuals to complete job}}{\text{Time it takes individual B to do the job alone}} = 1$$

Solution:

Let *w* equal the time it will take Jewel and Alexis to paint the fence working together. Set up the general work equation with the information provided:

$$\frac{w}{4} \quad + \quad \frac{w}{3} \quad = \quad 1 \text{ complete job}$$

↑	↑
4 hours represents Jewel's time working alone	3 hours represents Alexis's time working alone

Multiply through by 12 to eliminate the denominators and then solve the equation:

$$3w + 4w = 12$$
$$7w = 12$$
$$w = \frac{12}{7} = 1\frac{5}{7} \text{ hours}$$

Grid-in $\frac{12}{7}$ or 1.71.

Note: The answer to work problems in this format is always going to be a value in between half of the faster individual's time (in this case, $1\frac{1}{2}$ is half of Alexis's time) and half of the slower individual's time (in this case, 2 is half of Jewel's time):

$$1\frac{1}{2} \quad < \quad 1\frac{5}{7} \quad < \quad 2$$

↑	↑	↑
Half	ANSWER	Half
of		of
faster		slower
individual's		individual's
time		time

Use this as a guiding principle if you ever have to guess.

Mathematics
Chapter 7
Practice Problems

❏ Practice Problems

❏ Answer Explanations

**7A: Practice Problems Set
(Algebra & Number Operations)**

1. If r and s are integers such that $3 < |r| < 7$ and $2 < |s| < 10$, what is the least possible value of $r + s$?

    (A)   -17
    (B)   -15
    (C)   -5
    (D)   7
    (E)   11

2. Which of the following is the graph of the solution set of $|2x + 1| \le 9$?

    (A)

    (B)

    (C)

    (D)

    (E)

    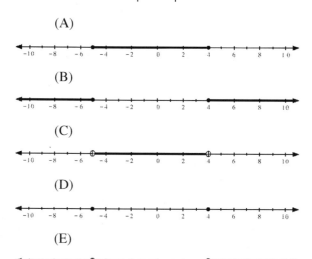

3. If $\dfrac{3x-1}{x+2} = 6$, which of the following is the value of x?

    (A) $-\dfrac{13}{3}$

    (B)   -3

    (C)   -1

    (D) $\dfrac{5}{2}$

    (E)   3

4. In the equation $7\sqrt{x} - 2 = 12$, what does x equal?

    (A) $\dfrac{12}{7}$

    (B) $\dfrac{100}{49}$

    (C)   4

    (D) $\dfrac{144}{25}$

    (E)   49

5. If $2\sqrt{3x} = \sqrt{9x+15}$, what does x equal?

    (A)   -5

    (B) $-\dfrac{13}{6}$

    (C)   -1

    (D) $\dfrac{5}{7}$

    (E)   5

6. *GRID-IN PROBLEM*

    If $x^{-3} = \dfrac{1}{8}$, what is the value of 5^{2x}?

7. *GRID-IN PROBLEM*

    y varies inversely with x. If $y = 180$ when $x = \dfrac{2}{3}$, what is the value of y when $x = \dfrac{3}{4}$?

8. If a function is defined as $f(x) = |x^2 + 2x + 1|$ and the domain of the function is $-4 \le x \le 0$, what is the function's range?

    (A) $0 \le y \le 9$
    (B) $0 \le y \le 16$
    (C) $0 \le y \le 25$
    (D) $4 \le y \le 9$
    (E) $4 \le y \le 16$

9.   Let $f(x) = \dfrac{x^2}{\sqrt[3]{x}} + 2x$. If m is a positive real number, what is the value of $f(m^3)$?

(A) $8m^3$

(B) $5m^3$

(C) $2m^3$

(D) $m^6 + 2m^3$

(E) $m^5 + 2m^3$

10.   Let $f(x) = -|x|$. Which of the following is true?

(A)   the function's domain is the set of all real numbers ≥ 0

(B)   the function's domain is the set of all real numbers < 0

(C)   the function's range is the set of all real numbers ≤ 0

(D)   the function's range is the set of all real numbers ≥ 0

(E)   the function's range is the set of all real numbers < 0

11.   The following represents a geometric sequence in which each of the blanks represents a positive integer:

2, ___, 18, ___, 162

Which of the following is the 4th term of the sequence (represented by the second blank)?

(A)   20

(B)   32

(C)   36

(D)   48

(E)   54

12.   A small town doubled in population every 4 years. If the original settlement consisted of 1,200 people, which of the following expresses the population at the end of y years?

(A) $1,200 \cdot 2^{4y}$

(B) $1,200 \cdot 4^{y-1}$

(C) $1,200 \cdot 2^{\frac{4}{y}}$

(D) $1,200 \cdot 2^{\frac{y}{4}}$

(E) $1,200 \cdot 4^{\frac{y}{4}}$

13.   M = {Odd integers less than 20}
       N = {Multiples of 3}

How many elements are contained in $M \cap N$?

(A)   2

(B)   3

(C)   4

(D)   5

(E)   6

14.   *GRID-IN PROBLEM*

Let the function f be defined by $f(x) = x^2 + 12$. If n is a positive number such that $f(3n) = 3f(n)$, what is the value of n?

15.   Which of the following represents the domain of the function $f(x) = \dfrac{2x-1}{x-3}$?

(A)   the set of all real numbers $\neq 0$

(B)   the set of all real numbers $\neq \dfrac{1}{2}$

(C)   the set of all real numbers < -3

(D)   the set of all real numbers $\neq \pm 3$

(E)   the set of all real numbers $\neq 3$

16.

$$C(w) = kw + a$$

A college offers a study abroad retreat in which a set number of students lives and studies in Athens. The college has calculated the cost C of the retreat as a constant k times the length w, in weeks, of the retreat added to the cost a of airplane tickets to get to and from Athens, as shown by the function above. The study abroad group stayed in Athens 4 weeks longer than planned. How much more did the longer retreat cost than the originally scheduled retreat?

(A) $4k$

(B) $4w$

(C) $4a$

(D) $w(k-4)$

(E) $k(w-4)$

17.   If $x > 0$ and $x^{-2} = 16$, then $2x^{\frac{1}{2}}$ equals:

(A)   -4

(B)   1

(C)   2

(D)   4

(E)   8

18.

x	$f(x)$
-1	3
3	2
5	9
6	12
7	4

According to the table above, for what value of x does $f(x) = 2x - 1$?

(A)   -1

(B)   3

(C)   5

(D)   6

(E)   7

19.   If $f(x) = \dfrac{1}{3x} + x^2$, what is the value of $f\left(-\dfrac{1}{3}\right)$?

(A) $-\dfrac{10}{9}$

(B) $-\dfrac{8}{9}$

(C) $-\dfrac{1}{9}$

(D) $\dfrac{7}{9}$

(E) $\dfrac{10}{9}$

20. y varies directly with x, and $y = 30$ when $x = 5$. When $x = 30$, $y =$

(A)   5

(B)   6

(C)   12

(D)   50

(E)   180

ANSWER EXPLANATIONS:

1.   (B)

PROBLEM   TYPE: ABSOLUTE   VALUE INEQUALITY

$3 < |r| < 7$

$|r| = 4$, 5 or 6, so r can equal 4, 5, or 6 as well as -4, -5, -6

$2 < |s| < 10$

$|s| = 3, 4, 5, 6, 7, 8$ or 9, so s can equal 3, 4, 5, 6, 7, 8 or 9 as well as -3, -4, -5, -6, -7, -8 or -9.

The least possible value of r is -6.
The least possible value of s is -9.

$(-6) + (-9) = -15$

2.   (A)
PROBLEM TYPE: GRAPH OF AN ABSOLUTE VALUE INEQUALITY

Write a compound sentence between -9 and 9:

$-9 \leq 2x + 1 \leq 9$

$-10 \leq 2x \leq 8$ Subtract 1 from each expression
$-5 \leq x \leq 4$ Divide each expression by 2

This solution set is depicted by the graph in answer choice (A).

3.   (A)
PROBLEM TYPE: RATIONAL EQUATIONS

$\dfrac{3x-1}{x+2} = 6$

$3x - 1 = 6(x + 2)$ ←cross multiply

$3x - 1 = 6x + 12$

$-13 = 3x$

$x = -\dfrac{13}{3}$

4.   (C)
PROBLEM TYPE: RADICAL EQUATIONS

$7\sqrt{x} - 2 = 12$
$7\sqrt{x} = 14$
$\sqrt{x} = 2$
$(\sqrt{x})^2 = 2^2$
$x = 4$

Check:

$7\sqrt{(4)} - 2 \overset{?}{=} 12$
$7(2) - 2 = 12$ ✓

5.   (E)
PROBLEM TYPE: RADICAL EQUATIONS

$2\sqrt{3x} = \sqrt{9x+15}$
$(2\sqrt{3x})^2 = (\sqrt{9x+15})^2$ ←square both sides

$4(3x) = 9x + 15$
$12x = 9x + 15$
$3x = 15$
$x = 5$

Check:

$2\sqrt{3x} \overset{?}{=} \sqrt{9x+15}$

$2\sqrt{3(5)} \overset{?}{=} \sqrt{9(5)+15}$

$2\sqrt{15} \overset{?}{=} \sqrt{60}$

$2\sqrt{15} \overset{?}{=} \sqrt{4} \cdot \sqrt{15}$
$2\sqrt{15} = 2\sqrt{15}$ ✓

6.   625
PROBLEM TYPE: RATIONAL EXPONENTS

$x^{-3} = \dfrac{1}{8}$

$\left(x^{-3}\right)^{-\frac{1}{3}} = \left(\dfrac{1}{8}\right)^{-\frac{1}{3}}$ ←Raise both sides to the $\left(-\dfrac{1}{3}\right)$

$x = 8^{\frac{1}{3}}$
$x = 2$

Then:

$5^{2x} = 5^{2(2)} = 5^4 = 625$

7.   160
PROBLEM TYPE: INVERSE VARIATION

Set up the inverse variation in the form $x_1 \cdot y_1 = x_2 \cdot y_2$:

$$\frac{2}{3} \cdot 180 = \frac{3}{4} \cdot y_2$$

$$120 = \frac{3}{4} \cdot y_2$$

$$y_2 = 160$$

8.   (A)
PROBLEM TYPE: DOMAIN & RANGE

Make a table reflecting domain & range values:

x	$f(x) = \lvert x^2 + 2x + 1 \rvert$
-4	9
-3	4
-2	1
-1	0
0	1

For the specified domain, the range's least value is 0 and its greatest value is 9.

9.   (E)
PROBLEM TYPE: EVALUATING FUNCTIONS

Replace x with m^3: $\dfrac{\left(m^3\right)^2}{\sqrt[3]{m^3}} + 2m^3 = \dfrac{m^6}{m} + 2m^3 = $

$m^5 + 2m^3$

10.   (C)
PROBLEM TYPE: DOMAIN AND RANGE

Because the range of $f(x) = \lvert x \rvert$ is the set of all real numbers ≥ 0, the range of $f(x) = -\lvert x \rvert$ is the set of all real numbers ≤ 0.

11.   (E)
PROBLEM TYPE: GEOMETRIC SEQUENCE

If x represents the number that goes in the second blank, the following ratio expresses the relationship among the first three terms:

$$\frac{2}{x} = \frac{x}{18}$$

$x^2 = 36$ x is a positive, so $x = 6$.

$6 \div 2 = 3$ ← The second term divided by the first term = 3, which is the common ratio.

$162 \div 3 = 54$ ← The fifth term divided by the common ratio will provide the fourth term, which goes in the second blank.

12.   (D)
PROBLEM TYPE: EXPONENTIAL GROWTH

"Paint by Numbers": Assign a number for y and determine what the population will be at the end of that many years.

Let $y = 12$ years, a multiple of the 4-year increments by which the population doubles.

Time	Number of People
Beginning	1,200
End of 4 years	2,400
End of 8 years	4,800
End of 12 years	9,600

Choice (D)'s expression $1{,}200 \cdot 2^{\frac{y}{4}}$ yields 9,600 when $y = 12$.

13.   (B)
PROBLEM TYPE: SETS

M = { 1, 3, 5, 7, 9, 11, 13, 15, 17, 19}
N = {3, 6, 9, 12, 15, 18, 21...}
M $\cap$ N = {3, 9, 15}

14.   2

PROBLEM   TYPE: VARIATIONS   OF   A   FUNCTION

$$f(3n) \quad = \quad 3f(n)$$
$$\downarrow \qquad\qquad \downarrow$$
$$(3n)^2 + 12 = 3(n^2 + 12)$$

$$9n^2 + 12 = 3n^2 + 36$$
$$6n^2 = 24$$
$$n^2 = 4 \qquad\qquad n \text{ is positive, so } n = 2.$$

15.   (E)

PROBLEM TYPE: DOMAIN OF A FUNCTION

The denominator of a function cannot = 0; therefore $x \neq 3$.

16.   (A)

PROBLEM TYPE: FUNCTION APPLICATION

If the retreat lasts 4 weeks longer, then:

$$C(w + 4) = k(w + 4) + a$$

Cost of extended   Cost of originally
retreat   planned retreat
$\downarrow$ $\downarrow$
$$(kw + 4k + a) \quad - \quad (kw + a) = 4k$$

The cost of the extended retreat exceeds the cost of the originally planned retreat by a quantity of $4k$.

17.   (B)

PROBLEM TYPE: INTEGER AND RATIONAL EXPONENTS

$$x^{-2} = \frac{1}{x^2} = 16 \qquad x^2 = \frac{1}{16}$$

$$x = \sqrt{\frac{1}{16}} = \frac{1}{4}$$

$$2x^{\frac{1}{2}} = \quad 2 \bullet \left(\frac{1}{4}\right)^{\frac{1}{2}} = 2 \bullet \sqrt{\frac{1}{4}} = 2 \bullet \frac{1}{2} = 1$$

18.   (C)

PROBLEM TYPE: EVALUATING A FUNCTION

$$f(x) = 2x - 1 \qquad 9 = 2(5) - 1$$

19.   (B)

PROBLEM TYPE: EVALUATING RATIONAL EXPRESSIONS

$$f(x) = \frac{1}{3x} + x^2$$

$$f\left(-\frac{1}{3}\right) = \frac{1}{3\left(-\frac{1}{3}\right)} + \left(-\frac{1}{3}\right)^2 = -1 + \frac{1}{9} = -\frac{8}{9}$$

20.   (E)

PROBLEM TYPE: DIRECT VARIATION

In this direct variation, $\dfrac{y}{x} = k$, which leads to the following ratio: $\dfrac{y_1}{x_1} = \dfrac{y_2}{x_2}$

$$\frac{30}{5} = \frac{y_2}{30}$$

Solve for y_2 through cross multiplication:

$$30 \bullet 30 = 5 \bullet y_2$$

$$900 = 5 \bullet y_2$$

$$180 = y_2$$

7B: **Practice Problems Set**
        (Plane & Coordinate Geometry
        and Graphs)

1.

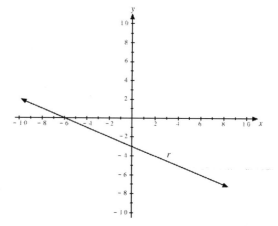

The slope of the line *r* in the graph above is:

(A)   -3

(B)   -2

(C) $-\dfrac{1}{2}$

(D) $\dfrac{1}{2}$

(E)   2

2.   *GRID-IN PROBLEM*

If *f* is a linear function and if $f(4) = 7$ and $f(2) = -1$, what is the slope of the graph of *f* in the *xy*-plane?

3.   If $f(x) = x^2$ and $g(x) = |x|$, which of the following statements are true?

    I. $f(x)$ and $g(x)$ have the same domain and range.

    II.   The graphs of $f(x)$ and $g(x)$ intersect in exactly 2 points.

    III. $f(2)$ and $g(-4)$ yield the same *y*-value.

(A)   I only

(B)   II only

(C)   III only

(D)   I and II

(E)   I and III

4.

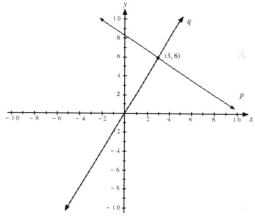

In the *xy*-coordinate system above, the lines *p* and *q* are perpendicular. If the point $(n, -9)$ is found on line *p*, what is the value of *n*?

5.   A circle's center has coordinates (1, 4). If *XY* is a diameter of the circle and *X* has coordinates $(-2, \dfrac{1}{2})$, what are the coordinates of *Y*?

(A) $(0, \dfrac{3}{4})$

(B) $(-1, \dfrac{9}{2})$

(C) $(-\dfrac{1}{2}, 3)$

(D) $(4, \dfrac{15}{2})$

(E) $(3, 2)$

6.   In isosceles $\triangle ABC$, $\overline{AB} \cong \overline{AC}$. If point A has coordinates $(3, 4)$ and point B has coordinates $(-3, 1)$, which of the following could NOT be the coordinates of C?

(A) $(9, 1)$
(B) $(-3, 7)$
(C) $(0, -2)$
(D) $(2, -1)$
(E) $(6, -2)$

7.   Which of the following represents the graph of $3x - 2y \leq 4$?

(C)

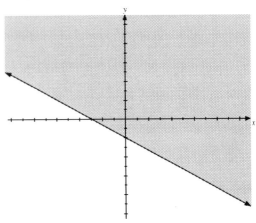

(A)

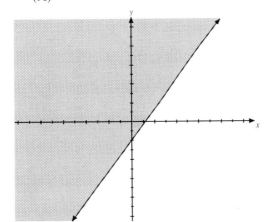

(D)

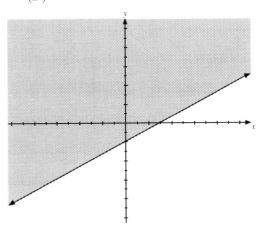

(B)

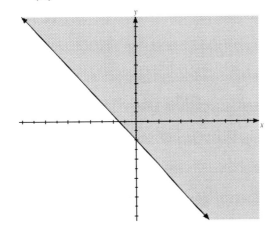

(E)

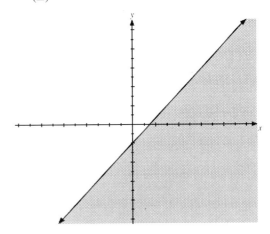

8.

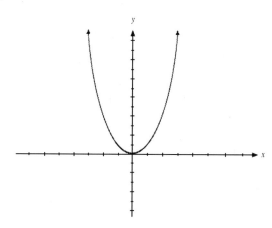

If the graph above represents $f(x) = x^2$, which of the following is a graph of $f(x) = (x - 4)^2 - 1$?

(A)

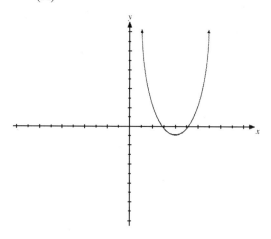

(B)

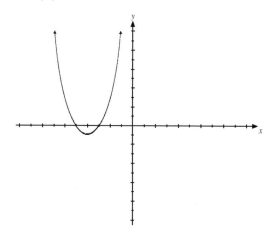

(C)

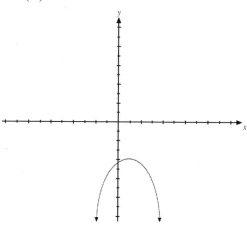

(D)

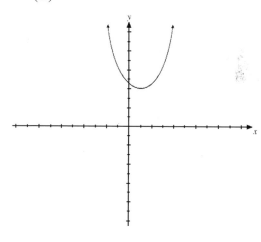

(E)

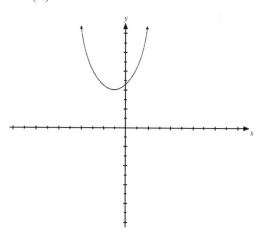

9.

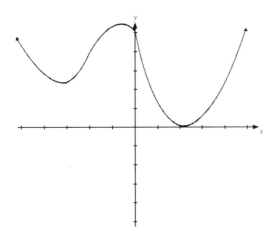

In the figure above, a section of the graph of a polynomial function $f(x)$ is shown. Which of the following statements are true?

I.   For the section of the graph shown, the range of the function does not contain any negative values.

II. For the section of the graph shown, $f(2) = 0$.

III. For the section of the graph shown, $f(1) > f(0)$.

(A)   I only
(B)   I and II
(C)   II and III
(D)   I, II, and III
(E)   None of the statements are true

10.   A snail can climb a wall a constant rate of 30 inches per hour. Suppose a child picks the snail and places it on the wall at a height of 2 feet from the ground at noon. Which of the following best represents the mathematical model for the snail's distance from the ground in feet at a given time t in hours after noon?

(A) $f(t) = 2 \bullet \left(\dfrac{5}{2}\right)^{t}$

(B) $f(t) = 30t + 2$

(C) $f(t) = \dfrac{5}{2}t + 2$

(D) $f(t) = \dfrac{5}{2}t$

(E) $f(t) = \left(\dfrac{5}{2}\right)^{t} + 2$

11. If a vehicle travels 40 miles from city *A* to city *B* and then travels to city *C* at a constant rate of 60 miles per hour, which of the following represents the graph of the vehicle's distance from city *A t* hours after the vehicle has left city *B*?

(A)

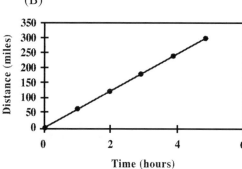

(B)

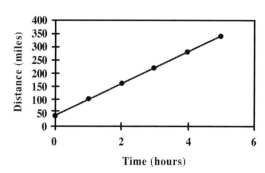

(C)

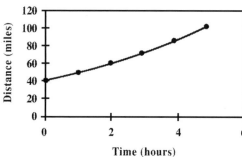

(D)

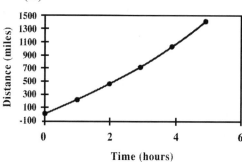

(E)

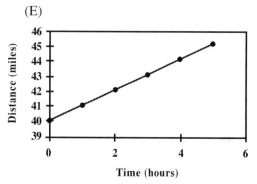

12.

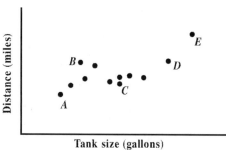

An automobile manufacturer is performing a mileage efficiency test on all models of its cars. Each data point in the scatterplot above reflects a particular car's tank size in gallons as well as the number of miles the car could be driven on a full tank of gas. Which point on the scatterplot above corresponds to the car with the best fuel efficiency?

(A)   A
(B)   B
(C)   C
(D)   D
(E)   E

13. The center of a circle in an *xy*-plane has the coordinates (3, 5). If the circle is tangent to the *y*-axis, which of the following are the coordinates of another point on the circle?

(A)   (5, 6)
(B)   (3, 8)
(C)   (2, 3)
(D)   (-2, 5)
(E)   (8, 5)

14. If ∠*ABC* measures 180°, then which of the following statements must be true?

    I.   *A*, *B*, and *C* are collinear
    II.   *A* is the vertex the angle
    III. $\overline{AB} \cong \overline{BC}$

(A)   I only
(B)   II only
(C)   III only
(D)   I and III
(E)   I, II, and III

15. *W*, *X*, *Y* and *Z* are distinct coplanar points such that $\overrightarrow{YZ}$ does not pass through *W*, $\overline{XY} \perp \overline{YZ}$ and $\overline{XY} \perp \overline{YW}$. All of the following statements must be true EXCEPT:

(A)   The measure of ∠*XYZ* is 90°

(B)   Points *W*, *Y* and *Z* are collinear

(C)   If the slope of $\overline{XY} = 2$, then the slope of $\overline{YW}$ is $-\dfrac{1}{2}$.

(D) $\overline{YZ}$ and $\overline{YW}$ have the same slope

(E) $\overline{YZ} \cong \overline{YW}$

16.

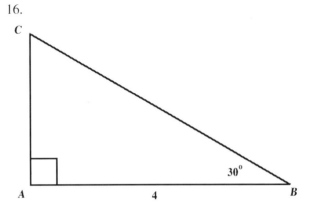

In Δ*ABC*, if *AB* = 4 then *BC* =

(A) $\dfrac{4\sqrt{3}}{3}$

(B) $\dfrac{8\sqrt{3}}{3}$

(C)   8

(D) $8\sqrt{3}$

(E)   16

17. In right Δ*XYZ*, hypotenuse *XY* = 20 and *XZ* = *YZ*. *YZ* equals:

(A) $4\sqrt{2}$
(B)   10
(C) $10\sqrt{2}$
(D) $10\sqrt{3}$
(E) $20\sqrt{2}$

18.

Annual Budget for Recreational Center

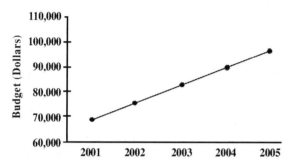

The graph above represents the annual budget to operate a city's recreational center. Based on the graph, what was the projected operational budget for 2006?

(A) $ 92,500

(B) $ 97,500

(C) $102,500

(D) $105,000

(E) $110,000

19.

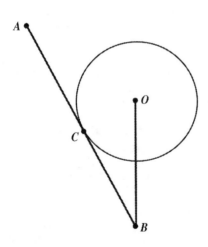

In the figure above, $\overline{AB}$ is tangent to $\odot O$ at point C, and C is the midpoint of $\overline{AB}$. If $AB = 20$ and the radius of the circle is 5, what is the length of OB?

(A) $3\sqrt{5}$

(B) $5\sqrt{5}$

(C)   8

(D)   10

(E)   15

20.   A circular emblem is inscribed in the bottom of a square-shaped fountain. If a coin is randomly tossed into the fountain, what is the probability that the coin will NOT land on the circular emblem?

(A) $1 - \dfrac{\pi}{4}$

(B) $\pi - 2$

(C) $\dfrac{2}{\pi}$

(D) $1 - \pi$

(E) $\dfrac{\pi}{4}$

ANSWER EXPLANATIONS:

1.   (C)
PROBLEM TYPE: LINEAR EQUATIONS – SLOPE

The line crosses the x and y-axes at (-6, 0) and (0, -3). Use the slope formula:

$$\text{slope} = \frac{y_2 - y_1}{x_2 - x_1} = \frac{0 - (-3)}{-6 - (0)} = -\frac{1}{2}$$

2.   4
PROBLEM TYPE: SLOPE OF A LINE

If $f(4) = 7$ and $f(2) = -1$, these two points in the coordinate plane are (4, 7) and (2, -1) respectively.

$$\text{slope} = \frac{y_2 - y_1}{x_2 - x_1} = \frac{7 - (-1)}{4 - 2} = \frac{8}{2} = 4$$

3.   (E)
PROBLEM TYPE: FUNCTIONS & THEIR GRAPHS

I.   The domain of both $f(x)$ and $g(x)$ is the set of all real numbers, and the range for both functions is the set of all real numbers ≥ 0. Statement I is TRUE.

II.   The two graphs intersect at 3 points, (-1, 1), (0, 0), and (1, 1). Statement II is FALSE.

III. $f(2) = 4$ and $g(-4) = 4$, therefore the two functions yield the same y-value. Statement III is TRUE.

Because statements I and III are true and II is false, the answer is (E).

4.   33

PROBLEM TYPE: SLOPES OF PERPENDICULAR LINES

Slope of line $q = \dfrac{y_2 - y_1}{x_2 - x_1} = \dfrac{6 - 0}{3 - 0} = 2$

Slope of line p perpendicular to line q will be the negative reciprocal of 2, or $-\dfrac{1}{2}$.

If point $(n, -9)$ is found on p, then: slope of line $p =$

$$-\frac{1}{2} = \frac{6 - (-9)}{3 - n}$$

Cross multiply to solve for n:

$-1(3 - n) = 2(6 + 9)$
$-3 + n = 30$
$n = 33$

5.   (D)

PROBLEM TYPE: MIDPOINT OF A LINE SEGMENT

The center of the circle $(1, 4)$ is the midpoint of diameter XY. Let the coordinates of Y be (x_2, y_2). Use the midpoint formula:

$$\left(\frac{-2 + x_2}{2}, \frac{\frac{1}{2} + y_2}{2} \right) = (1,\ 4)$$

Find the x-coordinate: $\dfrac{-2 + x_2}{2} = 1$

$-2 + x_2 = 2 \qquad x_2 = 4$

Repeat for the y-coordinate: $\dfrac{\frac{1}{2} + y_2}{2} = 4$

$\dfrac{1}{2} + y_2 = 8 \qquad y_2 = \dfrac{15}{2}$

$Y = (4, \dfrac{15}{2})$.

6.   (D)

PROBLEM TYPE: DISTANCE BETWEEN TWO POINTS

Apply the distance formula to find AB:

$$d = \sqrt{(x_2 - x_1)^2 + (y_2 - y_1)^2}$$

$$AB = \sqrt{(3 - (-3))^2 + (4 - 1)^2} = \sqrt{(36) + (9)} = \sqrt{45} = 3\sqrt{5}$$

Since $\overline{AB} \cong \overline{AC}$, AC also $= 3\sqrt{5}$.

Substitute each answer choice into the distance formula to find the one that will not yield a value of $3\sqrt{5}$.

(A) $\sqrt{(3-9)^2 + (4-1)^2} = \sqrt{36 + 9} = \sqrt{45} = 3\sqrt{5}$

(B) $\sqrt{(3-(-3))^2 + (4-7)^2} = \sqrt{36 + 9} = \sqrt{45} = 3\sqrt{5}$

(C) $\sqrt{(3-0)^2 + (4-(-2))^2} = \sqrt{9 + 36} = \sqrt{45} = 3\sqrt{5}$

(D) $\sqrt{(3-2)^2 + (4-(-1))^2} = \sqrt{1 + 25} = \sqrt{26}$

(E) $\sqrt{(3-6)^2 + (4-(-2))^2} = \sqrt{9 + 36} = \sqrt{45} = 3\sqrt{5}$

(D) is the only answer choice that does not yield $3\sqrt{5}$.

7.   (A)

PROBLEM TYPE: IDENTIFYING THE GRAPH OF A LINEAR INEQUALITY

Place the inequality in $y \geq mx + b$ form:

$3x - 2y \leq 4$ becomes $y \geq \dfrac{3}{2}x - 2$

(Remember to invert the inequality sign when multiplying or dividing by a negative number).

The symbol "$\geq$" in the $y \geq mx + b$ format indicates that the graph will include a solid line with shading above it. The line's slope is $\dfrac{3}{2}$ and its y-intercept is -2.

8.   (A)

PROBLEM TYPE: GRAPH TRANSFORMATION

Use your graphing calculator to input the graph of $f(x) = (x - 4)^2 - 1$. You will see that this graph has shifted down one unit and four units to the right with respect to $f(x) = x^2$. The answer is (A).

9.   (B)

PROBLEM TYPE: GRAPH PROPERTIES

I.   All of the y-values for this section of the graph are greater than or equal to zero. Statement I is TRUE.

II. The only point on the graph for which the x-coordinate is 2 is (2, 0). Statement II is TRUE.

III. $f(1) = 3$ and $f(0) = 5$. Statement III is FALSE.

Because statements I and II are true and III is false, the answer is (B).

10.   (C)

PROBLEM TYPE: FUNCTIONS AS MODELS

Find the first several data points. The snail's initial location at noon ($t = 0$) is 2 feet above the ground, so $f(0) = 2$. To find the snail's distance for each successive hour, add thirty inches (2.5 feet) per hour:

t (hours after noon)	$f(t)$ (feet from ground)
0	2
1	4.5
2	7
3	9.5

Enter the equations for each of the answer choices into the equation editor of your graphing calculator and use the table feature to compare the values for each equation with those shown above. The table reveals that the equation in (C) matches the values above.

11.   (A)

PROBLEM TYPE: FUNCTIONS AS MODELS

After the vehicle travels 40 miles, it continues at a constant rate of speed. This means that the correct graph is that of a linear function, so choices (C) and (D) can be eliminated. Because the vehicle starts 40 miles away from city A, answer choice (B) can also be eliminated, as the graph in (B) incorrectly indicates that the vehicle is 0 miles away from city A at time zero. Answer choice (E) can also be eliminated because this graph indicates that the vehicle is moving at only one mile per hour; the problem, however, specifies that the vehicle moves at 60 miles per hour. Answer choice (A) correctly reflects the initial 40 miles traveled followed by the vehicle's constant speed of 60 miles per hour.

12.   (B)

PROBLEM TYPE: SCATTERPLOT

For each car, the mileage per gallon is calculated by dividing the capacity of the fuel tank by the distance driven; this quotient equals the slope of the line that passes through the origin and the data point representing that particular car. The greater the slope of a line passing through the origin and a specific data point, the greater the mileage per gallon for the corresponding car. Draw a line from the origin through each labeled point. The slope through point B is the steepest.

13.   (B)

PROBLEM TYPE: COORDINATE PLANE GEOMETRY APPLICATION (DISTANCE/POINT OF TANGENCY)

Draw an xy-axis in the margin and plot the center of the circle and the point of tangency:

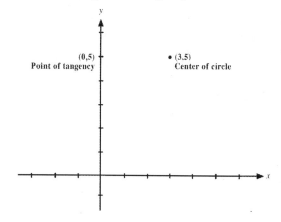

The circle has a radius of 3. Plot a few more points that are 3 units from the radius and identify those points.

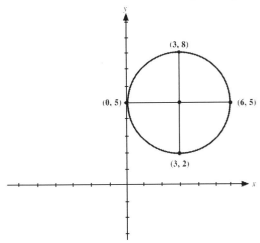

The point (3, 8) is found in (B).

14.   (A)
PROBLEM TYPE: GEOMETRIC NOTATION

I.   Any angle measuring 180° is a straight line. Statement I is TRUE.

II. The notation ∠ABC indicates that the vertex of the angle is B, not A. Statement II is FALSE.

III. The two segments indicated do not necessarily have to be the same length. Statement III is FALSE.

Because statement I is true and statements II and III are false, the answer is (A).

15.   (E)
PROBLEM TYPE: GEOMETRIC NOTATION/ PROPERTIES OF PERPENDICULAR LINES

The information presented in the problem leads to the following diagram:

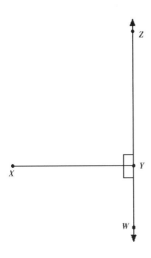

This diagram shows that the statements in answer choices (A) – (D) are true. The answer is (E), because $\overline{YZ}$ and $\overline{YW}$ are not necessarily congruent.

16.   (B)
PROBLEM TYPE: 30°-60°-90° TRIANGLE

Find the "short leg" (opposite 30°) by dividing the "long leg" of 4 (opposite 60°) by $\sqrt{3}$:

$$\frac{4}{\sqrt{3}} = \frac{4\sqrt{3}}{3}$$

Multiply the "short leg" by 2 to find the hypotenuse:

$$2 \bullet \left(\frac{4\sqrt{3}}{3} \right) = \frac{8\sqrt{3}}{3}$$

17.   (C)
PROBLEM TYPE: 45°-45°-90° TRIANGLE

The problem presents an isosceles right triangle (45°-45°-90°).

The hypotenuse is given.
Divide the hypotenuse (20) by $\sqrt{2}$ to find the length of either one of the legs:

$$\frac{20}{\sqrt{2}} = \frac{20\sqrt{2}}{2} = 10\sqrt{2}$$

18.   (D)
PROBLEM TYPE: FUNCTIONS AS MODELS

Careful study of the graph shows that the annual budget is increasing by approximately $7,500 per year. Extending the graph's trend line shows that in 2006 the operating budget equaled approximately $105,000 ($97,500 in 2005 plus $7,500).

19.   (B)
PROBLEM TYPE: TANGENT LINES

A tangent line forms a right angle with the radius at the point of tangency, so $\overline{OC} \perp \overline{AB}$. C is the midpoint of $\overline{AB}$, so $CB = 10$. Because the radius of the circle is 5, $OC = 5$.

$$10^2 + 5^2 = (OB)^2$$
$$125 = (OB)^2$$
$$OB = \sqrt{125} = 5\sqrt{5}$$

20.   (A)
PROBLEM TYPE: GEOMETRIC PROBABILITY

Sketch the bottom of the fountain:

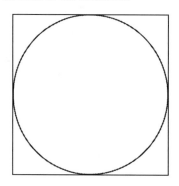

Probability that coin will fall outside of the circular emblem =

$$\frac{\text{(Area of square fountain bottom)} - \text{(Area of circular emblem)}}{\text{Area of square fountain bottom}}$$

Let the side of the fountain (the square bottom) equal 10 feet, which will be equal to the inscribed circle's diameter. Subtract the area of the circular emblem from the area of the square.

Area of square fountain bottom = $10 \cdot 10 = 100$

Area of circular emblem = $\left(\dfrac{10}{2}\right)^2 \cdot \pi = 25\pi$

Substitute these numbers into the probability ratio stated above:

$$\frac{100 - 25\pi}{100} = \frac{100}{100} - \frac{25\pi}{100} = 1 - \frac{\pi}{4}$$

7C: Practice Problems Set
(Mixed Practice)

1.   If $Y = \{$numbers that are perfect squares $< 100\}$ and $Z = \{$positive odd integers$\}$, how many elements are in $Y \cap Z$?

(A)   0
(B)   2
(C)   4
(D)   5
(E)   7

2.   If $f(x) = \dfrac{3x - 1}{x^2 - 16}$, what is the domain of $f(x)$?

(A)   the set of all real numbers
(B)   the set of all real numbers $\neq 3$
(C)   the set of all real numbers $\neq \pm 4$
(D)   the set of all real numbers $\neq 16$
(E)   the set of all real numbers ≥ 0

3.   In a 30°-60°-90° right triangle, the hypotenuse has length 12. What is the area of the triangle?

(A)   12
(B) $12\sqrt{3}$
(C) $18\sqrt{2}$
(D) $18\sqrt{3}$
(E) $36\sqrt{3}$

4.   What is the slope of a line perpendicular to the line represented by the equation $2x - 5y = 4$?

(A) $\dfrac{2}{5}$

(B) $-\dfrac{2}{5}$

(C) $\dfrac{5}{2}$

(D) $-\dfrac{5}{2}$

(E) $-\dfrac{4}{5}$

5.   If $f(x) = (x + 4)^2$ and $g(x) = (x - 2)^3$, which of the following is the smallest integer for which the value of $g(x)$ is greater than the value of $f(x)$?

(A)   5
(B)   6
(C)   7
(D)   8
(E)   9

6.   If $|2x - 1| \leq 5$, which of the following is true?

(A) $-3 \leq x \leq 2$
(B) $-2 \leq x \leq 3$
(C) $0 \leq x \leq 5$
(D) $-5 \leq x \leq 5$
(E) $x \leq -3$ or $x \geq 2$

7.   If the slope of line r is $\dfrac{3}{7}$, which of the following equations describes a line that passes through the point $(0, -1)$ and is parallel to r?

(A) $7x + 3y - 1 = 0$
(B) $7x - 3y - 7 = 0$
(C) $3x - 7y - 7 = 0$
(D) $3x + 7y - 1 = 0$
(E) $3x - 7y - 21 = 0$

8.

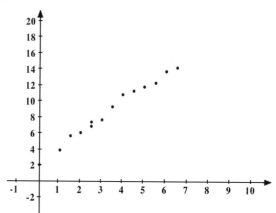

Which of the following equations best describes the points shown in the scatterplot above?

(A) $y = \dfrac{1}{2}x + 2$

(B) $y = x + 2$

(C) $y = x - 2$

(D) $y = 2x + 2$

(E) $y = 2x - 2$

9.   If $\angle CDE$ is a right angle, which of the following are true?

    I. $\overline{DE}$ is the hypotenuse of $\triangle CDE$
    II. $CE > CD$
    III. $\overrightarrow{DC} \perp \overrightarrow{CE}$

(A)   I only
(B)   II only
(C)   III only
(D)   II and III
(E)   None of the above

10.   If $11 - 6\sqrt{x} = 2$, $x =$

(A) $\dfrac{3}{4}$

(B) $\dfrac{3}{2}$

(C) $\dfrac{9}{4}$

(D) $\dfrac{11}{4}$

(E) $\dfrac{11}{2}$

11.

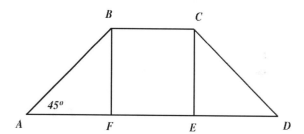

Area of square $BCEF = 36$
Perimeter of Isosceles trapezoid $ABCD =$

(A) $9 + 12\sqrt{2}$
(B) $24 + 6\sqrt{2}$
(C) $24 + 12\sqrt{2}$
(D) 48
(E) $16 + 2\sqrt{3}$

12.   The range of the function $f(x) = x^2 - 3$ is:

(A)   the set of all real numbers
(B)   the set of all real numbers > 3
(C)   the set of all real numbers ≥ 3
(D)   the set of all real numbers > -3
(E)   the set of all real numbers ≥ -3

13. y^2 varies directly with x, and $x = 12$ when $y = 2$. If $y > 0$, what is the value of y when $x = 75$?

(A)   3
(B)   5
(C)   6
(D)   25
(E)   225

14.

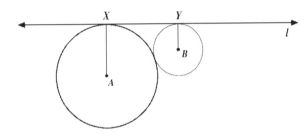

In the figure shown, line l is tangent to $\odot A$ at point X and to $\odot B$ at point Y. If the radius of $\odot B$ is r and the radius of $\odot A$ is $2r$, what is the length of XY?

(A) $r\sqrt{3}$

(B) $\sqrt{6}\,r$

(C) $2\sqrt{2}\,r$

(D) $3r$

(E) $2\sqrt{3}\,r$

15.   If x varies inversely with y^3 and $x = \dfrac{1}{9}$ when $y = 9$, then the positive value for which $x = y$ is which of the following?

(A) $\dfrac{1}{3}$

(B)   2

(C)   3

(D)   27

(E)   81

16.

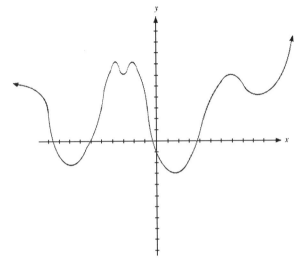

The section of graph above shows the function $f(x)$. What is the value of $f(4)$?

(A)   -2
(B)   1
(C)   0
(D)   3
(E)   6

GRID-IN RESPONSE QUESTIONS:

17.   If $9^{4x} = 27^{2x+3}$, what is the value of x?

18.   What is the 8th term of the following geometric sequence:

-81, 27, -9…

19.   A cone is sliced parallel to its base at a point half the distance from the top of the cone to the base. What is the probability that a point randomly selected from the interior of the original cone would also be found inside the newly created smaller cone?

20.   If $f(x) = \dfrac{1}{x^2} - 2x$, what is the value of $f(-\dfrac{1}{2})$?

ANSWER EXPLANATIONS:

1.   (D)

PROBLEM TYPE: INTERSECTION OF SETS

The question is asking for the elements that sets Y and Z have in common.

The following are perfect squares less than 100: 1, 4, 9, 16, 25, 36, 49, 64, 81

The odd integers in this group are 1, 9, 25, 49 and 81.

The answer is 5, or (D).

2.   (C)

PROBLEM TYPE: DOMAIN OF A FUNCTION

The domain cannot include any value that will set the denominator equal to zero.

$x^2 - 16 \neq 0$
$x^2 \neq 16$
$x \neq \pm 4$

3.   (D)

PROBLEM TYPE: 30°-60°-90° RIGHT TRIANGLE

Hypotenuse = 12
Short leg (opposite 30° angle) = 6
Long leg (opposite 60° angle) = $6\sqrt{3}$

Area of triangle = $\dfrac{b \bullet h}{2} = \dfrac{6 \bullet 6\sqrt{3}}{2} = \dfrac{36\sqrt{3}}{2} = 18\sqrt{3}$

4.   (D)

PROBLEM TYPE: SLOPE OF PERPENDICULAR LINES

Re-arrange the equation of the line into slope-intercept form:

$2x - 5y = 4$ becomes $y = \dfrac{2}{5}x - \dfrac{4}{5}$

The slope of this line is $\dfrac{2}{5}$. The slope of any line perpendicular to this line would have the negative reciprocal slope of $-\dfrac{5}{2}$.

5.   (C)

"Throw it in Reverse," but start with answer choice (A) (the least) to find the smallest number that produces a greater $g(x)$ than $f(x)$ value. The answer is (C), 7:

$f(7) = (7 + 4)^2 = 121$ and $g(7) = (7 - 2)^3 = 125$

6.   (B)

PROBLEM TYPE: ABSOLUTE   VALUE INEQUALITY

$|2x - 1| \leq 5$

$-5 \leq 2x - 1 \leq 5$ ← Write the inequality as a compound sentence between -5 and 5
$-4 \leq 2x \leq 6$ ←Add 1 to each expression
$-2 \leq x \leq 3$ ←Divide each expression by 2

7.   (C)

PROBLEM TYPE: LINEAR EQUATION/SLOPE OF PARALLEL LINE

The equation of this line has y-intercept (0, -1) and slope $\dfrac{3}{7}$ (same slope as r):

$y = \dfrac{3}{7}x - 1$

$7y = 3x - 7$ Multiply through by 7
$3x - 7y - 7 = 0$ Write in standard form

8.   (D)

PROBLEM TYPE: SCATTERPLOT

The y-intercept for the graph is 2, so eliminate choices (C) and (E). Draw a line through the origin (0, 0), (1, 1) and (2, 2). This is the line for which $y = x$ with slope 1. Because the points in the scatterplot represent a line with a slope steeper than 1, eliminate choices (A) and (B). The answer is (D).

9.   (B)

PROBLEM TYPE: GEOMETRIC NOTATION

Draw right $\angle CDE$:

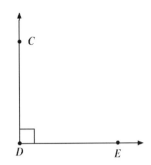

I. $\overline{DE}$ would be a leg in $\triangle CDE$, not the hypotenuse. Statement I is FALSE.

II.   Regardless of the placement of point E on $\overrightarrow{DE}$, CE will always be longer than CD. Statement II is TRUE.

III. $\overrightarrow{DC}$ is $\perp$ to $\overrightarrow{DE}$, not to $\overrightarrow{CE}$. Statement III is FALSE.

Only statement II is true.

10.   (C)
PROBLEM   TYPE: SOLVING   RADICAL EQUATIONS

$$11 - 6\sqrt{x} = 2$$

$$-6\sqrt{x} = -9$$

$$\sqrt{x} = \frac{-9}{-6} = \frac{3}{2}$$

$$x = (\sqrt{x})^2 = \left(\frac{3}{2}\right)^2 = \frac{9}{4}$$

11.   (C)
PROBLEM   TYPE: APPLICATION   OF   A 45°-45°-90° RIGHT TRIANGLE

Any side of square $BCEF = \sqrt{36} = 6$
$BC = CE = EF = FB = 6$

Because $BCEF$ is a square, $\triangle ABF$ is a 45°-45°-90° right triangle with $AF = BF = 6$ and $AB = 6\sqrt{2}$

$\angle A = 45°$, so $\angle D$ also $= 45°$
(definition of an isosceles trapezoid)

$\triangle CDE$ is also a 45°-45°-90° right triangle with $CE = ED = 6$ and $CD = 6\sqrt{2}$

Perimeter of the trapezoid = Base$_1$ + Base$_2$ + 2 • (leg)

Base$_1$ = the length of AD = AF + FE + ED = $6 + 6 + 6 = 18$

Base$_2$ = BC = 6
Leg AB = leg $CD = 6\sqrt{2}$

$2 \cdot (\text{leg}) = 2 \cdot 6\sqrt{2} = 12\sqrt{2}$

$18 + 6 + 12\sqrt{2} = 24 + 12\sqrt{2}$

12.   (E)
PROBLEM TYPE: RANGE OF A FUNCTION

The minimum point of the graph is at (0, -3); this is the graph's vertex. The range will include -3 and all y-values greater than -3.

13.   (B)
PROBLEM TYPE: DIRECT VARIATION

In this direct variation, $\dfrac{y^2}{x} = k$, which leads to the following ratio:

$$\frac{(y_1)^2}{x_1} = \frac{(y_2)^2}{x_2}, \text{ so } \frac{2^2}{12} = \frac{(y_2)^2}{75}$$

Cross multiply: $12 \cdot (y_2)^2 = 2^2 \cdot 75$

$$(y_2)^2 = \frac{2^2 \cdot 75}{12} = 25 \qquad y_2 = \sqrt{25} = 5$$

14.   (C)
PROBLEM TYPE: TANGENT LINES

Because line *l* is tangent to $\odot A$ at point *X* and to $\odot B$ at point *Y*, radius $\overline{AX}$ of $\odot A$ and radius $\overline{BY}$ of $\odot B$ are both perpendicular to line *l*.

Imagine that $\overline{XY}$ is shifted so that point *Y* coincides with point *B* and point *X* is shifted to point *X'* located *r* units from *A*. $X'B = XY$, and a right triangle is formed with vertices *X'*, *A*, and *B*. The hypotenuse of this right triangle is $\overline{AB}$:

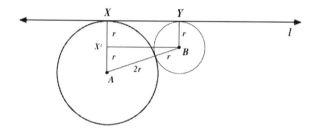

$AX' = r$
$AB = r + 2r = 3r$
$XY = X'B$

Use the Pythagorean theorem to solve for *X'B*, which equals *XY*:

$$r^2 + (X'B)^2 = (3r)^2$$
$$r^2 + (X'B)^2 = 9r^2$$
$$(X'B)^2 = 8r^2$$
$$X'B = XY = \sqrt{8}\,r$$
$$XY = 2\sqrt{2}\,r$$

15.   (C)
PROBLEM TYPE: INVERSE VARIATION

In this inverse variation,

$$x_1 \bullet (y_1)^3 = x_2 \bullet (y_2)^3$$

Because *x = y*, replace x_2 with y_2:

$$x_1 \bullet (y_1)^3 = (y_2)^4$$

Substitute the stated values for *x* and *y* as x_1 and y_1:

$$\frac{1}{9} \bullet 9^3 = (y_2)^4$$
$$81 = (y_2)^4$$
$$\sqrt[4]{81} = y_2 = 3$$

16.   (B)
PROBLEM TYPE: QUALITATIVE BEHAVIOR OF GRAPHS & FUNCTIONS

Find the point on the graph at which *x* = 4. Identify the point's corresponding *y*-value, which is 1.

17.   9/2 or 4.5
PROBLEM TYPE: RATIONAL EXPONENTS

Change the base on both sides by changing both the 9 and the 27 to a power of 3:

$$(3^2)^{4x} = (3^3)^{2x+3}$$
$$3^{8x} = 3^{6x+9}$$

Set each set of exponents equal to each other and solve for *x*:

$$8x = 6x + 9$$
$$2x = 9$$
$$x = \frac{9}{2} \text{ or } 4.5$$

18.   1/27 or .037
PROBLEM TYPE: GEOMETRIC SEQUENCE

The common ratio for this sequence is $-\frac{1}{3}$:

$$\frac{(-9)}{27} = -\frac{1}{3} \qquad \frac{27}{(-81)} = -\frac{1}{3}$$

4th term: $-9 \bullet \left(-\frac{1}{3}\right) = 3$

5th term: $3 \bullet \left(-\frac{1}{3}\right) = -1$

6th term: $-1 \cdot \left(-\dfrac{1}{3} \right) = \dfrac{1}{3}$

7th term: $\dfrac{1}{3} \cdot \left(-\dfrac{1}{3} \right) = -\dfrac{1}{9}$

8th term: $-\dfrac{1}{9} \cdot \left(-\dfrac{1}{3} \right) = \dfrac{1}{27}$

19.   1/8 OR .125
PROBLEM TYPE: GEOMETRIC PROBABILITY

Let the radius of the original cone equal 2 and the height of the original cone equal 2. Then the radius of the second smaller cone would be 1 and its height would be 1, as the base of the smaller cone is halfway between the original base and the tip of the cone.

Volume of original cone $= \dfrac{1}{3}\pi r^2 h = \dfrac{1}{3}\pi 2^2 \cdot 2 = \dfrac{8\pi}{3}$

Volume of smaller cone $= \dfrac{1}{3}\pi r^2 h = \dfrac{1}{3}\pi 1^2 \cdot 1 = \dfrac{\pi}{3}$

Probability that point will be found in smaller cone =

$$\dfrac{\text{Volume smaller cone}}{\text{Volume larger cone}} = \dfrac{\pi/3}{8\pi/3} = \dfrac{1}{8}$$

Grid-in $\dfrac{1}{8}$ or .125.

20.   5
PROBLEM TYPE: EVALUATING FUNCTIONS

Substitute $-\dfrac{1}{2}$ for x and simplify:

$$\dfrac{1}{\left(-\dfrac{1}{2} \right)^2} - 2 \cdot \left(-\dfrac{1}{2} \right) = \dfrac{1}{\dfrac{1}{4}} + 1 = 5$$

**7D: Practice Problems Set
"Math Hall of Fame" for the SAT
(Classic SAT Math Problems)**

1.   Point X on a number line has coordinate 4 and point Y has coordinate -12. If point Z is $\frac{3}{4}$ of the distance from X to Y, Z's coordinate is:

(A)   -8
(B)   -4
(C)   0
(D)   4
(E)   8

2.   A triangle in an xy-plane has vertices (-2, 5), (4, 5) and (1, 9). What is the area of the triangle?

(A)   6
(B)   8
(C)   9
(D)   12
(E)   24

3.

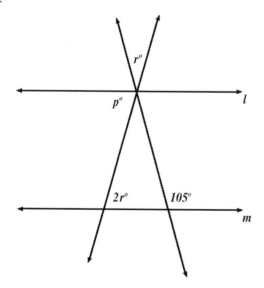

Line l is parallel to line m. In the figure shown, $p° =$

(A)   52.5°
(B)   60°
(C)   70°
(D)   75°
(E)   105°

4.   If $1 - s = t + 1$, then $\frac{s}{t} + s$ equals

(A) $\frac{1}{t}$
(B) $s + 1$
(C) $1 - s$
(D) $s - 1$
(E) s

5.   If $x^2 > x > x^3$, then x must be:

(A)   a positive number less than 1
(B)   a number greater than 1
(C)   a negative number greater than -1
(D)   a number less than -1
(E)   there is no real number that makes this expression true

6.   Of 200 passengers on a plane flight, 40% of the 20 first class passengers, 20% of the 60 business class passengers, and 60% of the remaining economy class passengers watched the movie. What percent of all passengers watched the movie?

(A)   40%
(B)   46%
(C)   60%
(D)   72%
(E)   92%

7.

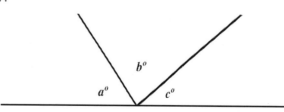

Note: Figure not drawn to scale.

$a{:}b{:}c = 3{:}4{:}2$ $b =$

(A)   60°
(B)   64°
(C)   72°
(D)   80°
(E)   84°

8. The average of five numbers is 7. The average of two of those numbers is 4. What is the average of the three remaining numbers?

    (A)   8
    (B)   9
    (C)   10
    (D)   11
    (E)   12

9. Sugar costs s dollars per pound, and p pounds of sugar are required to bake d dozen cookies. What is the cost in dollars of sugar per cookie?

    (A) $\dfrac{12d}{sp}$

    (B) $\dfrac{12sp}{d}$

    (C) $\dfrac{spd}{12}$

    (D) $12spd$

    (E) $\dfrac{sp}{12d}$

10. If y is an integer and $\dfrac{y-2}{3}$ is also an integer, which of the following must be true?

    (A) y is odd

    (B) $y > 2$

    (C) y is a multiple of 5

    (D) $\dfrac{y+1}{3}$ is an integer

    (E) $y - 2$ is divisible by 6

11. The supplement of an angle is four times the complement of an angle. What is the measure of the angle?

    (A) $30°$
    (B) $45°$
    (C) $60°$
    (D) $75°$
    (E) $120°$

12.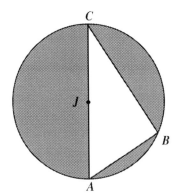

    Radius of $\odot J = 5$ $AB = 6$
    Area of the shaded region equals:

    (A)   1
    (B) π
    (C) $25\pi - 24$
    (D) $5(5\pi - 6)$
    (E) $25\pi - 36$

13. During the month of April, a class of s students sold 250 tickets to the school play. Starting May 1st, each student in the class sold an average of t tickets per week for w weeks. Including the month of April, how many total tickets will the class have sold d days after May 1st?

    (A) $250 + \dfrac{swd}{7t}$

    (B) $250 + \dfrac{7st}{d}$

    (C) $250 + \dfrac{7st}{w}$

    (D) $250 + \dfrac{std}{7}$

    (E) $250 + \dfrac{std}{7w}$

14.   Mariana has 18 coins consisting of dimes and nickels that have a total value of $1.45. How many dimes does she have?

(A)   3
(B)   5
(C)   7
(D)   9
(E)   11

GRID-IN PROBLEMS:

15.   The spokes for the seats on a Ferris wheel are 15° apart. How many seats are there on the Ferris wheel?

16.   Lauren wishes to enlarge a photograph from 3" x 5" to 4" x 6". The area of the original photo will be what percent of the area of the enlarged photo?

17.   The sum of 5 consecutive odd integers equals 105. What is the sum of the next 5 consecutive even integers?

18.   If a number n is increased by 4, the square of that sum is 80 more than the square of n. What is the value of n?

19.   Morgan paddled a canoe upstream in 5 hours and then returned the same distance downstream in 3 hours. If his rate was 12 miles per hour in still water, what was the rate of the stream's current?

20.   If the average (arithmetic mean) of four different positive integers is 95 and one of the integers is 200, what is the greatest possible value of one of the remaining integers?

ANSWER EXPLANATIONS:

1.   (A)
PROBLEM TYPE: DISTANCE ON A NUMBER LINE

Find the distance from X to Y by taking the absolute value of the difference of the two coordinates.

The distance from X to Y is:

$$|{-12} - 4| = 16$$

Find $\frac{3}{4}$ of this distance:

$$\frac{3}{4} \cdot 16 = 12$$

Counting 12 units from 4 in the negative direction:

$$4 - 12 = -8$$

2.   (D)
PROBLEM TYPE: AREA OF A FIGURE IN A COORDINATE PLANE

First, sketch the triangle:

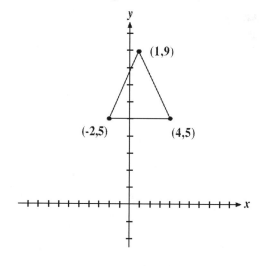

The length of the triangle's base connecting (-2, 5) and (4, 5) is $|(-2) - 4|$ or 6. The height of the triangle from this base to the point (1, 9) is $|9 - 5|$ or 4.

$$\text{Area} = \frac{1}{2}(b \cdot h) = \frac{1}{2}(6 \cdot 4) = 12$$

3.   (C)

PROBLEM TYPE: PARALLEL LINES

Vertical angles are congruent, so the angle opposite $r°$ also equals $r°$.

The sum of the measures of two interior angles of a triangle equals the measure of the remote exterior angle.

$$r° + 2r° = 105°$$
$$\uparrow \quad \uparrow \qquad \uparrow$$

Two   Remote
interior   exterior
$\angle$s $\angle$

$$3r° = 105° \qquad r° = 35°$$

If two parallel lines are crossed by a transversal, alternate interior angles are congruent.

The angles labeled $p°$ and $2r°$ are alternate interior angles. This means:
$p° = 2r°$
$p° = 2 \cdot 35° = 70°$

4.   (D)

PROBLEM TYPE: ALGEBRAIC EXPRESSION

$$1 - s = t + 1 \qquad -s = t$$

Because $-s$ equals t, then $-\dfrac{s}{t} = 1$ and $\dfrac{s}{t} = -1$

$$\dfrac{s}{t} + s = -1 + s = s - 1$$

5.   (D)

PROBLEM TYPE: PROPERTIES OF EXPONENTS

Substitute numbers for each answer choice to determine which is true.

Try $\dfrac{1}{2}$ for choice (A):

$$x^2 \quad > \quad x \quad > \quad x^3$$
$$\downarrow \qquad\qquad\qquad \downarrow$$
$$\left(\dfrac{1}{2}\right)^2 \qquad\qquad \left(\dfrac{1}{2}\right)^3$$

$$\dfrac{1}{4} \;<\; \dfrac{1}{2} \; but \; \dfrac{1}{2} \;>\; \dfrac{1}{8}$$

(A) is incorrect.

Try 2 for choice (B):

$$x^2 \quad > \quad x \quad > \quad x^3$$
$$\downarrow \qquad\qquad\qquad \downarrow$$
$$2^2 \qquad\qquad\qquad 2^3$$

$4 > 2$ *but* $2 < 8$

(B) is incorrect.

Try $-\dfrac{1}{2}$ for choice (C):

$$x^2 \quad > \quad x \quad > \quad x^3$$
$$\downarrow \qquad\qquad\qquad \downarrow$$
$$\left(-\dfrac{1}{2}\right)^2 \qquad\qquad \left(-\dfrac{1}{2}\right)^3$$

$$\dfrac{1}{4} \;>\; -\dfrac{1}{2} \; but \; -\dfrac{1}{2} \;<\; -\dfrac{1}{8}$$

(C) is incorrect.

Try -2 for choice (D):

$$x^2 \quad > \quad x \quad > \quad x^3$$
$$\downarrow \qquad\qquad\qquad \downarrow$$
$$(-2)^2 \qquad\qquad (-2)^3$$

$4 > -2 > -8$

(D) is correct.

6.   (B)

PROBLEM TYPE: PERCENT APPLICATION

Use a "Number Sentence" to determine the number of passengers in each group who watched the movie:

40% of the 20 first class passengers equals?

$$\downarrow \quad \downarrow \quad \downarrow \qquad\qquad\qquad \downarrow$$
$$.40 \quad \bullet \quad 20 \qquad\qquad\qquad = 8$$

20% of the 60 business class passengers equals?

$$\downarrow \quad \downarrow \quad \downarrow \qquad\qquad\qquad \downarrow$$
$$.20 \quad \bullet \quad 60 \qquad\qquad\qquad = 12$$

Determine the number of economy class passengers by subtracting the number of other types of passengers from the total:

200 total passengers – (20 first class) – (60 business class) = 120 economy class passengers

60% of the 120 economy class passengers equals?

$$\downarrow \quad \downarrow \quad \downarrow \qquad\qquad\qquad \downarrow$$
$$.60 \quad \bullet \quad 120 \qquad\qquad\qquad = 72$$

Determine the total number of passengers who watched the movie:
8 + 12 + 72 = 92

Determine the percentage of total passengers who watched the movie:

$$\frac{92}{200} = 46\%$$

7.   (D)
PROBLEM TYPE: ANGLE RATIOS

Angles that lie in a straight line add up to 180°.
$a° + b° + c° = 180°$

Write an equation utilizing the ratio relationships of the angles:
$3x + 4x + 2x = 180°$
$$\uparrow \quad\; \uparrow \quad\; \uparrow$$
$$a° \quad b° \quad c°$$

$9x = 180°$
$x = 20°$
$b° = 4x = 4 \bullet 20 = 80°$

8.   (B)
PROBLEM TYPE: FINDING AN AVERAGE

Find the sum of the five numbers:

Number of Numbers • Average = Sum of Numbers
$$\qquad \downarrow \qquad\qquad\quad \downarrow \qquad\qquad \downarrow$$
$$\qquad 5 \qquad\quad \bullet \qquad 7 \quad = \qquad 35$$

Sum of the five numbers = 35. The average of two of those numbers is 4, which means their sum is 8. Subtract 8 from 35 to determine the sum of the remaining three numbers:

35 – 8 = 27

27 is the sum of the three remaining numbers; divide 27 by three to find the average of those three numbers:

27 ÷ 3 = 9

9.   (E)
PROBLEM TYPE: WORD PROBLEM ("PAINT BY NUMBERS")

"Paint by Numbers:" Assign numbers for *s, p* and *d* and determine what the cost of sugar per cookie would be using those numbers. Choose numbers that will work well with a dozen. Assume that sugar costs $3.00 per pound and that 4 pounds of sugar are needed to bake 10 dozen cookies. That means that it will cost $12.00 to buy the sugar to make 120, or 10 dozen) cookies; this comes out to $.10 per cookie ($12.00 ÷ 120). In each answer choice, replace *s* with 3, *p* with 4, and *d* with 10 to see which answer choice produces .10:

(A) $\dfrac{12 \bullet 10}{3 \bullet 4} = 10$ *(DO NOT CONFUSE THIS WITH .10)*

(B) $\dfrac{12 \bullet 3 \bullet 4}{10} = 14.4$

(C) $\dfrac{3 \bullet 4 \bullet 10}{12} = 10$ *(THE SAME WRONG ANSWER AS IN CHOICE (A))*

(D) $12 \bullet 3 \bullet 4 \bullet 10 = 1,440$ *(A VERY EXPENSIVE COOKIE!)*

(E) $\dfrac{3 \bullet 4}{12 \bullet 10} = .10$ ***(THE ANSWER)***

10.   (D)
PROBLEM TYPE: PROPERTY OF INTEGERS

(A) NO Let $y = 8$ (an even integer): $\dfrac{8-2}{3} = 2$

(B) NO Let $y = -1$ (an integer < 2): $\dfrac{-1-2}{3} = -1$

(C) NO Let $y = 8$ (not a multiple of 5): $\dfrac{8-2}{3} = 2$

(D) YES Because $y + 1$ is 3 units greater than $y - 2$, $y + 1$ will always be divisible by 3 if $y - 2$ is divisible by 3.

(E) NO Let $y = 11$: $\dfrac{11-2}{3} = 3$, an integer. But $11 - 2 = 9$, and 9 is not divisible by 6.

The answer is (D).

11.   (C)
PROBLEM TYPE: COMPLEMENTARY AND SUPPLEMENTARY ANGLES

Let the measure of the angle = a.
Let the complement of the angle = $90 - a$.
Let the supplement of the angle = $180 - a$.

$4(90 - a) = 180 - a$
$360 - 4a = 180 - a$
$180 = 3a$
$a = 60$

12.   (C)
PROBLEM TYPE: AREA OF A SHADED REGION IN A CIRCLE

Any Δ inscribed in a semi-circle is always a right Δ; the hypotenuse of the triangle is always a diameter of the circle. The hypotenuse of ΔABC is AC. The radius of $\odot J$ is 5, so $AC = 10$.

Use the Pythagorean Theorem ($a^2 + b^2 = c^2$) to find the length of BC:

$6^2 + (BC)^2 = 10^2$
$(BC)^2 = 64$
$BC = 8$

Area of a right $\Delta = \dfrac{1}{2}(\text{leg}_1 \cdot \text{leg}_1) = \dfrac{1}{2}(6 \cdot 8) = 24$

Area of a circle = $\pi r^2 = 25\pi$

Area of shaded region = Area of a circle – Area of right Δ
$= 25\pi - 24$

13.   (D)
PROBLEM TYPE: WORD PROBLEM ("PAINT BY NUMBERS")

"Paint by Numbers": Momentarily ignore the 250 tickets sold in April found in each answer choice. Assign numbers for s, t, w and d and determine how many tickets would have been sold in May using those numbers. Assume that there are 10 students (s) in the class, each of whom sells 5 tickets (t) per week. That would make 150 tickets. Let $d = 14$ days and $w = 2$, representing the first two weeks of May. After 14 days, the students would have sold 100 tickets.

In the algebraic expression, replace s with 10, t with 5, w with 2, and d with 14 and find the answer choice that produces 100 :

(A) $\dfrac{10 \cdot 2 \cdot 14}{7 \cdot 5} = 8$

(B) $\dfrac{7 \cdot 10 \cdot 5}{14} = 25$

(C) $\dfrac{7 \cdot 10 \cdot 5}{2} = 175$

(D) $\dfrac{10 \cdot 5 \cdot 14}{7} = 100$ *(THE ANSWER)*

(E) $\dfrac{10 \cdot 5 \cdot 14}{7 \cdot 2} = 50$

14.   (E)

PROBLEM TYPE: WORD PROBLEM ("THROW IT IN REVERSE")

"Throw it in Reverse:" Start with answer choice (C) and solve backwards:

(C)   7   If there were 7 dimes, there would be 11 nickels (to make 18 coins in all) for a total of .70 + .55, or $1.25. Because this is <u>less</u> than $1.45, it can be concluded that 7 is TOO SMALL to be the number of dimes. Try a BIGGER ANSWER CHOICE; proceed to (D).

(D)   9   If there were 9 dimes, there would be 9 nickels (to make 18 coins in all) for a total of .90 + .45, or $1.35. Because this is still less than $1.45, it can be concluded that 9 is also TOO SMALL to be the number of dimes. The only remaining larger answer choice is (E), and that must be the answer.

(E)   11   If there were 11 dimes, there would be 7 nickels (to make 18 coins in all) for a total of 1.10 + .35, or $1.45.

15.   24

PROBLEM TYPE: DEGREES IN A CIRCLE

There are 360° in a circle.

360° ÷ 15 = 24   There are 24 seats on the Ferris wheel.

Be aware that this solution would not be correct if the question were posed as follows:

> *If a 360-foot length of ground were to be fenced with a post placed every 15 feet, how many posts would be needed?*

In this case, 25 fence posts would be required, not 24. On the Ferris Wheel, the spoke located at 0° is the same as the spoke located at 360°, but for non-circular arrangements such as linear fencing, the first post does not occupy the same position as the last and an extra post is needed!

16.   62.5

PROBLEM TYPE: RATIO (FRACTIONAL PART)

$$\text{Answer} = \frac{\text{Area of original photo}}{\text{Area of enlarged photo}}$$

$$\frac{3 \cdot 5}{4 \cdot 6} = \frac{15}{24} = \frac{5}{8} = .625 = 62.5\%$$

17.   150

PROBLEM TYPE: CONSECUTIVE INTEGER

Set the sum of five consecutive odd integers equal to 105:

$$n + n + 2 + n + 4 + n + 6 + n + 8 = 105$$

$$5n + 20 = 105$$
$$5n = 85$$
$$n = 17$$

The greatest integer, $(n + 8)$ will equal 25. The next 5 consecutive even integers will be 26, 28, 30, 32 and 34.

$$26 + 28 + 30 + 32 + 34 = 150$$

18.   8

PROBLEM TYPE: WORD PROBLEM WITH A QUADRATIC EQUATION

Convert the information in the problem into a number sentence:

$$(n + 4)^2 = 80 + n^2$$

Expand the left side of the equation:

$$n^2 + 8n + 16 = 80 + n^2$$
$$8n + 16 = 80$$
$$8n = 64$$
$$n = 8$$

19.   3

PROBLEM TYPE: DISTANCE/RATE/TIME WORD PROBLEM

Apply a variation of the distance, rate & time equation. d = distance r = rate t = time c = current

Going upstream, the current is subtracted from the rate, as it slows down the rate of travel: $d = (r - c) \cdot t$

Going downstream, the current is added to the rate, as it speeds up the rate of travel: $d = (r + c) \cdot t$

Upstream: $d = (12 - c) \cdot 5$
Downstream: $d = (12 + c) \cdot 3$

Use substitution: replace the "distance" in the second equation with the "(rate + current) • time" from the first equation. Then solve for "current" in the new equation.

$(12 - c) \cdot 5 = (12 + c) \cdot 3$
$60 - 5c = 36 + 3c$
$60 = 36 + 8c$
$24 = 8c$
$3 = c$

The current is moving at 3 miles per hour.

20.   177

PROBLEM TYPE: GREATEST POSSIBLE VALUE/AVERAGE

Assign the variables x, y and z for the missing integers and set up the basic equation for averages:

$$\frac{x + y + z + 200}{4} = 95$$

Let z represent the "greatest possible integer." If this is the case, then x and y both have to be the smallest possible different positive integers that exist. For z to equal to the largest value it can be, x and y will have to equal 1 and 2 respectively:

$$\frac{1 + 2 + z + 200}{4} = 95 \qquad 1 + 2 + z + 200 = 4 \cdot 95$$

$z + 203 = 380$
$z = 380 - 203 = 177$

The answer to grid-in is 177.

About the Author

Lisa Muehle is a co-founder and director of Cambridge Academic Services & Consulting, Inc., Laguna Beach, California. Ms. Muehle originated the *Colloquium Test Prep Course for the SAT*, a long term SAT training program for 7th – 11th grade students, in 1992. Three of Ms. Muehle's students have posted perfect SAT scores. Because of the unique long-term nature of the Colloquium program and its phenomenal score results, Lisa Muehle and the *Colloquium Test Prep Course for the SAT* have received extensive media coverage, including:

- *PBS Frontline* documentary "Secrets of the SAT" (aired Oct. 5, 1999)
- *CBS Early Show* feature "Kids and the SAT" (aired May 2, 2002)
- Los Angeles Times half-page feature in the Metro section, "Scoring SAT Tutors" (published Oct. 12, 1998)
- USA Today editorial (published July 11, 2000)
- Orange County Register front-page feature article, "For SAT, Even Young Teens Know the Score" (published Saturday, January 31, 2004)

978-1-58348-013-7
1-58348-013-7